Praise for *Crackers*

"The funniest book I've read in a decade."—Harry Crews

"[*Crackers* contains] pop zest and folk wisdom, . . . deep-dish country humor and acute sensibility. . . . Like Mark Twain, [Blount] pits the sagacity and saltiness of the cracker barrel against the smooth, evasive rhetoric of the soapbox."—*New Republic*

"[*Crackers* is] funny, not just witty, but out-and-out, downright funny."—*New York Times*

"[With *Crackers*] Blount establishes himself as a major humorist."—William F. Buckley Jr.

"[*Crackers*] serves as a springboard for all manner of wild, outrageous, incisive, iconoclastic observations about the South in particular and the American Reality in general."—*Library Journal*

Praise for Roy Blount, Jr.

"The funniest person I know."—Dave Barry

"It's downright refreshing to read somebody who has taste, intelligence, style, and, oh, bless you, wit—qualities that Blount has in abundance."—*Newsweek*

"Roy Blount is Andy Rooney with a Georgia accent, only funnier."—*Washington Post Book World*

"Page for page, Blount is as funny as anyone I've read in a long time."—Norman Mailer

"Blount [is] in serious contention for the title of America's most cherished humorist."—*New York Times Book Review*

"Blount is good company whatever he's writing."—*Time*

"Blount's reports from the odd corners of human existence are more than funny—they are illuminating. . . . One can say of many humorists, 'Nothing is sacred to him.' For Roy Blount, nothing is mundane."—*Nation*

"Blount writes in the grand tradition of such American humorists as Mark Twain and Will Rogers: he makes us laugh, sure enough, but he also makes us think about what it is we're finding so funny."—*Library Journal*

"Blount's light touch and sense of bemusement combine with arch intellect to give him the versatility to publish in *Organic Gardening* and *Country Journal* one day and *Harvard Magazine* the next."—*Chicago Tribune*

Crackers

Crackers

Roy Blount, Jr.

Brown Thrasher Books

THE UNIVERSITY OF GEORGIA PRESS

Athens & London

Published in 1998 as a Brown Thrasher Book
by the University of Georgia Press
Athens, Georgia 30602
© 1977, 1978, 1979, 1980 by Roy Blount, Jr.

Printed and bound by the Maple-Vail Book Manufacturing Group
The paper in this book meets the guidelines for permanence and durability
of the Committee on Production Guidelines for Book Longevity of the
Council on Library Resources.

Printed in the United States of America

02 01 00 99 98 P 5 4 3 2 1

Library of Congress Cataloging in Publication Data

Blount, Roy.
  Crackers / Roy Blount, Jr.
  p. cm.
  "Brown thrasher books."
  Originally published: New York : Knopf, 1980.
  ISBN 0-8203-2060-9 (pbk. : alk. paper)
  1. Carter, Jimmy, 1924– . 2. Carter, Billy. 3. Carter, Jimmy, 1924– —Family.
  4. Southern States—Civilization—20th century. 5. United States—Civilization—1970–
  I. Title.
  E873.B56 1998
  975'.043—dc21   98-3852

British Library Cataloging in Publication Data available

Crackers was originally published as *Crackers: This Whole Many-Angled Thing of Jimmy, More Carters, Ominous Little Animals, Sad-Singing Women, My Daddy and Me.*

Part of "Smack Dab in the Media" was originally published in *The New Yorker* as "The DiLiberto Times." "Early Billy" originally appeared in somewhat different form as "Chairman Billy" in *Playboy*. "The Love Songs of Roy Blount, Jr.," "Things in the Wrong Hands" (originally, "Sticking with Your Local Merchant"), and "More Carters" (originally, "Carter's Country Cousins") were first published in *Esquire*. Other portions have appeared in different form in *Texas Monthly* and *Sports Illustrated*.

Acknowledgments:
Acuff-Rose Publications, Inc.: Excerpt from "The Wreck on the Highway" by Dorsey Dixon. © Copyright 1946 Renewed 1973 by Acuff-Rose Publications, Inc. Used by permission of the publisher. All rights reserved.
The Atlanta Journal/The Atlanta Constitution: Article from the Atlanta *Constitution,* 7/19/77; Jimmy Townsend in the Atlanta *Constitution,* 7/16/79; various articles by Hugh Park in the Atlanta *Journal.*
ATV Music Corp.: Excerpts from "Black Rose" by Billy Joe Shaver, © 1971 ATV Music Corp.; "I Been to Georgia on a Fast Train" by Billy Joe Shaver, © 1972 ATV Music Corp.; "Ain't No God in Mexico" by Billy Joe Shaver, © 1973 ATV Music Corp.
Farrar, Straus & Giroux, Inc.: Excerpts from *Collected Poems* by Allen Tate, copyright © 1952, 1953, 1970, 1977 by Allen Tate, copyright 1931, 1932, 1937, 1948 by Charles Scribner's Sons, copyright renewed 1959, 1960, 1965 by Allen Tate. Reprinted by permission of Farrar, Straus & Giroux, Inc.
Groper Music, Inc.: Excerpt from "Hill Country Rain" by Jerry Jeff Walker, copyright © 1972 Groper Music, Inc.
Harper's Magazine: Excerpt from "The Dixie Smile" by Johnny Greene, copyright © 1976 by *Harper's Magazine.* All rights reserved. Excerpted from the September 1976 issue by special permission.
Peer International Corporation and Southern Music Publishing Company Limited: Excerpt from "Blue Yodel #10" by Jimmie Rodgers, copyright 1932 by Peer International Corporation. Copyright renewed by Peer International Corporation. Used by permission. All Rights Reserved.
Liz Smith: Excerpts from columns by Liz Smith in the New York *Daily News,* 4/4/78 and 9/19/79. Used by permission of Liz Smith and C.T.N.Y.D.N. Syndicate.

To three Yankees:
Joan,
sine qua non,
and Ennis and Kirven,
who are cute little boogers

And to my mother,
who taught me how to read in Georgia

Contents

ACKNOWLEDGMENTS

Of all the people who helped me get this book written,
I can't help tripling out the Bells,
Jane Ritchie, and old Gordon.

Crackers

The Invocation

I don't know about you, but I have this voice that goes:

"What? NAW. That ain't no way to write a damn sentence! That's the limpest damn piddliest damn saddest-looking most clogged and whiney damn hitching-around piss-and-corruption-covered damn sentence I ever saw.

"Boy! Anybody can snuffle along through the pine straw! I want to see you down with your teeth in the dirt! Reaching and gnawing and chewing and gnashing on some *oak tree roots!* Right on down through to where the *juice* is. *Git* it. *Drive.* Show me something!

"Wait a minute. Wait a minute.

*"*Just look at that. You proud of that sentence? You want your mama and daddy to read that sentence? You want your son or daughter to trustingly come upon that sorry-ass sentence someday buried way back deep in the public liberry and have to say my daddy wrote that? My daddy wrote that pore shitty sentence sitting there with no more grain nor solace in it than a old damn *half-cooked canned sleazy puffy-ass artificial god damn depressing-looking so-called biscuit?* Hunh? Hunh?

"Gah, ah ahhhhhhd, *damn.*

"Scratch that out. Scratch some *more* out. Stick your head in there and *scratch. Dig.* BEAR DOWN.

"I know *you. You* fraid you going to have to say something hard. You fraid you not going to be *able* to say something hard. I *told* you! I *told* you you wouldn't be able to call on the stuff you need right now to write that sentence right if you picked it up the trashy half-ass way you did. Reach . . . back . . . for it and it . . . ain't . . . *there,* is it? Hunh?

"Whud I *tell* you, boy? You can't suck *no* blood from a *dead* squirrel. *NAW!*

"*Aw!* You just flailin and wallerin! NAW. *Drive.* NAW. *Move.* NAW. *Hit. NAW!*

"SCRATCH. DIG. HEAVE. *NAW.*

"Do it again."

I can't pin down the source of that voice in my case. It probably has various coaches and sergeants in it, and Mrs. Methvin, my fifth-grade teacher, and the Old Testament. My daddy never spoke to me that way—as far as I know, he never said "damn"—but he grew up in the hardscrabble South and was hard to impress.

What I know is, I grew up pissing that voice *off.* Constantly. And just as constantly being lifted by mysterious updrafts.

I grew up in Georgia. President Jimmy Carter grew up in Georgia. Surely he too must hear that voice, must feel those surges. So why has his administration been identified with shilly-shally and polls? Why does the first President from my home state keep bringing me mortifying flashes of myself achieving popularity in the seventh grade and losing it (Why? What did I do? I was still the same little old boy) in the eighth?

You may not realize how rousing a moment it was for me, ethnically, when Daddy King stood up there in Madison Square Garden in 1976 at the behest of a by-God-country-white Southerner and led all the states in singing "We Shall Overcome." A Southern Baptist simple-talking peanut-warehousing grit-eating "Eyetalian"-saying Cracker had gotten the strongest and most nearly leftward party to nominate him for President. Of the United States. He had won the trust of Dr.

Martin Luther King's daddy, lieutenant, and spiritual constituency; and he had had a white hat popped on him by the
national media. George Wallace, Richard Daley, George Mc-
Govern, and who knows—probably Huey Long and Daniel
Webster—were up there with Daddy King and Jimmy, singing
to the nation a revolutionary soul-power song. Woooo. *Mercy!*

I was sitting in Manhattan watching this great musical
event on TV with my Georgia sister Susan, my Massachusetts
wife Joan, my New York friends Roland and Lois Betts, my in-
terracial goddaughter Margaret, and my brother-in-law Gerald
Duff, who is from East Texas. It was Gerald who sounded the
right note for the Southerners among us. Even though we
were all brought up clean and decent; even though, when the
Ku Klux Klan came down the aisle of my great-granddaddy's
church and deposited a bag of money in with the collection,
my great-granddaddy picked it up and handed it back to them;
and even though Gerald had just returned from a year of
teaching English in England—even so, Gerald hit the right
note, I think, when he sprang up from the sofa and hollered,
"We ain't trash no more!"

Jimmy has provided a few other high points since then.
Like when Menachem Begin told him, "You have written
your name in the history of two ancient peoples." Think of it:
Salome, Cheops, and old Jimmy. I nearly cried. And early in
the Iran crisis, when Jimmy was coming on as the head of a
more mature civilization than Persia—that was something.
Furthermore, I will defend Jimmy on many of what have been
perceived as his low points. The god damn *rabbit* incident, for
instance.

Still, I have had a hard time figuring out what he has been
up to, overall. He is from *my own state* and I have trouble
telling where he is coming from! I want him to show 'em! I
want him to show *me.* I want him to demonstrate how a
Georgia person can get down and *chew the roots.* Former
Governor Marvin Griffin is an old segregationist who couldn't
lead the nation in singing "Turkey in the Straw," but he hit it

about right when he told me, in the course of my researches, "Jimmy is like the feller who is wearing a blue serge suit and he pees in it. He has a warm feeling, but nobody else knows what is going on."

I am from Georgia and I am determined to decipher what has been going on. Decipher it, preferably, in a way that makes me proud. I come from people who have been blithely called rednecks, Crackers, white trash, Snopeses, and peckerwoods, people who have been put down from without and within. I want *vindication*.

Well, I mean, *some* vindication. I'm not saying . . .

"Wphph . . . WHAT? *Listen to you!*

"BOY! DAMN! *That ain't no way to write the god damn Invocation!*"

More Carters

Velveeta Carter, 36, Bird Swale, Tennessee. "Wail, there's no dat abat it, we're jis trash. Not mean hateful trash, jis people that don't amant to a whole lot. My daddy caint read, my momma don't wash, my brothers just kind of stand arand and say things lack 'shithook' to each other and peek at me in the bathroom and spit down between their feet till it forms a pool. And, wail, as far as me, wail, I had a Mexican baby. I don't know *how*, in this *world*, but I did.

"There he is over there chewing on the fly swatter! Jaime, quit that! Give that to Momma. That child, I declare, I don't know. That's the filthiest thang in this *house* he could chew on. Jaime, you ain't being raised to chew on no fly swat!

"But he's a precious little thang and I love him to death and I don't see where people got the right to look down on us and all. Daddy always taught us, one thing is—we may not have much but we're good as anybody. We've got prad, and we've got roots—course I'm the first generation ever to run into a crad of Mexicans. But my daddy's people been right here since years and years and years. Course, too, they didn't have nowhere to go.

"And now ar distant relative there is the President. It jis seems lack a dream. Didn't you lack it when he told that story down in Mexico abat Monterzumer's Revenge? Lord, we laughed. We was prad that he knew enough histry to know abat a Mexican king. Must've learned that in the Navy. I wouldn't've known *what* to say. I would've sho Lord lacked to go down there with him though."

Pissing and Moaning

There was no longer the faintest sign of vitality in M. Valde-mar; and concluding him to be dead, we were consigning him to the charge of the nurses, when a strong vibratory motion was observable in the tongue.
                                                                    —Poe

One thing about country life, even in Massachusetts, where I live now, you can take a leak most anywhere you want to, if you don't freeze to death. Particularly gratifying is to take one on the compost heap: according to *Organic Gardening*, human urine hastens the composting process, and it personalizes the garden issue in my own mind. Also, when you ask a team doctor whether athletes benefit from the handfuls of vitamins they eat, he will tell you, "Americans have the richest urine in the world." To waste anything that you can't write a song about wasting (well, maybe you *could* write one: "What's Urine Is No Longer Mine") would be a shame.

Compost is the kind of born-again we can all believe in—Vigoro out of corruption. One night my sister's husband Gerald and I were being ethnically overbearing toward my Northern wife Joan. She had said something sanguine about life. We hocked and spat and groaned and told her she didn't know what Southerners knew—what Poe knew, Gerald said: " 'The brute reality is a rotting corpse.' "

People of the South are full of compost. That doesn't rule out culture. A lot of Northern people probably think that if Poe had had the chance to be as optimistic as Longfellow, he would have jumped at it. Or if Hank Williams could have been Der Bingle. (I am working on a song that touches upon the problem of not knowing how to go on since Crosby died, called "Bing and Nothingness."] No, Hank and Poe wouldn't have. They had things of their own to jump at.

What would Poe have thought about Jimmy Carter? I imagine he would have gotten more of a charge out of Nixon. So did we all. What I think about the Carter presidency is that we should at least get some good compost out of it.

As a Georgian, I have never expected to have a major ongoing role in the thought of my time, nationwide. I don't imagine my relatives will every now and then have the pleasure of noticing in the paper where I have revealed something seminal: that white people were brought to this earth by UFO slave ships; that investment income is carcinogenic; that there is a new, heretofore unnoticed particle right in the middle of the atom in the form of a white-bearded big-breasted little Africo-Eurasian-featured character sitting on a tiny golden throne.

But I always figured an occasion would arise when I could water some small corner of the national pile. If having a President who is a Georgian Libra Jr. and who parts his hair on the right side (or did until he changed it), all of which I also am or do, is not that occasion, then I don't know what it is.

A person who is from Georgia, if he ever gets anywhere very far out of Georgia, is forever saying or thinking, "Well yeah, I'm from Georgia, *but* . . ." or "Sure, I'm from Georgia, what's so cute about that?" or "I'm from Georgia and I feel just as good as a pig in shit about it," or "I'm from Georgia, and if you were from Georgia you'd realize what kind of fool you are, but you aren't and don't, so I guess I'll just have to operate on two different levels at once," or "I'm from Georgia, and I guess I better leave my mind open to the possibility that I am missing something here or at least that people will assume I am—and now I've got to decide whether it'll be more worthwhile to go out of my way to *determine* that I'm not missing anything, or to go out of my way (casually) to *indicate* that I'm not missing anything, or to just let those who assume I am missing something go ahead and assume it and thereby miss something themselves, which will tickle me to death," or "That's right, I'm from Georgia, but (*and*) I have a sense of irony about it. But not for *your* benefit."

A person who is a Libra (if you believe in signs—on balance, I think most Libras probably do and don't) is always weighing and balancing everything, on the one hand, on the other hand, on both hands at once—making sure his left lobe knows what his right lobe is doing, and vice versa, and saying "and vice versa" to excess.

A person who is a Jr. probably grew up being called *Little* Jimmy, to differentiate him from Big Jimmy; and probably feels like he wants to make some kind of *departure*, because there is no such thing as *two* Big Jimmys; but he doesn't want to make *such* a departure that either he himself or Big Jimmy will wonder whether there is any such thing as *one* Big Jimmy.

A person who parts his hair on the right probably had a moment when he was a boy in a barbershop when the barber said, "You part it on the *right?* That's verry unyusyal. *Girls* part it on the right"; and he thought to himself, *"What!?* I'm eleven years old and just finding this out now? I had to find it out in the *barbershop?* I've got a *female part!* Is there an *operation* or something . . . ?" (That, of course, was before I read where Faulkner said that in every great writer there is a touch of the androgyne. I'm just glad it was Faulkner said it.)

In other words, a person who is from Georgia, a Libra, a Jr., and grew up parting his hair on the right is probably not the most likely person in the world to enact bold new sweeping programs.

He is, instead, a person of our time.

Hey: we are in a time when the most sweeping program is "Laverne and Shirley." When you can buy artificial gravy entailing "beef-style granules." When "comparison shopping" is not considered redundant. When somebody will sell you a bad wristwatch and shoes and tell you, "So sue me," and if you do, your lawyers will charge you an arm and a leg by the hour to negotiate what time it is, which turns out to be the time they all knock off to go jog. A time when big corporations have to make obscene profits—no, that's not all of it, the truth is their obscene percentage of the obscene *increase* in profits has to *improve* obscenely—because if it doesn't, investors won't invest, because investors have to reap obscene income in order to keep up with the obscene price increases it takes to make obscene profits keep mounting obscenely. A time when slavery and the Holocaust entertain millions of viewers, when the dollar is funnier than the zloty, and when fudgesicles and tomatoes taste about the same.

Remember all the frequently gala wildness that went on in the sixties in protest of supposedly pervasive repression? Now we don't need anything to repress us; all we want to do is seethe. Union, Jewish, and *student* influences are tending in various ways toward the reactionary. Sluggish as we are, we feverishly consume waning energy, and we have *fooled around with the nucleus* to the point that it may decide to destroy us by blowing up, leaking through, or improvising monster viruses. In 1978 a youth in Weymouth, Mass., stepped to the microphone at his high school graduation ceremony, said, "This is the American way," drew a pistol from under his gown, and shot himself. Lying down, he said, "There are too many issues in America today."

You want a little guy from Georgia who had to appeal to the whole audience of "Laverne and Shirley" *and* lawyers *and* the fudgesicle-corporation investors *and* the nuclear-power industry *and* the recombinant unions, Jews, and students in order to get elected *and* whose wife's hairdresser has him parting his hair on the left side all of a sudden after fifty-four years (that's the way I figure it, anyway, in spite of White House insistence that it was the President's own decision and his wife's hairdresser didn't even *notice*) to *solve all that* for you?

But, hey, I don't want to be putting myself in the President's shoes. I want to be casting aspersions on him. I want to assail him. That's what a President is for.

I was listening to the radio out of Hartford the other night, a talk show, just as sterile as all Connecticut. (On a *Georgia* talk show a while back I heard a discussion of fertility pills. A lady said, "I'd be just the one to have a horse." And then a man called in and said, "Since my wife and I were in an accident in our home so early in our marriage and then anyway too she may have damaged herself carrying a flagpole jammed back up against herself you know how they do in the high school band and we haven't been able to have children—and we had two dogs and a cat around the house and altered all of them, so I don't feel too confident to speak on this topic. I'd like to speak about all this talk of changing the state bird. Wonder if you have any thoughts on that.") On this *Hartford* talk show, a caller was saying about the President, "The *man* is *in* . . . *com* . . . petent. The man is a com . . . *plete* in . . . com . . . petent. His foreign *pol* . . . icy, his do . . . *mes* . . . tic . . ."

A little later, the caller revealed that he was a florist.

The son of a bitch was a *florist*. A Connecticut florist! Sends out ferns to strangers all day and then comes home and wants to issue judgments on the *com*petence of somebody who's got to deal with Russians, megacorporations, Mexicans, Israelites, unions, economists, congressmen, cartels, meltdowns, embryos-in-the-garbage-can-with-little-perfect-feet partisans, and polls! I don't care if he's a *hell* of a florist.

There I go, sympathizing. You can't expect anybody to have any sympathy for a presidential sympathizer.

> I got the redneck White House blues.
> The man just makes me more and more confused.
> He's in all the right churches,
> and all the wrong pews.
> I got the redneck White House blues.

More Carters

O. S. "Giblet" Carter, 39, who helps out around Hub and Dr. Bob Spangler's fireworks, stuffed baby alligator gifts, and country ham stand on Route 108 out here half a mile or so the other side of Fermit, Georgia, and is only about eighteen inches tall.

"Hooo, I tell folks I'm exactly the highth of one of Jimmy's ties, you know, I mean the part down below the neck when it's tied. Rilly though I'm prolly a little longer. Unless he wears a tie real long. I don't know. Jimmy come in the place back in '66 when he was arunning for governor. Hoo, yeah. I jumped up and said, 'Heeyyyo, Jimmy, you know weuz *related!*' He said why fine and kep looking around for where my voice was coming fum, thought it was just a *pupp*et or somewhat of that order, I 'magine. Folks'll do that when they ain't been around me long.

"M'little feet are s'small, law-dee. Why I can stand on a carrot. Could use me for Jimmy on the TV a lot, when they're in the close-ups. I'm about his size on the average person's screen, and you know with a small man, there's not the distortion as when you're trying to bring somebody large way down to fit the picture. And you know there's a favorance. You mighta thought I *was* Jimmy at a distance or something, wouldn't you? I can sound like him, too. Can't I do Jimmy—hey, Dr. Bob, can't I . . . ?"

"*Git* down off 'at table, Giblet, and run 'em mice. Like I *tode* you, now."

Nyah

Earl Lindquist of Houston, a 54-year-old contractor, is affront-ed by what he regards as the "packaging" of the President: "I'm telling you, it doesn't matter how Jimmy parts his hair or shakes his fist, the Government is beneath words."
                                  —THE NEW YORK TIMES

The power of the word! I'd be the last to dispute it. What would I dispute it with? This may confound your stereotype of Georgians, but I don't own any firearms. Mind you, I wouldn't want to live anywhere where there were no bullet holes in the road signs. But I don't feel it is my role to shoot them there.

There must be many people who aren't surprised that Jimmy Carter has produced few truly *elevated* sayings. When Pete Hamill writes in the New York *Daily News* about some Southern lady, "Her voice was slow and Southern, but there was something cultured about it too," you realize that there are those who don't associate high eloquence with my part of the country.

I would have thought, though, that a former Georgia governor would have a way with words. It was former Georgia governor Marvin Griffin who, when asked if he would go to jail to prevent integration, said, "Being arrested kindly crimps a governor's style." It was former Georgia governor Lester Maddox who said, "They call me a clown. But what's wrong with being a clown once in a while? Clowns are happy, humorous, and witty; and I don't know any in prison."

Jimmy Carter has even failed notably in quoting the elevated sayings of others. When he tried to psych the nation up for the energy crisis by invoking William James's "moral equivalent of war," people started referring to his "meow" speech. It is a good thing that in 1760, when James Otis proclaimed that "taxation without representation is tyranny," James Otis didn't say instead that "taxation without equity equals tyranny," because people might have started referring to it as James Otis's "tweet" speech, and the Revolution would have fizzled.

It's a shame that Jimmy hasn't been better verbally. Because a good saying will carry a man a long way. For instance, just as this book was going to press, I was lucky enough to obtain an interview with the " 'Nihilate Yo Andy Hardy" man.

"You know the story—well, how it started, this bunch of Arabs, three Arabs, come down out of the sky in a hot-air balloon, onto my property. And they just kind of stood there looking disorientated, and I told 'em, if they didn't get off my land I would 'nihilate their Andy Hardy. I said if they didn't believe it, try me. My thought was, I had 'em where I wanted 'em—which was funny, I tell people now, because I had 'em where I didn't want 'em, too. In my yard. The truth is, I tell people now, looking back on that moment, actually I wouldn't have fired. That was just something my daddy used to yell at us boys, 'I'm 'ona 'nihilate yo Andy Hardy.' I don't know no more about it than that, really. Whether he got it from his daddy, or what. And when I grew up and had boys of my own, why I kept it in the family.

"But these Arabs, they picked right up on it. Said if I wouldn't shoot they'd give me $1.4 million, and the balloon. And they did, too, spot cash money, mister. Bim bim bim. And .3 million more for my Plymouth, to get out of there in. Hell, I guess it didn't mean anything to them. They had just took off on a lark—it was some young Arabs, going around seeing the country. But $1.4 million looked like awful good money to me then, being I owed $16,000 on a $14,000 house—yeah, you heard that, yeah—and part of it had fell in.

"Was about the extent of my finances then. Yeah, fell in all over us one night when my wife June was screaming and yelling about something, and there was a bad hailstorm. Listen, I used to have some rough nights back before I came into my own.

"But, anyway, the first thing was these Arabs, and, you know, after that a lot of things just sort of seemed to snowball and multiply. Featured in the AP, *Us* magazine, 'Good Morning, America,' then the various spots—Donahue, 'Love Boat'—and we got the *Newsweek* cover, that was a big factor, and my major recording contract, and the Milwaukee Brewers wanted to pay me $3.4 million for eight years of playing ball. Not that I could necessarily play that well—you know, I'd *played* ball, in high school—but just purely for the draw. I thought that was a testimonial. And NBC paying me 3.5 million not to appear on ABC or CBS, and ABC paying me 4.5 not to appear on CBS or NBC, and CBS paying me 5.5 not to appear on NBC or ABC, and some little syndicate outfit out of Raleigh-Durham paying me I think it's .8 million not to appear on any of the networks. You remember, there was that first big scramble there.

"And, they're making the action doll of me and everything, and I bought a 4,000-acre ranch with Thomson's gazelles and mouse deer on it, and I endorse the snack cakes, the chicken parts, the dog shampoo—I can still be in *commercials* on the networks. My agent says that's one thing an American can't sign away, his right to be in commercials. And then just for getting together with some major clients of three or four of the various big corporations every once in a while, at functions—I just mainly talk, they line up, and I pose shaking hands with 'em, and I drink liquor and eat shrimp—for that I'll have $2.65 million coming in, staggered, over a period of time. I specify this certain kind of chili sauce. I got it one time in a Monsanto hospitality tent, and that stuff—it don't have to be shrimp, I could dip anything in that stuff and enjoy it.

"And then this one over here is packaging the book of my

story, and this one over there putting together the movie deal of it, and this other one just a-churning out the posters. And course all it is in the world is just a story of pure D exposure. You know, fame. A man who came from where hardly anybody would admit they recognized him, even on his own street, to where I guess, well, I know I can't go into the K-Mart to pick up some jumper cables any more but what I'll just be mobbed.

" ' 'Nihilate yo Andy Hardy.' I don't know, it came at a time, I believe, when basic values was being questioned, and people seemed like they were looking for something. So many of the sports teams used it, and I've had a many a parent to write me that it worked on their child. And too I was always just natural, and open too about my home life. People appreciate that. And, hell, I didn't care. Another thing, I never told this before but the feddle government paid me a good amount of money and kind of laid back on some of my deductions, you know, if I would make a tape for the arm services.

"I guess too it was the *way* I said it. But I'm going to let you in on something now: I get tired of repeating it. *'Tell us what you told the A-rabs.'* I have some other good sayings Daddy used to use, and then I make up several. But people are never satisfied, it looks like, but what they've got to hear the 'nihilate one. *'Tell us what you'd say to a bunch of women libbers.'* Or what I'd say to 'the interests' or 'OSHA.' Or 'Howard Cosell.' Or 'a damn old gouging doctor' or 'the power company' or whatever. From my lips.

"But, you know, I will say this. I don't believe everybody would have handled it the way that I have. I have pretty much kept right on the same beam, pretty much. And I've still got that old full-choke 12-gauge gun, and my same piece of property, only course I got a $895,000 home on it now, and I'm pretty well set. I got lifetime security for my family, which was the main thing, and got rid of June, and I think—I really think if some other folks ever light down on my yard like that, why this time I'll kill 'em. I just wish Daddy would be here to see it. My daddy couldn't have afforded to shoot anybody's *lawyer*, much less anybody."

Of course, it's easy enough for me to criticize the President's language; I haven't had to write any of it. In the fall of '79—when Jimmy seemed to be in urgent need of rearticulation—I got word that a Carterite familiar with my verbal work was looking to hire a new presidential speechwriter. For a minute I thought: Maybe I ought to volunteer and see if I can script those old boys a new Crackro-American Camelot.

But then I thought: Naw.

I decided it would probably turn out to be one of those experiences whose only real consolation is, as the feller said who was placing a call on the beach when a hurricane blew up and carried him out to sea in a phone booth, "Well, at least there's a book in it." And I already had *this* book going.

Writing presidential speeches is probably like writing network TV programs: if you ever wrote one that truly got down and chewed the roots, everybody in America would run out into the streets yelling and foaming and scared half to death. Also, the only way I know to dig and bear down in my writing is to be willing to let personal references creep in.

Jimmy would be on the phone hollering, *"What's this stuff about 'my brother-in-law Gerald'? I don't have any damn brother-in-law Gerald!"*

"Excuse me, Mr. President," I'd say. "That should be 'my aide Roy's brother-in-law Gerald.' "

I can hear Jimmy now. "I don't want one more word about *anybody's* brother-in-law!"

I won't be spoken to that way by a man the world calls inept.

What I have done, on my own initiative, is write a song that I'd be glad for Jimmy to use in any further campaigns:

> Let's have no more malaise, exacerbating
> Tensions, finding fault and Cracker-baiting.

This tendency to *épater les cous-rouges*
Won't solve our problems, they are too huge.
And, after all, he came from humble origins,
And something you should know concerning Georgians . . .

"What!? What kind of a damn campaign song . . . ?"

More Carters

Mrs. Glory Burnette Carter Louvins, 51, Fuel City, Texas. "I wouldn't call on him. I wouldn't dream of it. Back here when my daddy was so crazy and slipping out hiding in amongst the cows and wouldn't come in for dinner and howling in the night, if I was going to go to the President anytime it would've been then.

"Oh, and after that, Lord, he thought he had died and been returned as a palameener horse, but 'cept with the powers of human speech. Only it was *different* speech. I don't know, it didn't *sound* like Daddy.

"Ohhhh, I tell you, I didn't know *what* I was going to do with Daddy. And then dobbin his pore old body with chili sauce and all."

Yazoo

The first time I flew over town in an airplane, coming back from college, I looked down on the top of a water tank, and a sign on it said YAZOO CITY. *That was the first time it ever occurred to me that those letters together look funny.*

—SPENCER GILBERT

From the very beginning, I had no designs on a post. Consultant, secretary of something, sportswriter laureate, confidant, anything like that. Well, I might have considered putting in a few months as confidant. Confidants can probably cultivate an impressive if-these-old-lips-weren't-sealed sort of air. But I would begin to feel stopped up as a confidant, hanging around giving myself deep background.

And I don't know anything about investments.

I saw a man standing behind Jimmy on television, not long after the inauguration, whose role I could have gotten into. The title for it might be Surface Background. He was smiling and rocking back on his heels and working a cigar and winking, first in one direction and then the other. I don't know who he was, but *he* clearly did, for the time being, and he was *in on* things, at some level.

See, you may not be from Georgia, like I am. For a while it was good, writing for a newspaper in Atlanta, you could achieve a measure of significance just by standing opposed to the forces of hate. And the forces of hate were probably not going to be able to get back at you, because the Chamber considered them bad for business. But the truth was, Southern liberalism had about been mapped out and settled. And yet, people would occasionally take their money out of my daddy's savings and loan because of things I'd written.

In 1968, when Jimmy was just another state senator, I took off North. How was I supposed to know that a *white Baptist* was going to arise in *South Georgia*, a hotbed of the hate forces, and lead us out of the wilderness?

Of course, I had, by exposure to Northerners, learned the same lesson Jimmy had, that people *outside* Georgia weren't so damn hot (I might add "either," but I'm not going to). But when Jimmy and Daddy King led the nation in "We Shall Overcome," I watched it on TV with my mouth hanging open. I was like a man who goes from being half eat up with hookworms to catching nice speckled trout with them. I was damned if I was going to miss out on the entire Jimmy era.

I didn't expect anything much in the way of wealth, honor, patronage, or fame. No more in the way of lasting glory than maybe a footnote in history.

[1]Though he received scant attention at the time, Phosper's meticulous steel engravings of frogs springing (always shown off the ground, though sometimes just *barely*) are among the few works of the period that still provide pleasure.

[2]Among the few contemporary defenders of the Address was frontier educator Eural "Pow Wow" DePerry, who later toured the country advocating the use of reason in Indian-fighting.

[3]One of the region's earliest settlers, Thigpen also raised experimental vegetables, fought five duels, edited a weekly newspaper, *The Calumniator*, and carried on a correspondence in Greek verse with John C. Calhoun. On a visit to Boston in 1886, he was shot in the foot by a disgruntled advocate of nude masques, who was aiming at William Dean Howells. Injured only slightly, Thigpen in later years would go around with the foot bare in good weather and refer to the scar, misleadingly, as "old Santyanny's autograph."

I paid my dues. I *put up* with being from Georgia, not to mention *in* Georgia, during my formative years, when my ethnic group was being represented in the national eye by Bull Conners and Sheriff Leroy Raney. Wouldn't *you* feel entitled to get in on a little of the table-turning later? I don't want to have to hem and haw when my grandchildren ask me what I was doing while my home boy was leading, however uncertainly, the Free World.

So in '77, when I heard that Jimmy was getting ready to go to the new high school gym in Yazoo City, Mississippi, and answer questions from the townspeople on national TV, I went there to see how I could get plugged in. "*Please* get some new shoes," my mother asked me, but as it turned out I doubt the President ever saw my feet, much less connected them with my family. I came *close* to a couple of footnotes, though.

I wasn't going into Yazoo cold. For one thing, I knew Jerry Clower, the country comedian, a Yazoo City resident who, I had heard, was to play a role in the President's reception. When I pulled into town the night before the big event, I got an inkling of the size of that role.

Jerry weighs a good deal over two hundred fifty pounds, I would say, and he is tall too, and has a head the size of a squared-off basketball. In the face, he looks a little like John Wayne and a little like Buddy Hackett. He filmed a chain-saw commercial once that the company wouldn't run because, according to Jerry, "I overpowered the saw."

I sighted Jerry wearing a huge red suit, waving his arms, whooping and serving as host at a watermelon-cutting in the town triangle, which is what Yazoo City has instead of a town square.

Jerry began his professional storytelling career while selling fertilizer for the Mississippi Chemical Corporation in Yazoo. He enhanced his sales talks with stories of growing up poor but hearty in the Mississippi Delta south of Yazoo. These stories of coon hunts, rat-killings, and cat's-head biscuits caught on so well, independent of the fertilizer, that he has gone on to fame and fortune as a "Grand Ole Opry" regular, a recording star, and the life of state fairs North and South.

In Jerry's stories, somebody is always fighting a lynx in a

tree or devouring more than one huge watermelon single- and bare-handed or taking apart a beer joint with a chain saw. Jerry can make some of the finest rooting, squalling, and hollering noises you ever heard from a dais, and he is not withdrawn offstage, either. At the risk of alienating his audience, Jerry has even stood tall as a racial progressive. He not only defended the beleaguered desegregated public schools in Yazoo City but also called all those who failed to support them racists. He is an outspoken, born-again, teetotaling, work-ethic Baptist. And he is not satisfied yet with the extent to which he has impressed himself upon the nation.

"There is nothing formal you got to do here," he was telling the town-triangle crowd, "except *love each other*. You are just as welcome here as a *ripe watermelon* on the *Fourth of July*." He made the watermelon sound like four gret big uns and the day sound like it was hot and juicy to the point of explosion. Jerry was standing on a wooden stage in front of a big banner reading "Yazooans Welcome President Carter."

But then he right away yielded the stage to a black singing group from the local high school. As they sang "Why don't you reach out and *touch* . . . somebody's haaand?" and other selections, Jerry conferred with three White House aides, introduced me to nine people, and told a radio interviewer about his uncle Versy Ledbetter.

"Uncle Versy was outside in the yard one day when his wife Aunt Pet Ledbetter asked him would he like to come inside and have a piece of apple pie with the church ladies. Uncle Versy said he believed he would.

"Now, one of the church ladies had told Aunt Pet about a new way of serving apple pie, where you served it *hot*.

"And Uncle Versy never had had apple pie hot. He'd always had it cooled. So he came in there to the parlor and took a big old bite of that pie right into his mouth, and WAAAWWWW, it like to have burnt the whole roof of his mouth *off*, and AWWWWWW, Uncle Versy gathered that big old mouthful of pie up in his mouth and went WOWR . . . *phoo*. And spit.

"And there was a great big quivering *gob* of steaming hot apple pie right out on Aunt Pet's best tablecloth in front of the church ladies.

"And Uncle Versy said, 'You know there's a many a damn fool woulda *swallered* that.' "

I have enthusiastically retold that story to non-Southerners who have looked sick and called it regional at best. I'd say they're the ones being regional. As Lenny Bruce was to sexuality, Jerry Clower is to digestion. Only he's less self-conscious about it. "Hooooooo, this town is fizzlin like a big Alka-Seltzer," he told the radio man. Then he took the stage to exclaim some closing remarks:

"Now lately network television has had to show some bad things.

"Looting and things.

"Tomorrow afternoon at the airport the President's going to be coming in.

"And I'm going to be there to welcome him.

"And we want to show the country some positive people.

"With *smiling, happy* expressions on their faces.

"*Thanking God our President is alive!*

"*And I'm gonna be the FIRST THING HE SEES when he gets to Mississippi.*"

I could see the likelihood of that. I could also see the likelihood that any footnotes achieved within two hundred yards of Jerry were going to be achieved by *him*. I was getting a little anxious. People were bustling around, fulfilling their roles. For instance there were a number of men with the same length of hair and with suits and ties on. People were coming up to them and asking, "Y'all Secret Service?" And they were saying, "We can't say."

Willie Morris the writer was there covering for *Time* and the Washington *Star*. It was his home town. I couldn't compete with him in Yazoo-ology.

Barry Jagoda, the Carter TV man, was there. When I asked him what his role was, he had the answer right away: "To make sure everything looks the way it really is." That was a role a person could get his teeth into. "The gym is a gym," he explained. "It's a good . . . gym. We don't want anybody turning it into their idea of a boutique." A gym for Jimmy.

Harriett DeCell, another progressive Yazooan, was on hand, showing off the local library, of which she was proud: "It's the only place in town where you can have whiskey *and* black people."

My own role was not clear yet. Fortunately I had another connection.

Jerry wasn't my only connection. There was Spencer Gilbert, a Yazoo City lawyer and native, an old boy I'd gone to Vanderbilt with. And, lo and behold, it turned out that Spencer's father-in-law was Owen Cooper.

That was Owen Cooper, the retired president of Mississippi Chemical. Owen Cooper, the bulwark in Mississippi of that radical social program Headstart. Owen Cooper, the nationally eminent Baptist. Owen Cooper, the man at whose house in Yazoo City Jimmy Carter was going to spend the night!

Now, Spencer is a self-effacing but active lawyer who deals in contract litigation and things like that but who also works for liberal causes. He has organized legal-aid services for the poor, he has defended a professor who lost his job at Jackson State College for showing an R-rated movie, and he has helped force the rerouting of Interstate 10 to preserve the habitat of the world's last surviving sand cranes. (The sand crane is a bird. A Biloxi newspaper showed how popular Spencer's side in the I-10 controversy was by publishing a recipe for sand cranes across its front page.) But for me at the time, all these credentials of Spencer's were overshadowed by the fact that I figured Spencer had access to the President's bedroom.

That chamber was already famous by the time I reached Yazoo City. That afternoon TV crews had been lined up for hours, filming each other, waiting for Mrs. Cooper to get the new drapes, new carpet, and new bedspreads ready for the national limelight. Gossips were estimating that the Coopers had spent up to $4,000 on the new furnishings. "I love Mrs. Cooper," said one townsperson, "but I think it's tacky they're giving the President that room with the two little old single beds and they're keeping their big bed."

Hmm. *Two* little old single beds. And Rosalynn wasn't coming down with him. *Did anybody have dibs on the second bed?* I could just be lying there under the covers when he came in, and I'd say, "Mr. President . . . Jimmy, I know you're tired but I'm doing a book and I'd just like to chat with you for a minute before you doze off."

But I guess I'm not pushy enough. I never brought up the question of that second bed while being shown the room, by Mrs. Cooper's daughter, a fine-looking pregnant woman of spirit, named Fran Miles. "This is it," she said. "But the other press saw the bedroom. Here, you can see the bathroom."

At last, an exclusive angle. A john for Jimmy. A pearl-grey phone had been installed by the sink. "You could pick that up right now and the White House would be on it," Fran said.

But hell if Jimmy was going to see to it that the government couldn't cut into my phone, which is something he said he was going to see to, then I ought not to cut into his. Some other way for me to take advantage of this access would surely arise.

Shhhhhhhhhhhh.

Any homeowner has heard that sound. A toilet that won't stop flushing. A President can't rest easy with that in his ear.

I regarded the apparatus. I lifted its lid. All the innards were brand-new. "The plumbers have been here all day," Fran sighed. I raised my hand in a mind-resting way. I manually bent, slightly, the float arm.

Silence.

"There," I said. At this point Spencer, however, intervened. Heretofore he had held back. He could afford to: he had already met Jimmy way back before the primaries. He had asked Jimmy what he could do to help his campaign.

"Help me get some money," Jimmy had said.

Furthermore, Spencer was going to participate in the Coopers' family prayers with the President. "I'm going to wear a bow tie, so I'll stick out," he had said.

But now he felt called upon to improve on my adjustment. It was his in-laws' presidential bathroom, after all, not mine. And then, you know lawyers. He added a little bend of his own.

Shhhhhhhhhhhhhhhh.

"Spencer," I said, "please." The arm was getting crooked now, but I bent it in a clever compensating way. Again, the noise ceased. The float stood firm, holding back the flow.

The float was made of Styrofoam.

Now. It happens that I *love* writing on Styrofoam with a felt-tip pen. If you have ever done it, you know what I mean. There is a sensual satisfaction to it. Many is the Styrofoam coffee cup I have decorated strikingly while waiting for something to happen on the news fronts of the world. My felt-tip pen was handy. Surely a brief note, "Hello, Mr. President," and my name, and "I am from Georgia," and an assurance that I didn't expect anything in return for my services, and then something like "Hang in there on the water projects" would not be out of place.

Then it hit me.

The trouble was, the President was unlikely to look into the workings of the toilet now that the toilet was fixed.

What I had done, I had turned this machinery that linked me to the seat of power into a perfect model of the unsqueaky wheel. Here I had been trying to squeeze some personal recognition out of the President's visit to the people. Yet in playing a constructive role, I had secured my anonymity. I was representative of millions. Selflessly, I replaced the gleaming porcelain slab that masked my contribution.

At a local party later that night, I took another tack. My hostess, Betty Raney, was looking for a question to ask the President the following night in the gym. Well, Willie Morris felt like he needed to change a few of the words of the question I came up with. As before, with Spencer in the lavatory, I could appreciate his position. But *essentially*, it was *my* question that Betty posed the next evening to the sopping-with-good-old-Dixie-sweat Chief Executive:

"What is there about your Southern heritage that led to your concern with human rights?"

Well, there was the actual President of America, from Georgia, up there on the stage, answering my question. He went on dubiously awhile about the libertarian virtues of Southern religiosity, and then he said:

"In the South we were guilty for many years of the deprivation of human rights to [sic] a large portion of our citizens. Black people didn't have the right to vote, seek an equal school, a good job or home. There has been in the South a change in that. That change is the best thing that ever happened to the South in my lifetime."

At that a big cheer went up from Mississippians, black and white. A milestone. On July 21, 1977, *Desegregation* was incorporated into the great Southern heritage of self-congratulation.

I enjoyed being in that crowd, all of us flapping our cardboard fans with the funeral parlor ads on them. Jimmy was a sign of the obsolescence of the old lurid Southland, which was stark enough to provide the nation with grounds whereon anyone with gumption could fight for or against the rights of man. Now maybe we could all, all God's children, black and white, North and South, get back to scratching, scuffling, ingloriously adjusting our float arms, and fighting for the right-of-way.

As people were filing out of the gym, I ran into Barry Jagoda and asked him whether the fans ("Southern self-propelled air conditioning," Jimmy had called them) had been his idea. Rather testily he pointed to the funeral parlor ads, as if funeral parlors always and spontaneously provide fans to presidential gym gatherings. He rushed away before I could confront him with my suspicion that the powerful electric fans in the gym walls had been kept off for the first half of the evening (Yazooans had tried to turn them on, but the White House opposed it) so that the President could work up a good sweat and take off his coat and roll up his sleeves for television. But I was willing to let that slide. I felt charitable—even necessary. Thanks to me the President was on his way to evening quarters where the toilet would not be an issue.

I spent that night at Jerry Clower's house. The President had cited Jerry by name on national TV. He said he admired him.

Jerry was tickled to death. "The President of the United States is an admirer of mine!" he cried while eating several large sausages and watching a TV replay of the affair. "If the President of the United States is, everybody ought to be!"

When Jimmy had landed in Jackson that afternoon, sure enough Jerry had been on the landing-strip podium to greet him. "He got off the plane," Jerry told me, "and I thought, 'Well, all that stuff about him being friendly is probably lies, and he'll come up all snot-nasty and BBD&O.' But here he come, and I asked him if I could hug him. And he said, 'Sure.'

"And then tonight, on television, the President of the United States said he admired *me!* I'm just human enough to get excited about that. You know, they talked for a while about me introducing him in the gym. But his people were afraid he wouldn't be able to follow me. My friend Charles Jackson told them, 'That's right, *Jimmy Carter* couldn't follow Jerry. He'd be like a goose in a high wind. But *President* Jimmy Carter, the power of the office, could follow him.' But they were afraid of it."

Jerry sighed. But then he brightened back up. "After he finished with the questions, you know, he picked a cricket off his shirt and thumped it right over at me."

The President had also had a good televised word for Willie Morris. For me, there had been no hugs, no plugs, no crickets thumped. But I knew what I had done.

I thought. As it turned out—well, a couple of days after the event, I called Spencer again. Asked him how the prayers and everything went. He said fine. I said I guessed the President got a good night's sleep and all, what with his toilet not going Shhhhhhhhhhhhhhh.

Spencer said that was probably true. "However," he said.

"*However?* " I asked.

The family had not been content, Spencer said, to let "our" work with the float arm stand. "They called the plumbers back in," he said. "They got it fixed professionally."

"Oh," I said, historically diminished. I said I guessed they knew what they were doing. It was their toilet.

"Well. But the only thing was . . ."

"The only thing was *what?*"

"The plumbers turned the water off to fix it, and they forgot to turn it back on. The next morning after the President left, it was discovered that he'd gone the whole night without a toilet that would flush."

All those new curtains, drapes, bedspreads. . . . Well, I left it at that. I didn't ask, "Uh, how . . . exactly . . . ?" I didn't ask any follow-up questions.

I guess it's just as well I didn't write my name on that Styrofoam float.

More Carters

Dr. J. E. M. McMethane Carter, 45, Rolla, Missouri, interdisciplinary professor at the Hugh B. Ferguson University of Plain Sense and Mysterophysics.

"Let me put it this way. I don't bleev there is any such thing as a black hole, however I do bleev there is a little about four and a half foot tall man named Bobby who is completely impossible to get in a wrestling hold. Because I saw that little son of a bitch *operate* one night outside a dance.

"I don't bleev that everything everywhere is all just little electrons whirling around each other with nothing in between, however I do bleev there is something seriously missing somewhere.

"I don't bleev that if you take and sail off around the world faster enough than light you will come back before you ever took and sailed off, however I do bleev that my distant cousin twice removed President Jimmy Carter can be coming from absolutely nowhere, and then suddenly going absolutely nowhere, and then suddenly coming from absolutely nowhere again, and always be nowhere in particular."

The Damnedest Thing

Children cannot be surprised by the extraordinary who have not been made aware of what is ordinary. A generation knowing top hats only as props for conjurers does not think it is so remarkable when rabbits emerge from them.
—Iona and Peter Opie, *The Oxford Book of Children's Verse*

Can't anybody wear a hat with a rabbit in it! For a short time!
—Kirven Blount

Let's talk about the rabbit incident. Jimmy probably should have kept his mouth shut about the rabbit, never mentioned to anyone but Rosalynn that it had attacked his canoe . . .

"Oh, Jimmy, are you all right?"

"Yes, I'm *all right*, but it was the damnedest thing."

"Jimmy. Honey. Are you sure it was a rabbit?"

. . . and that he had to fend it off with his paddle. But that's the kind of thing that happens to people in real life. You just seldom read about it in the newspapers. Unless you live in the South. A while back there was a front-page story in the Nashville *Tennessean* headlined "Disposing of Chipmunk Brings 100-Foot Tumble."

An elderly Inglewood woman was trying to toss a dead chipmunk over a bluff in her backyard yesterday when she lost her balance and fell 100 feet down the embankment, police said.

As Mrs. Herman W. Lawrence, 73, lay in a thick patch of underbrush, her small dog, Mystre, came scurrying down the steep embankment to help her mistress. The dog began barking.

Mrs. Lawrence then began yelling for help and her sister, Miss Mary Larkey, heard her.

"I ran over and called to her and I heard her voice but I couldn't tell where she was," said Miss Larkey, who had gone for a shovel with which to pitch the chipmunk over the bluff when her sister apparently decided she could throw it away.

"I asked her if she was all right," added Miss Larkey, "and she told me she was holding on to something and couldn't hold on much longer."

About an hour later [nice transition], with the help of Metro police, the Inglewood-Madison Fire Department, members of the Davidson County Rescue Squad and ambulance attendants from the Phillips-Robinson Funeral Home, Mrs. Lawrence was pulled to safety and on her way to Nashville Memorial Hospital.

She was X-rayed and examined at the hospital. Despite some bruises received from her fall, doctors said Mrs. Lawrence seemed to be in pretty good shape.

Metro Police Sgt. K. I. Wright said Mrs. Lawrence was lucky she fell onto a lodge [should be "ledge," I think], instead of plunging into the Cumberland just about 50 more feet away . . .

After a bath to remove the mud she encountered in her fall, she went to her room and went to sleep, hospital officials said.

"She was joking and laughing about it at the hospital," said Sgt. Wright. "She seemed to be such a good-natured lady."

Now there are probably some who wouldn't think that was a front-page story. But that is the kind of thing that happens to people. Bravo to the *Tennessean* for telling it, and to the reporter, George Watson Jr., for getting the spelling of the dog's name.

"Dog's name is Mister, huh? How do you spell that, Mrs. Lawrence?"

One time I was bitten by a rhea in the Memphis zoo. A rhea is a bird like an ostrich, and it strode right up and shot out this long hairy-looking neck and bit me on the index finger. There were a lot of other people around, but it showed no interest in anyone but me.

Not much of an anecdote, I know. But everything in life is not necessarily much of an anecdote. For a good while thereafter I kept wanting to talk about it. "The damnedest thing," I would tell people. "I didn't even know there was such a thing as a rhea. From Patagonia, I understand. Turns out the name probably comes from the mother of Zeus. She was named Rhea. And it just strode right up and . . ."

"What? A ray? *Whose* mother?" Nobody ever wanted to listen. But it relieved me to talk about it.

If I were President, though, and a rhea bit me and I told someone about it, there would immediately be little boxes in *Newsweek* and the cartoonists would be having a field day and Jack W. Germond and Jules Witcover would be writing:

"WASHINGTON—The story about the 'fed-up ostrich' that bit the President is, no doubt about it, funny.

"But it highlights a graver problem for this beleaguered Chief Executive. A sure sign that a politician is in trouble is when the voters start laughing at him. They see him as a well-meaning man whose mild manner invites even obscure Patagonian birds to take a nip . . ."

We would have the spectacle once again of the leader of the Western world "issuing clarifying statements"—which means that the press has been saying, "Mr. President! Mr. President! Tell us more, ah, *snk*, about the . . . ostrich."

Or in Jimmy's case, the rabbit. And the President being a good sport about it. He can't very well snap, "I am not issuing one more god damn word about that god damn *rabbit!*"

So: "It was just a nice, quiet, typical Georgia rabbit" (*The New York Times*).

And: "It was a fairly robust-looking rabbit who was swimming, apparently with no difficulty. I took the boat paddle and hit water at the rabbit and he eventually and reluctantly turned away and went to shore" (Boston *Globe*).

And: "I never did hit the rabbit. I just splashed toward him and he finally veered his course and went over to the bank and climbed up on the bank" (Atlanta *Journal*).

When you're a Cracker, you're always having something to disprove. *Everybody* in Western civilization has something to disprove, but not everybody realizes it. Everybody just realizes that the President is a Cracker who doesn't even have the propriety to be a mean one. "When a mind-set lodges itself in the public consciousness about a political figure," write Germond and Witcover, "any story or remark that can stretch good-natured laughter into ridicule can be damaging, by embellishing and exaggerating a routine flaw. . . . The fact that there is nothing about Jimmy Carter that makes rabbits think they can gobble him up won't curtail the ridicule he will endure now."

That's what political commentators do: inform voters as to what the voters' mind-sets are. Here are Germond and Witcover after several disreputable people (the more reputable ones came later) accused Hamilton Jordan of sniffing coke: "Once again, as was the case with Bert Lance and Andrew Young, the President has allowed himself to be depicted as a political leader tolerant to the point of being weak when those personally close to him are involved.

"The President does not see it that way, of course. What he sees is a friend who he believes has been unjustly accused, and a situation that demands his personal loyalty. And from that perspective, Carter can certainly do no less than stand behind Jordan. But the political price is high among voters who have already made a negative judgment on Jordan and aren't willing to await a fair finding in this matter."

What if books were reviewed that way? "This is an honest piece of work but the average reader doesn't realize it because the average reader is shallow and responds to shallow reviews, so the author has screwed up again."

What political commentators do is inform voters that a politician is an inhuman machine doing things just for votes—and then when he turns around and does something unpopular for a good human reason, *they* turn around and inform the voters that he is fecklessly costing himself votes. "Allowing himself to be depicted . . ." Of course, if he is trying to *control* how he is depicted, he is image-mongering—and if he won't allow himself to be depicted at all, then he is paranoid and boring.

I'll tell you one thing. Jimmy didn't deserve to be put down by Richard Nixon on account of the rabbit. Nixon was hosting a nostalgic reunion of his aides and supporters, to mark the end of his political exile. He admitted that his administration had had problems, but "at least we were never attacked by a killer rabbit." I kept expecting Hitler to return from the grave to observe, "*Wenigstens wurden wir nie von einem blutrunstigen Kaninchen angefallen.*"

Right about the time Jimmy was repelling the rabbit, scientists declared ecstatically that they had discovered a particle, the "gluon," that holds all matter together. (Just when so many political coalitions to the left of Richard Viguerie—who may even now be working out a way of harnessing phlogiston to serve the right-wing mailing-list industry—were coming apart.) You know and I know what really holds all matter together is being able *to tell somebody what is the matter*—even if you're the President and the matter is that all of a sudden there is a rabbit trying to get in your boat. Of course, now, Jimmy could have been more sympathetic to the rabbit, which at the time was one of the few living things trying to climb aboard with him. But what if the rabbit, once taken on, had jumped all over the President and made him swamp his canoe? *Then* what would the columnists have written?

"Once again, as was the case with Bert Lance and Andrew Young . . ."

It's hard being President.

> I know what they're saying 'bout me,
> I can read.
> You know, Oval Office occupants
> Also bleed.
> Even my own party's saying
> I can't lead . . .

You're an engineer and you find yourself pulled way down by a little rabbit and boosted way up by a bunch of ranting Iranians. How are you going to figure out how the machinery works?

More Carters

Arimethea Carter Burthen, 94, Old Grounder, Tennessee, who has maintained every day for the past fifty-seven years that she is going to "pass over" soon.

"My boy Courts, you know, I had him after I come under the shadow. He says Meemaw, says you'll outlive us all. Says you done outlived a many a one. But I don't know, this thing has just brought me down to where I believe sometimes . . . it's hard.

"Wail, naw, Jimmy's not real regular about calling, to be troofle. And course, I don't let on to him, I try to spare him what I can. But I told him back here Sunday, I said, 'Jimmy, you almost lost me this mawnin. I don't bleev I'll make it through to supper. I *declare* I don't.' He said, 'Now, Miss Arimethea, we all concerned with this problem. We all vitally concerned.'

"But it didn't give me no more lift than nothin."

Things in the Wrong Hands

I had an uncle who was afraid to fly. So he took a train and you know what happened? A plane fell on it. —ROGER MILLER

The trouble with the world today in my estimation is nobody has a handle on it. Hardly anybody. And just because I come from a part of the country whose idea of progressive legislation for many years was an occasional law against "flogging while masked" doesn't mean that I have no license to lay such a generalized charge.

Let me put it this way: *Every single case of anything with which I have ever had the least real iota of experience, personally, has turned out to be either a lot more complicated or a lot less complicated than it had been* (and would continue to be) *made out to be.*

I fault the media, even though I am in on it. (This is one of those cases where you can construe "media" in the singular. Because it makes you feel better.) I fault the society, even though I am willing to go so far as to admit that I am in on that too. I fault the way things have been handled, by nearly everybody, down through the years.

I thought having a President from Georgia might give me a grip on things. And sure enough, sometimes I think, "Whooee! Old Jimmy is going to *do something* with that presidency!" But more often Jimmy himself has seemed to function as nothing much more than a device for convincing everybody he's still *elected*, and that just barely.

I hate to see people too wrapped up in devices. I was talking to an old boy in New York City the other day and he told me:

"Hey, somese *products* out today. My sister is glued to the dry cleaners.

"*My sister is glued to the dry cleaners.*

"*Yeah.* This Wonder Glue they got out now. *One drop* of it holding the cowboy hat to this like overhanging tree limb, on the commercial, you've seen it, another drop the hat to the cowboy, you haven't ever seen it? Yeah, another drop cowboy the saddle, another drop saddle the horse, *horse is up off the ground!* It's *outrageous* man. And is the horse *pissed!* You know, trying to buck, kicking, catching just a little dirt with his hooves when he reaches way down, hey, this commercial is *out there.* This is not this little sentimental, you know, group of close friends at the beach enjoying a certain prestige brand of brew together—this is, you have to admit, it's some hairy television. I mean—and the cowboy, he's feeling *pressure,* you know. Waving his arms, whoopeeing, for a while, but, yeah, and then you see his lips going, Hey, Awright, How Much Longer, you know.

"So my sister walks into the dry cleaners—I mean this glue, what does it care? Who's hot, where's pressure—this glue would stick Sinatra to the Chinese army. I mean, so *sue* this glue. It could care less! It just happens to be *very good at its job.*

"So—and what I can't figure, how do they *make* this glue? I mean guys at the plant must be stuck to the walls, you know, and there's shoes stuck all over the floor people had to abandon them, gloves stuck to handles and then other gloves stuck to those gloves, guys are running along behind the delivery trucks yelling Stop! Slow down! glued to the tailgate. . . . All the workers, you know, spending half their day reporting to the infirmary stuck to each other, stuff stuck to their hands, gloves hanging down from their heads where they forgot, reached up to scratch. Breathing that stuff, you know, and years later comes time to remove their like gall bladder—no! Won't come out!

"And you know, it's like somese other things. What if they get in the wrong hands? Friends of mine, guys broke in their place tied them up wanted to know where were their valu-

ables. My friends are not rich, Dana is into shirts some way—
well not really *into* shirts, truthfully, but he works with this
company makes these kind of slippery shirts with scenes on
them you know, you see them in like singles bars? Like not a
pattern but one big scene, right? Deers running or, you know
the French picnic where the women are naked. He works in
the art department of this company, he finds these scenes for
these shirts. Looks in old magazines or something for scenes
for these shirts—he comes home at night, leaves it behind
him, man. He went to Pratt. And Robin is working on her
doctorate in social work, decided to go on and get it—only job
she could find when she finished her master's, she didn't like
the looks of the neighborhood, at all: Hey, life is too short,
she says. But they do all right, they got three and a half rooms
with a view of the entrance of the Holland Tunnel there, but
they don't have a lot of valuables, in the sense of the word,
you know, to begin with. And it so happens, their *complete*
sound system *and* their color TV *and* their pills just got
ripped off that morning. But the guys break in, they don't believe that. And, you know, put yourself in the guys' place:
you might not believe it either. I mean what are the chances
of that? The same day! Twenty to one?

"So what they do, they tie up my friends. Good thing they
don't come armed with Wonder Glue. But what they get, they
find in the kitchen, here's what I mean about wrong hands—
my friends have one of these Miracle Processors, you know.
For when they feel like gourmet, or just want to mush something up fast. Thing shreds/grinds/grates/chops/blends/slices/
dices/juices/pulps/purees/rotisses/foams milk for cappuccino.
Thing does everything but brown and serve. Thing's far out,
my friends've like got these ten or twelve big containers full
of stuff in the refrigerator they mushed up one night they really got into it, they're not sure what the stuff is any more, it's
all colors.

"So these break-in guys get ahold of that thing, and their
first idea, they're going to puree the cat. If my friends don't

tell them where are the valuables. But the cat starts to do this snarl and puffs up real big and goes, like, Puree Your Mama, and they back off. So, they're going to juice the hamster. But the hamster runs up one of them's sleeve and the guy is jumping around, threatening my friends they better call the hamster off—how are you going to call off a hamster? And the hamster eats out through the guy's Yankee jacket he's wearing and gets away.

"So—but now the cat is trying to get the hamster, which is eating way back up into this big batik cushion they entertain on you know, and the cat is reaching up in there dragging out all this foam vinyl stuff or whatever it is all over the floor, and meanwhile the guys that broke in, they're like pureeing, juicing, shredding, grinding my friends' schefflera bush and their spider plants and brownies and like all these cheeses from different countries, and the tongues from their good Adidases, and—my friends have this life-size reproduction of Maynard G. Krebs in their bedroom, just for smiles, you know, but . . . You remember, on the Dobie Gillis show, Dobie Gillis's friend Maynard G. Krebs—this isn't a cardboard, like a flat thing, you know, this is a like I don't know a *scale model*, it's got like all dimensions, how are you going to replace that today? And these guys pulled the nose off that and diced it—you know, personal things. And—they find their T-shirt collection. My friends have got this T-shirt collection you would not believe. Are you ready for this, they have got a Bob Zimmerman T-shirt. A T-shirt, before Dylan changed his name. I mean who knows how old that is, right, and this one guy is going to put their T-shirts in the processor.

" 'That ain't going to work,' the other guy says. 'You're just going to ruin that machine.'

" 'Naw, let's try it,' the first guy says.

" 'Let's take it home and try it,' the other guy says.

"So they just take the machine and the T-shirts, and the MegaStyle— I forgot, my friends have one of these new self-contained multi hair-stylers, it curls/waves/fixes/shapes/

shaves/straightens/Afroes/detangles/dries, you know, really powerful, in like seconds. Hand-held. Carry it in your backpack. It's got this setting, 'Zephyrize,' your hair looks like Art Garfunkel—or you can goof with it, get this kind of lumpy slick-down, like Nixon or your parents or somebody. The break-in guys were using that to *curl* all these things in the apartment. Curled all the pages in my friends' bound volumes of *Crawdaddy*, waved their records, got all their posters down off the walls and curled them up so strong they to this day can't unroll them right—make you cry. Frizzed up this sheepskin coat my friend Dana had—there's this 'Pre-Raphaelitize' setting, I think they used that, kind of looks nice, actually, but you know they conditioned all their macrame, it's just hanging limp; and my friends are going, Aw man, come on—we don't have any valuables, you know.

"Anyway, I was telling you my sister goes in to get her dry cleaning. And—she's lost her slip. Okay, so that means standing around in there while the dry-cleaning guy, looks like a vulture, you know, he's talking to his like eighty-year-old buddy he's always in there they're always like coming down hard on modern days, you know:

" 'That McDonald's.'

" 'I never been in one.'

" 'They got some sweethots in *there*.'

" 'All I got to do is, look in.'

" 'The lowest. The woist.'

" 'Who needs it?'

" 'We're in the last days now. It won't be long.

"You know, and all this is my sister's fault, right, because she lost her slip. So my sister's not going to stand there listening to all this, she starts filing her nails, right, she's got things to do—and she breaks one. So she gets out this Wonder Glue, going to fix it. That's one of the suggested features, this Wonder Glue. It fixes nails.

"So finally the dry-cleaning guy, he's talked about my sister bringing on the end of the world long enough, now he's going to look for her cleaning, got to go through everything on the rack. You know, he's got this moving rack, this conveyor, all the ready dry cleaning hangs on it in order by the slip numbers. Pushes a button, right, and nnnnn-nnnnnnnnnnnnnn-*k'lk*; nn'*k'lk*; nnnnnh-*k'lk*. And there's the right cleaning. It's this *long* conveyor goes way off into the back of the place back where the pressing machine is and this woman is always pressing, *FSHHH!*, and singing blues songs. Anyway, you see all the clothes moving around through there past her like soldiers or something, they kind of swing out like they're keeping their balance coming around the corners, then they nnnnnnnnnnnnnnnnnn, right up behind the counter. Lot of people go in there with their cleaning just so they can watch that thing move.

"So my sister is in the middle of gluing her nail, right, and she's carrying the Wonder Glue with her, going back behind the counter to the conveyor to identify her cleaning. Okay— *so*, in comes this foreign guy looks like he's from India, Iraq, somewhere, carrying an armload of sweaters and little carpets and all, you know, funny three-piece suits and caftans, I don't know, can't see where he's going, this big pile of strange stuff starts to shift, and he trips, cleaning guy sees it and jumps, hits my sister's arm, I don't know my sister don't know the exact sequence you know there was several stages to it I guess but she throws up her hand to catch herself and next thing she knows she's stuck to the conveyor and three, four like scratchy foreign vests and things and this really ugly like scatter rug, man, and all these hangers and clear plastic—well they got most of it off somehow except my sister's hand off the conveyor. She's still stuck there, been three days now and, sure, she and the dry-cleaning guy are suing each other but how's she going to talk to her lawyers you know the dry-cleaning guy is always right there listening! I mean they can stay back in the back as long as the conveyor isn't running, but it's hard to talk back there with *FSHHH!* and 'Gonna bah me uh pistol, Lawd Lawd, Gonna *bah* me uh . . .' you know and as soon as the dry-cleaning guy overhears my sister saying something about him he just pushes the button and brings her around—and he's butting in, arguing, 'Oh no! Oh no you don't! I'm forty-three years in one location!' he's yelling. And you know my sister's always going, 'You just stick to your business,' and he's saying, '*My* business! *My* business! Whose glue was it? Whose glue was it!' Says everything twice you know. And people coming in to pick up their cleaning and giving my sister these funny looks—you know, they're waiting for their cleaning to come around and nnnnnn-nnnnnnnnnnnnn, here comes my sister. With her lawyers running along beside her, when they're there. And the dry-cleaning guy is yelling at his customers, 'I don't even know this woman! I don't even know this woman!' Well, my sister has only been coming in there for like three and a half years is all. But he says he never saw her before, and 'Where is her slip!' he says. 'Where is her slip!' And he's hindering the efforts of the police rescue squad trying to cut a piece out of the conveyor because he claims the conveyor is a landmark! Says it's a landmark, his lawyer got out a temporary injunction, I mean there's no way that's going to hold up, but the rescue-squad guys don't like to cut in there with their saw anyway, there's all these wires and things and anyway it is a nice piece of machinery. And nobody's *seen* the foreign guy, he got away, and nobody can read the labels in his clothes. The lawyers say it opens up all kinds of questions. They're digging on all this. But that's doing my sister a lot of good."

You see? You see what I mean! What we need is to back off from devices and emphasize good shit and common life. A lot of people would be embarrassed to say that. But, hell, I don't care—I'm from Georgia.

More Carters

Martha Carter Kelvinator, 48, Bullard Dam, Georgia, who is married to a top-loading automatic washer. "Yeah, I got the durn thing back here a few years ago and it washed my things s'good, I, well, I just fell in love with it. And my daddy, he's Jimmy's fourth or fifth cousin and all, why he had me marry it. And I haven't regretted it one day in this world.

"Yeah, shore Jimmy come to the wedding, but I don't know what for. He hardly spoke a word to Kel, just stuck his head in at the reception like he had to get somers else. Jimmy's funny. I don't know. I don't think tell the truth Jimmy knows how to just *let loose.*"

Being from Georgia

There on the roads I read Buy your flour meal and meat in Georgia. And I knew that was interesting. Was it prose or was it poetry I knew that it was interesting. Buy your flour meal and meat in Georgia. —GERTRUDE STEIN

For a while after Jimmy arose there was talk about redneck chic, a phrase that reminded me of the expression "nigger heaven." The assumption seemed to be, you weren't going to have to do anything except be Southern to reflect the administration's glory. Persons wearing boots caked with South Georgia slops and pig dung were going to be whooping and rolling and snorting and dancing in the streets of Washington, slaughtering hogs and boiling up big vats of grits out back of the Sans Souci.

I never did think that idea was going to pan out.

"Where are you from?" Northern people ask me socially, with this little glint in their eye.

"Decatur, Georgia, just outside Atlanta," I say in as level a tone as I can.

"I th-o-o-o-*ought* I detected a little accent," they say, and it's the most irritating god damn thing in the world. They get a strange humorous look on their faces.

It's a peculiar sensation. I think I am confessing to something, in their eyes. Something largely amusing, but something which, if they weren't so broad-minded as to feel very nearly complicitous about it, they might feel entitled to describe as low-down.

But it's something they can *handle*—I mean they've seen people on television doing this Southern thing, they know we don't mean half the things we say, just a way we have of talking. ("I love to hear you talk," people have actually said to my *face*.)

I don't know what it is that I am confessing to. If I thought they thought I was confessing to hating niggers, I would tell them I would whip their ass, or get some of my black friends—ask some of my black—some of my friends who happen to be black—to whip their ass if they didn't take it back. If I thought they thought I was confessing to being barefooted, I would get right up there at the dinner table or wherever it is and show them my shoes. Not that I'm wearing shoes for any Northern person's benefit.

But don't worry, I ain't going to complain, that ain't my people's way. We don't let on. (We just send complete fools up to the Congress and let them get even for us.)

I am talking the way it feels right in my mouth. "Pore," for instance, is a lot better way of pronouncing the word *poor* than "pooor." When you say "pooor," you purse your lips like a rich person. When you say "pore," you say it the way poor folks and poor old souls and poorhouse residents say it when they say, "This is a pore excuse for living."

Certain Southern vowels are distinguished things. Have you ever heard Jimmie "The Singing Brakeman" Rodgers sing, in "Blue Yodel Number 10":

> I ain't no shiek man,
> Don't try to vamp no girls.
> I ain't no shiek man,
> Don't try to vamp no girls.
> It's my regular grinding
> Gets me by in this world.

Only he don't say "grinding." He says "griiiiiin-din." That long flat pure gristly semi-nasal *i*, like the French ending *-in*, only fuller-bodied, coming from hard up against the right rear corner of the roof of your mouth.

There are notes that can't be struck, things that can't be

said, in Northern, because Northern tends to throw a little bit of a long *e* in behind the *i*, so that "Well I be god damn" sounds like "Well i.e. be god damn."

The word "on" *deserves* to be pronounced "own," to rhyme with—therefore to help counterbalance—"moan," "bone," "alone." What satisfaction is there in crying "Get it *ahn*"? And in the pale lexicon of respectable English there is no such word as "caint." "Caint you see-ee ... that evenin sun go down ..." You want to say "can't" there?

On the other hand. I know. I knew it before I ever left Georgia: there are Southern vowels that to persons of intelligence are a pain in the bowels. "Wa'il, *yay*is" for "Well, yes": that kind of thing. However much you can't abide the self-satisfied self-ignorance that crops up in some Southern vowels, I bet you can abide it better than I can. You let me worry about that, and you go worry about the self-satisfied self-ignorance that crops up in some New York, Long Island, Boston, California, Ohio vowels.

I admit it, I have done some accommodating. I have about quit saying "faingers" for "fingers," and have gradually modulated a good ways from "git," on purpose—at least in such expressions as "Perhaps I am missing the point, but I can't quite put my finger on what you are getting at in this passage." It's a sad commentary on the way people judge people's minds, but it's true that if I were to say "my fainger on what you are gitting at," it might suggest that I actually *was* missing the point.

I have had people back down home accuse me of losing my accent. And then I get off the plane on the other end and people are saying, "You're not from the *city*, heeya. I *thot* I heard a little ..."

Maybe Northern people think I'm trying to sing when I talk. I know that everywhere I turn, Northern people in their twenties are trying to sound like Ray Charles or Mother Maybelle Carter. As if it were just a *sound* you can pick up and use. It used to be, people stood in their parlors in evening gowns and sang soprano solos about fairies in the bottom of their garden. Now they sit around cross-legged with guitars and try to sound like Southern people—niggers and rednecks, in other words—complaining that the boll weevil and the pater-rollers are going to get them. Listen, Northern people. The boll weevil and the pater-rollers aren't studying you.

And it isn't just amateurs. It's a lot of people you see performing in public. I'm not talking about the Beatles and the Rolling Stones ripping off Chuck Berry and all—they filtered it through Liverpool and hallucinogens and what have you, and, in a sense, advanced it. I'm talking about people who earnestly pooch their lips out and double their chins and twist their mouths all around so they sOWund lak sumbuddy who knows Jesus—I mean the old tough sweet Jesus—and drinks bad whiskey and has got grit in his or her craw.

Consider Janis Joplin. Janis Joplin didn't start getting good until she stopped trying to be an hysterical Bessie Smith, which was a contradiction in terms, and started sounding like her upbringing, brought up to date, on her last album, *Pearl*, notably in "Me and Bobby McGee." You had a real person singing in that album. She started out, you know, in Austin, Texas, singing "Silver Threads and Golden Needles" at Kenneth Threadgill's gas-station bar, which is closed now but where I once had such a good time listening to country music with hippies and professors and men in tractor-company caps, all mixed together, that I nearly got squashed underneath the bare hub of a Hungarian man in the seed business's car at two o'clock in the morning, helping him change his tire after I'd knocked his glass of whiskey over twice.

You're supposed to sound like the way you grow up. Advancing it along and remixing it, up to a point.

But why should I have to explain all that to everybody just because I'm from Georgia? In Harlem, I gather from the novels of Chester Himes, "to send someone to Georgia," or "to Georgia someone," means to take his money and still not fuck him, or to fuck her and still not give her the money.

That sounds about right. Georgia is a place you get sent to or you come from or you march through or you drive through. Convicts settled it. It's got some fine red dirt, hills, vegetables, and folks, but I don't believe anybody has ever dreamed of growing up and moving to Georgia.

But now the President of the United States is from Georgia. It's true that he has been snubbed by a freshman congressman from South Dakota, and it's true that he has a pretty mealy-mouth version of a Georgia accent. But he is the President, and he is from Georgia. And here I am in the state of Carter-busters, of Ted Kennedy and Tip O'Neill, of Massachusetts—a cold state, settled by Puritans, where it snowed so hard one day in *May* a few years ago that the snow piled up on the green leaves and blossoms and broke off big spring limbs all over town, *boom, boom, boom,* until it sounded like a war.

I missed the war, in Vietnam, the war which Southerners remained steadfastly in favor of, according to the polls, long after the rest of the nation had given up on the idea of destroying something to save it (although that is pretty much what the rest of the nation did to the South during the sixties and seventies of the *last* century). The war which a Texas President and a Georgia Secretary of State were able to maintain such an enthusiasm for. The war which was like pro football, in that mostly niggers and rednecks and Slovenians fought it and the rest of us watched.

Well, I say I missed it. I was in the Army when it started building up. I thought I had resisted the draft the only way a healthy American who didn't feel too spiritually pure could, by going through ROTC. I was from Georgia, I didn't know any better at the time. Don't get me wrong: I made bad grades in ROTC, I never shined my brass. But I think anti-military Americans ought to take part in their Army, so they can keep an eye on it.

The closest I came to fighting was in Georgia, Fort Benning, during basic training. We were simulating being on patrol in enemy territory and I was patrol leader. I was having a fairly good time tramping through the piney woods when somebody simulating a local alien farmer jumped out and started yelling in a simulated foreign language. If he kept it up, he'd alert the enemy. It was my job to deal with him. What I did was grab him around the shoulders and shake him, in a largely simulated way. He kept yelling. He looked highly dissatisfied, and probably wished that I were the one yelling and he the one doing the silencing. I tried to think of a way to argue with him. He was a big old country-looking boy with an Adam's apple that jerked.

I guess I was supposed to put my forearm across his throat from behind and throttle off his voice, something like that, but that went against my grain. I don't want to stifle dissent. I always want to hear what people are yelling. I'm afraid I'll miss something. Maybe I was supposed to simulate shooting him, but I hadn't anticipated doing anything like that, on such a personal basis, in the Army. This was a good while before anybody had heard of Lieutenant Calley, the Southern boy who was the GI Joe of his time.

"Well, god damn it, do *something*. Hit him, throw dirt on him, mail him to Houston," my interior voice exclaimed.

"*Sh!*" I said to the simulated farmer, and a disgusted observer appeared out of the bushes.

The next thing I knew I was part of the war effort in New York City, in the Quartermaster Corps, phasing out bases. Then I went back to Georgia to work for the Atlanta *Journal*, which wasn't a real activist institution.

It's true that there was a tradition at the Atlanta papers of anti-redneck editorials. I was proud one afternoon to receive a telegram that said: "COONLOVER [RALPH] MCGILL, COONLOVER [GENE] PATTERSON, COONLOVER [REESE] CLEGHORN, NOW COONLOVER BLOUNT. HELL WILL BURN YOUR TRAITOR SOULS." The old boys in the pressroom were always jibing at some of us writers for the liberalism in the slugs of type they had to set, looking us in the eye as one old boy to another and saying, "You know you don't *believe* that shit," sincerely assuming in some cases that we were being duped or bought off by Communists or Rockefellers. But when Reese Cleghorn left the paper to work in civil rights, certain old editorial hands were heard to say, "Well, Reese has got the nigger sickness." Said it sort of tongue-in-cheek but not entirely.

I got a column, and wrote favorably about Tom Hayden and Stokely Carmichael and unfavorably about white sheriffs and Senator Talmadge. I was dimly aware of Jimmy Carter as someone Lester Maddox had brushed off in a Democratic primary.

I wanted to go to New York. Writing for a Georgia outlet is like putting on skits for your parents: you can only go so far. I would sit there at my desk and pound out things which, though I knew they were insufficient to the historical moment, I knew would elicit hysterical phone calls anyway. And Mr. Jack Spalding, the editor, who had a whole lot of children, would stop by on his way home and say things in a fatalistic vein:

"I've got to go home and take charge of the unit. Marilyn and Charles have gone to the allergist to see what makes Charles sneeze, turn blue, and then purple—I mean John. I hope it's cats. Charles is the one that's down with the virus." And somebody would call up Hugh Park, who wrote columns of local anecdotes, country lore, and criminal-court scenes, and ask him what to do about a howling dog, and Hugh would answer, "Sqwu*eeeeze* his little lar-ynx." Most of us younger *Journal* staffers would chafe at how untroublesome to the white-business, Atlanta power structure the paper was, and it sure was. But some of Hugh Park's columns have held up better over the years than most issue-oriented reporting:

There was a clean neat woman with her hair drawn tidily back of her head and three of the sweetest-faced, saddest-eyed children you ever saw.

Testimony was that the husband and father, a florid man who wore double-lens glasses, had beaten his shy 16-year-old daughter while drunk and had called them all obscene names.

His wife's voice was broken-hearted as she talked to him. "Will you quit drinking, Daddy?" she asked. "Come back to us. We need you and you need us. You haven't had your medicine for a day and a half now."

She stroked the back of his neck while she talked. He held his head down, his face red with blood and his eyes glassy. He looked like he might suffer from high blood pressure.

"I did wrong," he said in a dead remote voice to no one in particular. "Did wrong . . ." He trailed off, staggered and almost fell. It was as if he had a small stroke.

"I'll let you go this time," said Judge Little hurriedly.

Paulding Countians became as alert as their pioneer ancestors, particularly at night, after hunters found what doctors believed to be a severed woman's hand.

The hunters, Spurgeon, Ralph and Bobby Lawrence, brought the hand to Sheriff J. K. (Bob) Shipp. "It looked just like the hand of a medium-sized woman," said the sheriff. "We were disturbed because a girl here . . . had been reported missing."

The sheriff drove to Atlanta . . . where the hand was examined by the state crime laboratory. There it was determined that it was the right rear foot of a bear.

Sounds incredible, doesn't it, that anyone would think for a moment that a bear's paw was a woman's hand? "The hair had come off," explained the sheriff, "and the flesh was pink and natural looking just like a woman's. The claws were also missing. Without claws, a bear's paw is the size and shape of a woman's hand."

Sheriff Shipp believes that the bear may have belonged to a Paulding County farmer who died not too long ago. "He raised them kind of like you would hogs," he said, "although I guess he considered them pets more than anything else. When he died I expect this bear escaped and either hunters shot him or dogs got him. Somebody or something got his claws. There is a little mystery there."

A stout black woman was accused of disrupting the rhythm of a dance floor by standing in the middle of it holding a butcher knife.

She said that people often took advantage of her. "One time," she declared, "my common law husband and his mother caught me when I was asleep and rooted my wig in my head."

Things like that were going on in Georgia during the war. I did walk in some marches and fault the war in the paper. Those activities were easier, and more gratifying and less mysterious, than trying to deal with a yelling simulated alien farmer. Often I felt bad about not having joined the counter-culture. But, I don't know, I had all these Oxford-cloth shirts I didn't want to throw away.

I was twenty-five or twenty-six and owned a forty-five-year-old house with a four- or five-year-old first marriage in it, and the house was up on concrete blocks, and so was the marriage, and I would crawl underneath the whole thing and lie on my back in the Georgia dirt ("I tell you what, boy. You ain't done *diddly* yet") and make up Georgia limericks, which I put in my column. The Georgia limerick proved popular with all stripes of Georgian. Its first line had to end with a Georgia town—Meigs, Clyo, Jakin, Gough, Luxomni, Subligna, Leaf, Elmodel, Relee, Tubize, Plumb, Climax, Glory . . .

> Wade L. McWilliams of Adel
> Remarked to his wife, "I'm afraid El-
>   Lenora that you've
>   Gone too far!" She said "Move
> Your feet and don't bother me, Wade L."

> A modern young pastor of Baxley
> Shepherds his flock rather laxly.
>   When one of his stewards
>   Took off for Lourdes,
> He said, "I don't care what he does, axly."

> A girl of the Marshes of Glynn
> Sank in them, as well as in sin,
>   One day when her boat

Would not stay afloat
with one hundred and twenty-four men.

There was an old lady of Peach
Whose grasp exceeded her reach.
　　She'd walk down an aisle
　　Of produce and smile
And walk out with three pounds of each.

A lonesome old soul of McRae
Sat home saying, "There ain't no wae."
　　Till a lady from Bimini
　　Slid down his chimini
And he granted, "Oh, well, there mae."

I was keenly aware that these clouded twenties of mine, more widely known as the sixties, lacked what people were calling relevance. I *kind of* got involved in the life of my time every now and then, but it never seemed to be of a piece with what everybody was sharing nationally in the media. It wasn't *in* the media. It was in *Georgia*.

With fellow Atlanta reporters, including David Nordan (to whom it was, years later, that Jimmy Carter would say about Ted Kennedy, "I don't have to kiss his ass"), I attended what was expected to be an urban disorder, but it didn't work out. I wore somebody's army helmet, the kind you call a steel pot, because all the hard hats were taken. But nobody threw anything at us, anyway. The scene was a housing project, Dixie Hills. I watched a SNCC field worker teach some of the residents how to do the power handshake, and heard him declare that the only good white man was Charles Joseph Whitman, who had shot a bunch of white men.

I admired SNCC. But I felt like a fool just standing there with my mouth hanging open, listening to somebody extol the shooting of a category of people into which I fell. "What about Schwerner and Chaney and Goodman?" was what I wanted to say. But I didn't feel like I deserved to invoke them. And I couldn't remember which two of them were white.

So I started arguing with the SNCC worker about Abraham Lincoln. The SNCC guy himself had brought Lincoln up, saying, "You think *he* was a good white man? He said he'd rather have a union with slavery than no union at all."

"People who get things done are always going to be saying compromising things," was the best I could think of to say.

It wasn't much of an argument, and who was I to be arguing with the Movement, anyway? But I wanted to argue with *somebody* besides white dumb-asses. Right before the rednecks shot Michael Schwerner, one of them asked him, "Are you the nigger-lover?" and he answered, "Sir, I understand how you feel." If I had been there—well, of course I like to think I would have been trying to stop the rednecks and getting shot myself, but I might have seized the opportunity to argue with Schwerner, to say: "You're in the *right* here, of course, but I'm not sure you do know how this old boy here *feels*."

Recently there appeared a TV drama about incidents from those years in the South. After watching this drama, a nine-year-old boy I was sitting with at a Formica table asked me, "Which were you in—the Klan or the FBI?"

"I was just in Georgia," I said.

Then one weekend in 1969 I went to visit my sister Susan—who is about half a generation younger than I am—at the University of Georgia. Word came that kids had been shot at Kent State, and we seized the university.

I didn't want the university. But there I was hunkering in the street outside the chancellor's house, blocking traffic and yelling, "One, Two, Three, Four, We Don't Want Your Fucking War" with everybody else, and having a big time.

When we surrounded the main administration building, the chancellor, who was originally a veterinarian, came out on the balcony to reason with us, and there was this girl student standing right next to him hollering "BULLSHIT" after every sentence he spoke. Right next to me was a youth who regarded me suspiciously because I looked a little old to be doing all this.

"Are you a teacher?" he asked.

I pointed to Susan and said, "No, I'm just a brother."

He said, "We are *all* brothers here."

I enjoyed it. But I didn't feel that it spoke to my needs. To tell the truth, I think anybody who sticks his head up within half a mile of National Guardsmen with rifles is as crazy as anybody who sends National Guardsmen with rifles to a campus in April.

But that's just me, I'm from Georgia. I never did want a revolution. I just wanted to stop feeling so *wrong*.

I wrote only one protest song during the sixties:

> It used to be so nice to be a white man,
> It looked like then the Lord was on our side,
> But I don't think I know a single white man
> Who hasn't recently sat down and cried.
>   Ohhhh. From De-troit to the Fertile Crescent,
>   I am feeling obsolescent.
>   Lift the white man's burden from me, Lord.
>   Welfare got Cadillacs
>   I got to pay for and
>   I can't pay for my Fooooord:
> Lift the white man's burden from me Lord.
>
> I thank the Lord our President's still a white man,
> But I don't think that he can pull us through.
> There must be fifty Nigros in the Congress
> And there is only one Spiro Agnew.
>   Ohhhh. From Ocean Hill to Yokohama,
>   Non-white powr's gonna get my mama,
>   Lift the white man's burden from me, Lord.

Think about China, all them
   millions and millions comin'
     at you in a hooooorde:
Lift the white man's burden from me, Lord.

They've just about took over athaletics,
'Cause whites can't run as fast or jump as high.
It always used to be we didn't need to,
But I'm afraid we're goin' to, by and by.
   Ohhhhhh. It started with the Brooklyn Dodgers,
      Now we're takin' colored lodgers,
      Lift the white man's burden from me, Lord.
      My boy Billy played
         four years of basket-
            ball and never scoooored:
Lift the white man's burden from me, Lord.

They're all you ever see now on the TV,
They've even got them reading us the news.
And I thought things was awful on the TV
Back when all we ever got was Jews.
   Ohhhhh. Bill Cos-by and Diahann Carroll,
      They've got white folks over a barrel.
      Lift the white man's burden from me, Lord.
      Lookin' all loosey and goosey and juicy, makin'
         whites look
            stiff as a boooooard:
Lift the white man's burden from me, Lord.

In Vietnam they're short and don't wear helmets,
And yet it seems we just can't win that war.
I think we ought to hit another campus,
For there we know just what we're fighting for.
   Ohhhh. From Amherst to the Mekong Delta,
      Lord, why don't you give me shelta?
      Lift the white man's burden from me Lord.
      Looks like to me you'd start

> comin' on in with that
> terrible swift swoooooord:
> Lift the white man's burden from me Lord.

It was the best I could do. I was in Georgia.

Then, all of a sudden in the seventies, a Georgian made a real before-God run at the White House, and I had an *interest*.

More Carters

A. Don and E. Don Carter, 39, who are the "Two-Headed Four-Armed Three-Legged Gospel-Singing Man" in a traveling show throughout most parts of the country.

"Aw, we ham't seen a sign of Jimmy since the big family union back in '48. I don't think Jimmy's too innersted in us. I say that 'cause, well, it's sorta cool between us. E. Don voted against him."

"I did not neither, A. Don."

"Well, yes, you sure as the H-word did. I tried to tell you, it can't hurt us in the bookings, having kin in the White House. Thought he might summon us on up to appear. Kindly showcase us. Done us a world of good nationally."

"*Well, I just liked Mr. Ford.*"

"Uh-huh, you liked him. I know. E. Don, he votes the man. But this time it wadn't *professional*, E. Don. We got to think of our*sef* sometime. Hear?

"And I tell you what else. I guarantee you—you think old Gerald R. Ford cares two diddlies whether you like him or not? Well? H'm? E. Don?

"I swanny, E. Don, sometimes getting something through to you is like . . . I don't know what."

South of the Border

We don't favor one region over another. We don't ever put a partisan cast on what we do. We just try to build coalitions.
          —ANN WEXLER, Carter Aide

You say Jimmy's administration has been just too tacky and awful.

I am tempted to say it hasn't been tacky and awful enough. Well, that's not right, either. What it hasn't been is *profoundly* and *tellingly* tacky and awful enough.

For instance, you probably agree with me that Jimmy shouldn't have gone down to Mexico and stood up before that country's President and leading citizens and reminisced about getting Montezuma's Revenge. That was just dumb. And yet not simple-minded enough to be graceful. I'm surprised someone didn't jump up and yell, in Spanish, "You want to see some *revenge*, motherfucker . . . ?"

But you probably think Jimmy should have come up with a quote from Unamuno or somebody, something classy in Spanish.

Curate de la afección de preocuparte como aparezcas a los demás. Cuidate solo . . . de la idea que de ti Dios tenga. [Cure yourself of the inclination to bother about how you look to other people. Be concerned only . . . with the idea God has of you.]

You're maybe thinking, "That ought to go over pretty well with some Mexicans." In other words, America is saying, "Hey, don't worry about how *we* think of you. Go ahead and just be Mexicans in the sight of the Lord. Or *Dios*, you call him."

No—see, you're not considering this, because you think

you've covered yourself by quoting Unamuno. But, in fact, that would be a *condescending* thing to say to a crowd of Mexicans, and that's just what we want to avoid. The thing is, we're very strong in the field of condescension-avoidance when we've got a Georgia President, because a Georgian hasn't got any real business condescending to anybody. As Jimmy showed, *sort of,* by making a more vulgar remark than any Mexican ever has, even in the movies.

But if he'd been more *vigorously* vulgar, he might have gone further toward making the point that America used to make internationally: that *nobody's* got any business condescending to anybody. Here's what I wish Jimmy had done. I wish he had shown no *hint* of Anglo *oblige.* I wish he had spoken more deeply from his roots and said, "Hey! Y'all think America has some kind of simply overbearing attitude toward people, but the truth is that a lot of Americans have been scared *shitless* by Mexicans. If you have never found yourself sitting on the ground outside a Mexican entertainment facility in the middle of the night *terrible* drunk and missing your wallet and all your friends and one of your shoes and here come five grimacing *federales,* you haven't had the full American *or* Mexican experience. Of course, I have never been in that situation myself but some friends of my brother Billy's have." Then Jimmy might have swung into a couple of snatches from Billy Joe Shaver's country song, "Ain't No God in Mexico":

> Ain't no God in Mexico
> Ain't no way to understand
> How that border-crossing feeling
> Makes a fool out of a man
>
> If I'd never felt the sunshine
> Hell I would not miss the rain.
> If my feet would fit a railroad track
> Then I guess I'd been a train.

Ain't no God in Mexico
Ain't no comfort in the can
When you're down in Matamoros
Getting busted by the man.

If I'd never felt the sunshine
Well I would not miss the rain
If I hadn't been railroaded
Well I guess I'd be a train.

What the hell. The Mexicans have got a lot of oil. See how *they* like being called "the man." Let's *us* be the pore crazy souls in the court of world opinion once in a while. Let everybody give *us* a little slack.

It's not as though we *aren't* pore crazy souls. Jimmy is one. I am.

And it's not just because we're both from Georgia.

More Carters

Anonymous Carter, somewhere in Delaware, telephone caller. "They ringing these little silver bells at me in the street, you realize. What I don't *know* is, is it tied in with this A-rab thing or not. I tell you what I bleev, I bleev it's stepped up since Jimmy come in. I hate to say that, but—I bleev Jimmy got me wired up and is listening to the A-rabs thoo me. Is what I *bleev*, now. Jimmy won't *tell* me that.

"And you know they *bought* Bert Lance's bank!"

A Many-Angled Thing

[Traditional Southern] ideas are slowly dying like a frog in warm water. You throw a frog in hot *water and he'll jump out of there. But you put him in* warm *water, and soften him up a little bit, and he'll just sit there while you slowly cook him.*

> —JAMES A. GRAHAM, North Carolina Commissioner of Agriculture, quoted in Fred Powledge, *Journeys Through the South*

People have offered all kinds of suggestions. "Maybe if he'd bring in a few less Georgians," said the proprietor of the Granite Candy Shop in the fall of '79, "and—I hate to say it—a few more intellectuals."

No, that wouldn't help. For one thing—talk about *strange times*—never have so many intellectuals, or *any* intellectuals, been willing to admit publicly that they didn't know what the President ought to do either, other than show more leadership.

For another thing—say Einstein is born again and brought into the administration. Einstein is not from Georgia, right? Einstein is an intellectual, right?

"Alfred, I am proud of you. Rosalynn and I both think the world of your theory. [President, Einstein embrace. Press is ushered out.]

"It's fine for we who are physicists. Now our task is to examine this great theory on all sides, so as to make an adequate, comprehensive assessment of how relativity will be perceived throughout our country. By the forces of labor. By Catholics. By the digital-watch industry, whose leaders have been of great help to me as your President, although when I lived in Plains they would not have given me the time of day.

"How it will be perceived, in short, by all the many different elements of our society that hold sincerely differing ideas of what is good for the country, and for our universe as well. We need a relativity, as I have said before, just as generous and unselfish and competent and fiscally sound as . . . I am. I invite you to confer with me and with Hamilton Jordan, and with Bob Strauss, and with Pat Caddell and Gerald Rafshoon, on this great question that is before us today. God bless you, Alfred."

The next thing you know—perhaps at a party for the cast of *Hair*, as Brzezinski is boogieing and asking anyone who will listen, "Who's Zbigniew name in national security affairs?"—Einstein gets smashed and launches an absolutist tirade. Washington abuzz; columnists taking cheap shots ("The latest chuckle along the Potomac is that Einstein thought he understood relativity until he met the President's relatives"); Einstein diminished, relativity compromised.

That seems to be the lot of a remarkable number of people who get involved with Jimmy Carter: some kind of reduction, some kind of fall. Remember when his Washington *pastor* was asked to resign for "alleged questionable conduct while giving spiritual counsel" to a young woman member of his flock? "It's rather complicated," said one of the church's deacons. "It's a many-angled thing."

I don't doubt for one minute it was many-angled. So is the whole question of the Jimmy presidency. *One* interpretation is that Satan or Godless Communism or the Trilateral Commission or the Bavarian Illuminati or whatever you want to call it said, "Hey! Here's something we could do. Take some poor son of a bitch from *Georgia* and make him President."

I don't believe in this Power myself. I feel not only that people these days have no control over their lives but that nobody else does either: "I think that Life's Too Sweet a Thing (to Know What It's Doing to Me)." But let's just theorize that a Power is at work in our society replacing good shit with bad shit—the Power that developed the Mammoth Disembodied

Corporation, which either supplies you with bad shit (sales) or treats you like it (service), and vouchsafes you no one to complain to who is exactly responsible, or even interested. The Power's corporations fill the stores, the ether, the prints, the landscape with fingerprintless fabrications; have just about ruined country music, family life, and groceries.

But the Power was a little bit worried about the South. The South has a way of *personalizing* things. *Literalizing* things. Its Baptists *talk to Jesus*; if they get a chance they will take a shot at converting the Buddhist President of South Korea. ("This is the kind of thing," Jimmy said after *he* urged the as-yet-unassassinated Park Chung Hee to consider finding Jesus, "that can happen between Presidents and everyone.") Its sorriest white people *parade around in white sheets*. That's a Southerner's idea of being faceless; wearing a hood. With a *point* on it.

How are you ever going to entirely denature a region like that? You might say that the dethronement of cotton, by polyester in the marketplace and by soybeans in the fields, might denature the South.

> I wish I wa-as in the land of soybeans,
> Justice there's just like Judge Roy Bean's,
> Look away, look away . . .

But I don't know. Many places down in the Delta that used to be cotton fields are now woods. That means deer roam where there used to be weevils. That's not bad. And recently in the window of a discount center in the Florida Panhandle, I saw a big sign that said: FASHIONABLE POLYESTER—$1.99 A YARD.

Only in the South would people think polyester was *fashionable*. That's almost enough to embarrass the corporations that wrap our populace in oily rags. They don't want you to get a *lift* when you pull on a cheap pair of pants. They want you to be thinking, "Well, I am wearing pants that feel like cheap seat covers but I guess that's all I deserve." Southern people can be thinking things like that and still be full of beans. I have known Southern people who gloried in, and on, cheap seat covers. There is probably an old boy somewhere in the South busy right this minute incorporating artificial fibers into a personal handwoven country song about his copious girlfriend:

> She's my Sugarbaby,
> She's my pride,
> She's all Polly Esther
> And a yard wide.
>
> I doubt she'll ever wrinkle bad,
> She's got a kind of shine,
> She's all Polly Esther
> And two-thirds mine.

So it took a special effort to drag the South into the order of things—to make sure Southern people got not only plenty of bad shit but along with it a sinking sensation. So, a Cracker President. A Mississippian would have been basest and best, but Mississippi is still a little far out. Georgia sounds almost as funky and is a good deal more malleable; it's got Corporate Atlanta in it.

So find a Georgia Candidate. A Georgia Candidate with a proudly no-account Georgia brother. A Georgia Candidate whose Georgia press relations man has the same first name as the boy in *The Yearling* and is actually more flip publicly than the press. A Georgia Candidate whose top Georgia lieutenant has the same last name as a holy river and is likely to take a few sips and act childish. A Georgia Candidate whose key black supporter is a Georgian who wears nice suits and says things like "When the lights go out, folks will steal." A Georgia Candidate whose Georgia banker friend pulls so-called money down out of the big-city air (where the Power wants to keep it) and turns it into liberal, actually spendable, confederate credit for his neighbors in Calhoun. Take a bunch of Georgians like that and *let them "run the country."*

When Jimmy got nominated I figured, oh boy, there was going to be a crying need for able young Crackro-American writers—who were *from* Georgia but *outside* Georgia, who could sort of intermediate, could tell Georgia about *anomie* and the rest of the world about rooster pepper sausage. It wasn't long, however, before the burden seemed to be on me to prove that a Georgian could do anything right.

"The Georgians around him," the newspapers call them. (Pete Hamill in the New York *Daily News* calls them "those hambones.") Around Nixon, it was Germans. Germans and white Southerners, of course, are the only ethnic groups left that you can, in all seriousness, respectably disparage. How would you like to be left alone in a category with a bunch of Germans! (Just kidding, Germans.)

The time when nobody in the *world* knows how to administer America *would* be the time when Georgians get a chance at it. Hey, let me just say this: Georgia produced Tyrus Raymond Cobb, Ray Charles, and Joanne Woodward. Oliver Hardy. Otis Redding. Margaret Dumont. James "Sex Machine" Brown.

(I might also mention that the President of Equatorial Guinea not long ago had a group of his enemies hanged while loudspeakers blared the tune "Those Were the Days." And people complain that *Jimmy* is tacky.)

You see, you take a white Southerner, ethnically identified with several forms of out-and-out good shit: manure, shit-kicking music, collard greens. And then you contrive to have him elected President by the votes not only of other Crackers but also of black Americans, who are perhaps the people in the world most likely to be believed when they say of something: "Hey. This is some *good* shit." You set up this richly, organically fecund mandate, and then, of course, you discredit it.

It helped that the Georgia President was *not a good old boy.*

The concept of "good old boy," I guess, is something we are going to have to thrash out.

I am not going to sit here and deny that there is something vulnerable about the expression "good old boy."

You wouldn't call Wayne a dunce
But he ain't got much grace.
He had a mustache once
But it didn't fit on his face.

But he's a gooooood ole bawy.
A gooooood ole bawy,
You just knawy
'S a good ole bawy
By th'expression on his face.
He's a gooooood ole bawy.
You just knawy
'S a good old bawy
And a credit to his race.

But among those who coined the phrase—as opposed to those for whom it is a pop derogation—the accent falls on "good" and "old" and "boy."

"You know what? He's a good . . . old . . . boy."

"He sho is."

It's like "good old wagon," or "good old dog." You might say, "He's a good old feller," or "a good old guy," or "a right good old worker," or "a pretty good old bail bondsman." Or, "He was a good old Daddy to us boys."

"Good old boy" means pretty much the same as "mensch." And properly speaking, it does not come welded together. You can say, "He's a pretty sorry old boy," or "I don't trust that old boy no more than a snake."

It's true that "old boy" is a unit. You might say, "When you give a horse some coffee, it affects him the way a couple of beers will an old boy." "Old boy" in redneck English is akin to "dude" or "motherfucker" in black English, only it is always male and human. Whereas you say, "I'm going to eat *all* this dude" or "*all* this motherfucker," referring to, say, a pie, you wouldn't say, "I'm going to eat all this old boy." (Not "*old* boy." You might say, "I'm going to eat all this boy.") But just as you would say, "Dude was walking down the street one day with his eyes closed and here come, *wham*, a full can of chili from somewhere," or "Motherfucker was walking down the street and here come, *wham*, a full can of chili from somewhere"—by the same token, you would say, "Old boy was walking down the road and here come, *wham*, a full can of chili from somewhere."

A term that is more generally equivalent to "dude" or "motherfucker" is "sumbitch": "I'm going to eat *all* this sumbitch." You can say, "He was a good old son of a bitch" (in the testimonial case, there is no contraction), just as you can say, "He was a good old motherfucker."

You will note that all three terms, "old boy," "sumbitch," and "motherfucker," are *filial*. The assumption in redneck English is that anybody who is a man appreciates being called a boy (and anybody who is a woman appreciates being called a girl, and anybody who is rich appreciates being called poor). So if somebody is a solid, reliable, unpretentious, stand-up, companionable, appropriately loose, joke-sharing feller, with a working understanding of certain bases of head-to-head equal footing, you say, "You know, he's a good old boy."

All right. In those bases of equal footing, limitations do abound. Generally speaking, it is harder to be recognized as a good old boy if you have a passion for racial justice, or an interest in, say, art, than if you have a passion for stock-car racing or an interest in, say, veterinary medicine—harder, even, than if you have a passion for racial *in*justice, or an interest in, say, getting drunk and bringing a live alligator into a public place to see what will happen.

But it is not entirely bad to have people around who forthrightly remind us that at the edge of everyone's world map should be written, "There Be Alligators." And at any rate, since "good old boy" is almost as flexible a term as "virtuous person," we lose something if we let it become a buzz word, a stereotype. (Forget about the alligator. I shouldn't have brought the alligator up.) A good old boy is not inevitably a dumb violent peckerwood, in national terms. There is demonstrably such a thing as a good old boy who is sharp and peaceable; and there is construably such a thing as a good old progressive, in national terms. Conceivably, a Cracker President might have confounded the Power by proving himself to be a good old rooted pluralist innovative libertarian boy—thereby panning out even better than the Cracow pontiff.

The trouble is, Jimmy is not as good an old boy as the Pope is. I don't know; for a while I thought maybe Jimmy was doing a Milo Pennington. Sometimes reporters will talk about "doing a Columbo," which means acting dumb like Lieutenant Columbo the TV detective, who is not as dumb as he acts. In Jimmy's autobiography, *Why Not the Best*, Milo Pennington appears as a man who is less inept than he acts. He is a Texas peanut farmer who goes around with Jimmy winning people for Christ in Lock Haven, Pa., right after Jimmy's first gubernatorial campaign has failed. Milo, Jimmy writes, "did the work and talking. It seemed to me he was the most inept person I had ever known in expressing himself. He fumbled and didn't know what to say and I thought, 'Oh, I could do much better. . . .' But he had done it before and he was a deeply committed person," and Milo Pennington converted fifteen or twenty whole Lock Haven families. So maybe Jimmy figured that ineptness was the new eloquence.

But it didn't work for him, so he started using hand gestures. "This was an extraordinary performance by this man," said Sam Donaldson of ABC News after Jimmy's '79 energy speech. "I mean, he gave it a heck of a shot. . . . He used gestures."

Well. There are theatrical good old boys, and bullshitting good old boys, Penningtonian good old boys, maybe even pontificating good old boys, and Lord knows there are good old boys who will gesture. But I don't think there can be a posturing good old boy.

Jimmy's mother is a good old girl—who went into the Peace Corps without losing her nature. I wanted to hug old Miss Lillian the morning after Jimmy won, when she appeared on TV waiting for her son the President down at the Plains depot, and she cried, "I'll have to leave the church!"

That's what Southern ladies jocularly cry when they do something quaintly scandalous. It's like saying, "This is the end of me!" What she was doing was wearing a JIMMY FOR PRESIDENT T-shirt out in public. It is refreshing in this day and age to hear someone acknowledge that a T-shirt with a message on it is a disreputable thing to dress in. But mainly I liked what she shouted out because I thought of it as a nice touch. All my life I have been staring dully at trumped-up white Southern characters in movies and on TV, and now here was a real one.

She was happy, full of herself, and justified. And evaluating things in personal local terms, terms indigenous to where she *lived*—not in terms of that unspoken presumably zeitgeisty cut-rate-liberal-tradition national-media mainstream of consciousness which shifts constantly—which alters when it alteration finds—but which is assumed by national mediasts and complaisant readers/viewers to be the drift of Understanding Up to This Moment.

Traditionally, Southern politicians have been bullfrogs on lily pads, or old mossy logs. Personally I prefer politicians to be bullfrogs and logs, as long as I don't have to apply to them for an easement. For some time I was confounded by Jimmy because he wouldn't hold still so that I, a media guy, could wash over him; he wouldn't wash; he was washing over me.

And over other people. Jimmy's ascendancy drained, permanently or temporarily, the juices from a lot of big frogs. He pointedly won without courting Mayor Daley or the Kennedys, although Jimmy had ridden a long way on his supposed resemblance to Jack. He diluted the influence of Senator Herman Talmadge, took over and neutralized the constituency of George Wallace, soaked up the legacy of Martin Luther King. He established the irrelevance of Hubert Humphrey. He deposed Henry Kissinger. (And his region caused the humiliation and shedding of Nelson Rockefeller.) Jimmy made capital out of Bob Dylan, the Allman Brothers, and the once-wonderful Cracker poet James Dickey *just* before it became generally apparent that they had shot their creative bolts. He upstaged Atlanta—which had thought it would produce whatever hot was going to come out of Georgia. He caught Hunter Thompson with his loathing down. He has served more or less as his own Billy Graham.

Through it all Jimmy has been Christopher Robin or David Copperfield or Charlie Brown or Pogo—a flat bland too-nice central figure, a good old cipher, around whom good old vivid faulty characters caper. Take Jimmy's director of management and budget. Bert Lance stood for something. He performed the great national service of personalizing—in a finally too-homey and therefore traceable way—exactly what is wrong with the economy. Take Jimmy's UN representative. Andrew Young gave Americans just what they either hoped or feared they would get if a black guy ever represented America to the world. Who has ever played to the hilt the role of President's Mama the way Miss Lillian has? And what kind of character was Sherman Adams compared with Hamilton Jordan?

Unfortunately, America has been so washed out by television that it can't stand real characters. Lance and Billy Carter and Young have all wound up involved, in different ways, with Arabs. Arabs have eventually been about the only people who would give them credit. We have come to know a lot of hairy new Arab characters during the Carter years.

A great thing about America is that it has so many movable parts. There's an impasse in some place like the Holy Land, and all of a sudden a dozen or so demonstrative black Baptist preachers, who've been at loose ends over here for a while, are over there in Arabia shifting the balance. Personally, I think that's fine. You hear a lot of people saying they'll never listen to black Baptist preachers again, after seeing them over there hugging on old Yasir Arafat. Well, I wouldn't hug the man myself. He looks like a Ku Klux to me. But you can't dismiss the Palestinians just because they have a leader who looks and acts like that. They've got to be worked into the perceived landscape somehow, and somebody needs to improve our picture of the Middle East by tuning in the Arab background behind brave Sadat. Black Baptist preachers are, insofar as anything is in public life, a familiar and dependable quantity. You see them over there hugging Arafat and if you've got any sense you don't start yelling, "They can't do that! They're embracing terrorism!" You say, "Hm. So that's what Arafat looks like, hugging black Baptist preachers."

A neighbor of yours, whom you don't always agree with, whose viewpoint lately may even gripe your ass, but whom you *know*, goes over there and hugs Arafat. It gives you a little perspective. But people don't want to look at it that way. Arabs don't fit into the Understanding.

Anyway, Jimmy was highly floatable by the Power for just long enough, long enough for him to get into office, and long enough to set him up as a great new *international* hope. "For the first time since President Kennedy died," wrote *The Times* of London in May of '77, "the Western World can feel that it has a leader—one who can both arouse the enthusiasm of people and inspire the confidence of statesmen."

"Far from being Southern bumpkins," wrote Charles Mohr of *The New York Times* from London, "they [Jordan and Powell] represent a kind of new chic."

Less than a year later, a White House aide was saying that Jimmy was "tired of being regarded as a wimp." And the world was ready to turn to another chic.

Things might have been different if the President had been a good old boy. If a person is not a good old boy, then disturbing possibilities open up: he may be a big old baby; a saint; unknowing: *too* knowing. You're not sure how to deal with him. A good old boy will take advantage of another good old boy when he has to, and will help him out when he can. He will also take some creative pride in the way he does the one thing and the other and mixes the two things together. The only way he can manage all this is by putting himself in the other old boy's shoes.

Old Frank Church was running for re-election in hawkish Idaho back in '62 just before the Cuban missile crisis. Now old Jack Kennedy knew that Church had a constituency that dearly loved to see its senators stand up to Russians. But it served Kennedy's purposes at the time to deny reports of Soviet missiles in Cuba. He used Church to confirm that denial, by sending him to Guantanamo, whence Church went to Idaho and denied the missile reports as he campaigned.

Then Kennedy confirmed the reports, leaving Church in a bind. But Kennedy sent a military plane to Idaho, with fanfare, to bring Church to Washington to confer on the problem, which made old Church look good to Idaho.

Now in '79, when Church was campaigning again, and supporting the *Carter* administration's denial of reports of a Soviet combat brigade in Cuba, the *Carter* administration, which doesn't get along too well with Church or any other old boys outside its inner circle, let Church make the *announcement* that the brigade was there, after all. It was just too good an opportunity for Church to pass up. He ran around Idaho hawking and spitting and saying he wouldn't let the SALT treaty pass till the brigade was out of there.

It sure wasn't a statesmanlike thing for old Church to do, but what did Jimmy expect? Maybe he didn't think anybody named Church would be so unchristian. Instead of putting himself in Church's shoes, he put himself in Church's hands. An old boy don't want another old boy in his *hands*, lying there expecting him to do the decent thing. He wants to be in a situation where he and the other old boy are calling each other sumbitch motherfucker and both of them doing a day's work and getting away with some good shit, although the papers might call it "questionable conduct while giving spiritual counsel."

However, in the long run Jimmy outflanked old Church. Jimmy's "backing down" before the Russians may have helped lead to the Afghanistan invasion, which helped him so much in the polls. And Church's roughrider posturing caused *him* to lose credibility at home and in the Senate. A person who is not a good old boy can be *dangerous.* You know that when a Georgia person isn't a good old boy his interior voice is raising holy disgusted hell with him, and there is no telling how he will respond. Hit him a good shot and he's liable to turn into a butterfly, a mirror, a tarbaby, a color in the air.

People think they know everything about a President. People who say they'll wait until they've walked a mile in her moccasins before they judge their Aunt Frances are tromping all around inside the President's psyche, looking out, waving, telling us what it's like in there.

But Jimmy is hard to figure. Maybe he's devising a way to outflank the Power. Maybe he's more of a character than he lets on.

More Carters

Sartrain Lolley Carter, 43, Whack, North Carolina, who is writing a book entitled *A Southerner's Account.* "I know what you're saying. You're saying, Lord help us, another book on the South. But this is the first one *I've* written. Look at it from that point of view.

"I tell you the truth, a lot of these other books, I haven't even read them. *The Mind of the South.* Boy, I tell you. *The Mind of the South.* People will take and just *write a book* about something, won't they?

"Where are you from? Say you're from Illinois. How would you like to read a book, *The Mind of Illinois?*

"Actually I did skim through Cobb and Ringling Fry's book they put out here lately, *The Looks Southern People Get on Their Faces.* But you know, it don't come off anywhere near as well in print as it does when Cobb and Ringling *tell* it, where they can demonstrate the expressions live. Cobb can do forty or fifty 'Pissed Offs' alone. He gets to doing them one after another till—well, one time Ringling broke in on him and said, 'Quit it, Cobb, and gimme a chance to do some "While Hummings" or some "Wondering About Some-things" '; and you should have seen the one Cobb gave him then. Ringling has just about completely given up on cutting in on Cobb when he gets going.

"I don't read books about the South, but I read *Southern books.* Hoooo, people cutting one another with scythes, steal-ing one another's wooden legs, setting fires, making tarbabies out of one another. I listen to Southern music, but I don't lis-ten to music about the South. As a matter of fact, I think the Frys entitled their book *The Looks People Get on Their Faces,* and it was the publisher that stuck in the *Southern.*

"I think mostly what I'll write about is women out in the woods nekkid. I never have run into any out there yet, but I've got an idea what it'd be like."

Trash No More

I cannot help having a deep interest in the welfare of the State of Georgia and of the South as a whole. Still I never go into that part of the country and come away without a certain sense of sadness. One can enjoy oneself superficially, but one must shut one's eyes. —ELEANOR ROOSEVELT.

The world has heaped contumely on my people, even on the one of us who is President. But do we try to make people feel guilty for the misunderstanding? No. Do we file anti-defamation suits? No. That ain't my people's way. We don't even like to *wear* suits. And when we piss and moan, we piss and moan *music*. Otherwise, we just go on about our business, and wait for you to come South and then sell you spiritually tainted souvenirs. That's right. Like those ashtrays you get along the highway that have a picture of an outhouse with a voice coming from inside it, saying,

I'm the Only Man in
GEORGIA
Who Knows What He's Doing

Those ashtrays have got a taint put on them, which—since you all don't know how to live with original sin—makes you nervous and irritable and rootless and in need of psychiatry.

That might explain a lot. That might explain why Jimmy Carter's Health, Education, and Welfare Department is trying to stamp out smoking and yet in the same breath, so to speak, Jimmy goes down to North Carolina and announces that he sees no conflict between tobacco production and national health goals. He calls for research to make smoking "even more safe than it is today." So safe you could probably drive without a seat belt while doing it. He says this on the same day that the American Medical Association issues a report that cigarettes can cause irreversible damage not only to your lungs but also to your arteries and heart.

See, he can't just completely close down smoking, because that would kill the tainted-outhouse-ashtray program. There's probably a similar reasoning behind his marijuana policy— come out for decriminalizing it and then poison it with parra-quat and then have your drug-program head, I believe they called him, tell reporters that your aides smoke it a lot. It's all designed to confuse the North, to get on the North's nerves. I guess. But, hell, I don't know.

Sometimes, I just don't know.

> I got the redneck White House blues.
> Look at him up there on the news.
> The President's from Georgia
> but still we owe dues.
> I got the redneck White House blues.

It was the spring before Freedom Summer, when flights of clear-eyed Northern late adolescents would go South to help prove to the world what dumb-asses my people could be (a crusade that would be physically brave, morally impeccable, and, if you don't mind my saying so, no more imaginative than dynamiting fish). It was the spring of '64, then, and I was in Harvard Graduate School studying English literature, which for the most part was like learning about women at the Mayo Clinic. And one afternoon this African got up in my favorite class, Difficult Fiction, and denounced William Faulkner for his treatment of "non-Western people."

Reading from a prepared text, in a way that struck me as unnaturally ... *crisp,* this African averred that all the non-Western people (which was to say, all the non-rednecks) in

Faulkner were rendered as savage, stoic, menial, or deranged, and none of them was seen from within—and how, then, could Faulkner be countenanced at Harvard?

"*Well, got DAMN it,*" was my reaction.

I stood up and spluttered.

Spluttered as cogently as a person can splutter who is trying to say something he always thought went without saying. In the name of art; of Faulkner; of Clytie; of Joe Christmas; of stoicism; of derangement; of savagery; of my interior voice; and of not presuming to get any further inside anybody than you can *feel* your way. And as I spluttered, I felt—more harshly than I ever had in the South while urging race-mixing or even pooh-poohing major football—a climate of opinion setting in around me.

I had managed to simplify my classmates' thinking, to raise a clear moral issue: this guy with the redneck accent is so dumb as to hate this passing African.

I *liked* this class. I liked Mr. Monroe Engel, who taught it, though he hadn't had much to say to me since he'd found out that I was going into the Army the following year. I liked not only *Absalom, Absalom!* but also *What Maisie Knew* and *The Good Soldier* and *Under the Volcano* and the other books we read. All my life I had wanted to be somewhere where people argued about books. (At Vanderbilt, where I had just spent four years, we had had grotesque race-relations arguments, punctuated by well-reared coeds' savage cries of "Would you want to take a *shower* with them?") And now that I had reached such a place, I found myself dismissed as a person with an incriminating accent. "Well, just kiss my ass, all of you all," I thought partly, but only *partly*.

> I got the redneck White House blues.
> Even when we win one, we lose.
> The President's from Georgia,
> > but he's wearing shoes.
> I got the redneck White House blues.

After class, I spoke with the African, who didn't seem to feel like he belonged there either, and we went and played some tennis, but he didn't play like any African I had imagined. He played with grimly classic strokes, whereas I whanged loose-wristedly the way I'd learned to hit a baseball on the red clay back home.

But I can't claim to have been what is known as "a country boy." My grandparents and great-grandparents were farmers and carpenters and railroad workers, but my daddy mobilized his way up to national prominence in savings and loan, and I was raised in a town of 28,000 right outside Atlanta. The only way I ever got my neck red was playing Little League baseball, or fishing for croakers on vacation, or catching bees in Mason jars with Sandy Penick and Sally Everett, or doing yardwork under duress. I only followed a plow once, and that was on a field trip with the Explorer Scouts. I broke about four and a half feet of new ground under the July afternoon sun and felt dizzy and went and hid behind some bushes with some other Explorers until the Scoutmaster, who had come up with this plowing idea, and who *had* been a country boy, came and dragged us out.

I can't even speak as one who was a real Boy Scout. I didn't much like to water ski or sleep in tents full of bugs. I wanted to be by myself and imagine I was playing major-league ball, which took place somewhere way off on a higher plane, where movies and the federal government and magazines came from and where they argued about books. I wanted to meet some Jews. We only had one in Decatur, and he was a Presbyterian. And I wanted to contribute to the media, from which I gathered that all the stuff I grew up with was low and corny.

Not quintessentially low and corny, which might have been sort of exciting. ("Hey, look here in 'Lil Abner,' there's a pitcher of Daddy!") But just for-all-intents-and-purposes low and corny. You might say I grew up sort of rosy-necked. Which means that if you were to call me that, I'd feel obliged to try to whip your ass (this is just talk, though) in a semi-detached way.

But I've put all that behind me, except in my mind. I have left the South, bodily, and have resided right happily on a fairly high-crime New York street and come to know Arnold Schwartzenegger, Gilda Radner, and Elaine. I have appeared in a photograph in the *Daily News* as part of a crowd watching a shoot-out, and I have written for the best magazine and the best newspaper in the world, and for a lot of other ones.

And up here on the national level I have often felt like a man who has been diagnosed crazy, and who has worried about it and resolved to improve, and then has visited a psychiatrists' convention, and finds himself saying, "Yeah, I sure am crazy. I'm extremely crazy," so nobody will take him for a psychiatrist.

But don't get me wrong. I'm a hard-core First Amendment boy. I'm always eager to be the first to amend something; and, too, I cling to the thought that people who put out publications have more sense, in some ways, than people who read them, or at least more than the ones who write letters to the editor. Still and all, one of the main things I have learned since leaving the South is that all those Northern institutions from which I gathered that my culture was low and corny and crazy have their own ways of being low and corny and crazy.

It's not so much my people who are crazy as it is the human mind. This is a hard thought, and one which my people have been instrumental in keeping off most people's minds for a number of years. My people have taken on the role of being crazy for *everybody*. Which is what I thought Jimmy would do, in a new and educational way.

But I'm having a hard time figuring out how he has.

I got the redneck White House blues.
I'm tired of all these synthesized views.
Half of him is Vance's,

the other Zbigniew's.
I got the redneck White House blues.

He don't look like much of a redneck, I know. Most of the time he looks, and sounds, like a man who's come down from a slightly higher level of church administration to give a talk to your congregation on good sound business reasons why you ought to tithe.

But he *said* he was a redneck, when he ran for governor. And I thought that might count for something when he got elected President.

I liked it when Senator Edward Brooke of Massachusetts complained, "When you get to the White House, the place looks physically dirty. People running around in jeans, it just doesn't look right."

"Lord!" I thought to myself when I read that. "We have done something now! This is a great day for both our peoples, when you think about it. We have established that a famous black man can be anal-repressive."

And I liked it when Mark Russell—the supposed Washington *satirist*, Lord help us, this is what they have in that town for a *satirist*—got offended by Hamilton Jordan's referring to Pennsylvania Avenue as Pennsylvania Street. "Now everybody knows about Pennsylvania Avenue and what it means to us here," Russell was quoted as harrumphing, in an in-depth story on the administration's shortcomings in *People* magazine.

You know what else I liked? I liked Jimmy in that *Playboy* interview. It sounded to me exactly like what an open, sincere Baptist who has seen something of the world through Baptist eyes *ought* to say in *Playboy*. That was a Baptist id and a Baptist ego and a Baptist superego out there wrestling in full view of the nation, and that is the kind of thing I think of as honorable exposure. It mixed piety and the flesh in the best tradition of country music.

I wish he'd come out with more of that kind of stuff. That's real-life stuff. Back during the campaign, when Earl Butz was quoted as saying that all black folks want is "a tight pussy, loose shoes, and a warm place to shit," I wish Jimmy had responded by saying it sounded like a set of priorities that a lot of people could identify with.

I liked it when Jimmy was giving Andy Young leeway to bring things out into the open. I don't want people to be *right* all the time. I want them to let us in on their thinking.

Of course, I guess that's hard to do when there are forty-four thousand cameras, note pads, printing presses, teletype machines, deadlines, headlines, commentators, potshotters, leakers, and layers of ignorance between you and the people you are talking to. But surely in the long run openness resists mistranslation better than secrecy does. That was in fact supposed to be a tenet of Jimmy's administration—and Jimmy's *subordinates*, for a while there, were working various veins of disclosure. But Jimmy himself got defensive; he seized up. And then he seized up the rest of them.

What if, instead of old Why Not the Best Jimmy, it had been Kissing Jim Folsom who came up out of the darkest South to be President? When Folsom was governor of Alabama, he used to appear in public forums barefooted, because that felt even better to him sometimes than loose shoes. He would lie down flat on sidewalks or auditorium stages barefooted, drunk, and in control of the situation, with no hint of *straining after image*. And he was liberal-minded. In his gubernatorial Christmas message in 1949, he said, "As long as the Negroes are held down by deprivation and lack of opportunity, all the other people will be held down alongside them." You notice he didn't say "all *us* other people." And he kept on talking that way through the fifties and sixties. He vetoed segregation bills and served Adam Clayton Powell whiskey in the governor's mansion. Once Kissing Jim had a whole lot of dignitaries out on his yacht watching a performance by the Alabama Air National Guard. He was bragging about all the new planes the Guard had and what they could do. Several of the planes took off and started looping around impressively, and then something went wrong with one of them, and it plunged into the water and exploded into fire and foam.

The first to break the silence was Folsom.

"Kiss my ass," he said, "if that ain't a show."

Now there may have been an element of apparent insensitivity in that, but sometimes a President has to seem hard. If old Jim had gotten to be Chief Executive, it might have bucked him up to the point that he wouldn't have let liquor cut into his effectiveness, and there is no telling what he would have accomplished in the way of relieving awkward national pauses.

> I got the redneck White House blues.
> The South's not gonna rise, but just diffuse.
> Have you heard that country album
>   by Julie Andrews?
> I got the redneck White House blues.

More Carters

The original Jimmy Carter, 78, Sarasota, Florida. "Good gracious alive I was Jimmy Carter before this character ever thought about it. I was answering up in school to it, signing up for various things with it, carving it on so many various wooden things, why I was known as Jimmy Carter nearly everywhere just about that I would go.

"Sure. Why it wasn't nothing for me to hear, 'Hey, Jimmy Carter!' 'Jimmy—Jimmy Carter, how are you? Just the man I wanted to see.' 'Well if it ain't old Jimmy Carter.'

"Sure. I've been hearing it for nearly eighty years now. It ain't nothing new to me. I'm just as much Jimmy Carter and American and a child of God as he is. And I'm sharp. Sure. Put me in a room with anybody. A-rabs. Russians. I'm ready."

Early Billy

His own place lay in a rougher territory, where there was some clay in the soil and it was not so productive. When he bought his land, he hadn't the money to buy on High Prairie, so he told his boys, when they grumbled, that if their land hadn't some clay in it, they wouldn't own it at all.
—WILLA CATHER, "Neighbor Rossicky"

Right away I knew there was one Carter I could come to terms with. I felt it incumbent upon me to spend some time with Billy, even if it meant drinking a lot of beer. In the spring of '77, I went down to see him in Plains, and on the way back, in the Atlanta airport, I was asked, "What is he *really like?*"

"Wonderful," I replied. "We drove all around, drinking beer and throwing the cans out the window and meeting veterinarians and talking about goats and monkeys and getting out to piss in the highway right near a billboard that said NAIL BEGGARWEED IN PEANUTS . . ."

"But how much of that," this guy asked, "was calculated?"

"Well," I said, "I know part of it wasn't. We were trying to piss on the shoulder."

That's the kind of Carter Billy is, you can understand what he's driving at. You should be able to, anyway. It looks like America has missed his point. I just wish the first Cracker White House were as entertaining as the Carter peanut warehouse was when Billy was in charge.

"There's that god damn invalid woman!"

"Billy, she's been waiting all day."

"I don't give a god damn. I don't care if she *is* a god damn invalid."

A middle-aged woman on a walker is making her way resolutely in a drizzling rain from door to window to window to door of the Carter peanut-warehouse offices in Plains, Georgia. She wants to meet old Billy, the President's brother, hero to beer drinkers and workingmen, who is trying to get some work done so he can get away and drink some beer.

Outside, in a street that never used to see any tourists except an occasional one who was seriously lost, people from all over America are hanging around, peering in, waiting for Billy to emerge. And now three old folks have just barged right in through the front door past the NO ADMITTANCE sign. "We've come all the way from Atlanta to see Billy," one of them announces.

"Lady," says Randy Coleman, Billy's office manager, "we have people come all the way from *Japan* to see Billy. But I can't give him to you if he's not here, can I?"

Billy is hiding in his inner office. The visitors peer around suspiciously. Finally, they leave, muttering, and Billy—chunky, blue-jeaned, intense—re-emerges into the anteroom, shaking his head and sucking in cigarette smoke that never seems to come back out. He looks a little like Opie, the kid on the old Andy Griffith show, grown up and considerably filled out and harried half to death. His expression eases when he picks up his bull-penis-in-*rigor-mortis* walking stick. "The other day, we had a lady in here holding it. She said, 'Ohhh, what's this made of?' " He goes "Heenh-heenh-heenh" in his distinctive, nervous, strangled, and infectious laugh.

"Dear Gussie," sighs Billy's big, blond, serene, ironically smiling wife, Sybil. She doesn't say it loudly enough to hurt the new visitor's feelings.

Another one has gotten in and he has caught Billy flat-footed. A spry Bermuda-shorted man from Cincinnati who wants Billy to pose holding a can of Cincinnati-brewed beer. "I saw the old gentleman your uncle over at his antique shop," the intruder says. "He said you'd be over here." At that, Billy's friend Tommy Butler, the Swift & Company salesman, known as Tommy B., begins to make faces and act like he's choking.

Glumly, silently, with the air of a dog being dressed up in baby clothes, Billy takes the beer and holds it up and the man snaps the picture and hands Billy his card and urges him to stop by the next time he's in Cincinnati and goes away happy.

Billy begins to chase Tommy B. around the room. "I didn't say anything," Butler whoops, dodging kicks. One thing that really riles Billy is to hear his cousin, Hugh Carter—an encourager of tourists and a frequent opponent of Billy's in local political matters—referred to as his uncle.

A thump is heard against the side door. The phone rings and Billy's secretary says, for the umpteenth time, "No, I'm sorry." At home, Billy's phone is off the hook. Too many bomb threats coming in. The listed phone at his gas station is off the hook, too. A while back, one college kid won forty-eight dollars in an afternoon of answering it, hanging up and betting another college kid that it would ring again within forty-five seconds.

Outside, a bus operated by one of the town's twelve tour services is passing. A megaphonic voice says, "There goes some of Billy's daughters!"

The daughter, Jana, eighteen, wearing a sweat shirt that says TWINKIE, bursts in to say, "Momma, one of the chickens has its head under another one and I think she's eating the eggs."

Sybil says, "Chickens don't eat the eggs. That's pigs that eat little pigs."

Jana is relieved. Someone mentions that a research organization is taking a survey at Billy's gas station to see what percentage of Americans are willing to show a stranger their belly buttons on request. "I wouldn't do that," says Jana, "but I'd throw 'em a moon."

"That old crazy man called," Randy tells Jana with relish.

"No! The one that chased me in Americus?" The police and Billy had had to be called. "What did he want?"

"He called asking for a job."

In an adjoining office, piles of strange tributes may be seen. A wood carving that reads, inexplicably, THERE'S A PORK CHOP IN EVERY BILLY. A cake, reading HAPPY BIRTHDAY TO SOMEONE WITH STYLE, mounted on four upright beer cans. Dozens of huge floppy hats made of beer cans crocheted together. Several cases of strange off-brand beers. "Four or five different cases come in every week," says Sybil. "We have to throw most of it away. You can't be sure what somebody might have put in it."

"This one's Guatemalan," says Billy. "Probably wash the bottles out with sewage."

Many people who, as Billy says, "claim they are women authors" have sent in copies of their vanity-press books, in response to his assertion on the Mike Douglas show that women could do some things well, but writing books was not one of them. This is not, of course, a defensible assertion, but the books that have been mailed in tend to bear it out. They come with inscriptions: "Maybe and God willing you will read this true BOOK even if written by a woman. You proply [sic] got an avelange [sic] of BOOKS through your talk shows . . ."

"Here's a poet wants you to autograph a poem so he can sell it," says Sybil. She is going through the day's big stack of fan mail. "This man says he has a thing for Jimmy about heating and if he's interested, to call him.

" 'I will send you round-trip bus fare. You can stay with my two boys and . . .'

" 'I sent your mother a life-size picture of Christ and she answered with a sweet letter, but your sister-in-law never . . .'

"This one's marked on the envelope, 'Mr. and Mrs. Billy Carter, Very Personal.' Then it begins, 'Dear sirs . . .'

"This man wants you to go into business with him. 'It wouldn't hurt your image to be the first person to strike oil in

Georgia. There are definite hydrocarbon deposits . . .' And he wants you to get them out."

"This lady asks which side you would have fought on in the Civil War."

"Tell her I'd probably hid out in the swamp," Billy says.

Sybil rolls her eyes. "One lady in Rome wrote to say she wanted a picture of Billy to replace one of the two Popes she had on her wall. People keep writing in to say we're real. Oh, how nice, I thought we were artificial."

"You can tell your brother to kiss my ass," Billy tells Randy, whose brother, a state legislator, has just voted for legalizing fourteen-foot-wide trailers on Georgia roads, something Billy is against because "Georgia roads are only sixteen feet wide."

"Your cousin Hugh was the one pushed it through," Randy says.

"I already told him—several times."

"What if somebody comes to take us hostage?" someone asks. "I'm getting a shotgun in here."

"I already got two," Billy says.

Randy is scanning the tourists with binoculars, looking for good-looking women among them. Various members of staff and family join him at the window.

"There's a man going to the bathroom."

"Where?"

"Look at that lady in that box there. What's she doing?"

"Selling tickets."

"To what?"

"To look at the man going to the bathroom."

Billy tells Sybil a friend of theirs has asked him to put in an appearance at a function the same day he's already been asked to be in several other places. "I don't know what to tell him."

"Tell him no, Billy."

"You call him."

"No, I'm not going to. You've got to learn to say no, Billy."

Billy sighs. "When I was on the 'Tomorrow' show, I drove to Albany and flew out of there at ten A.M. and back in at one-fifty the next morning. I must've spent four thousand dollars of my own money traveling to things before I started getting expenses. Anything to get away from Plains for a while. Plains is one big rip-off. You can't buy a quart of milk or a loaf of bread any more. Just Jimmy Carter souvenirs."

Billy takes a business call in his office. In a few minutes, muffled shouting can be heard.

Another of Billy and Sybil's six children, their daughter Kim, twenty-one, comes in.

"Who was that little writer, went back and wrote that I looked like Daisy Mae?" she asks after a while. "Said I walked off twitching my behind? Sat right over there on that couch. Little bitty man. And you all made me go off with him and show him around town."

Billy bursts out of his office, enraged by his phone call. "Do a favor for the man, and then he screws me out of two thousand dollars. One thing I can't stand is to have a man tell me I can't call him a god damn son of a bitch when that's exactly what I just finished doing. I think I'm going to go into Albany and hit a man and get throwed in jail!"

But here are some more people, another elderly threesome, strolling in. They want Billy to come out and pose on the doorstep with them.

"No, ma'am, I can't."

"We heard you were a good old boy."

Billy draws away to the far side of the room.

"Said you were the nicest person in the world."

"Yes'm."

"Well, you're not being too nice now."

There is a pained silence. Looking like people who have been denied a civil right, the tourists leave. It's noon! Boom! Billy and Sybil and Jana and Randy and Tommy B. and I dash outside and leap into the Blazer—tourists are banging on the sides, the lady on the walker is bearing down, she is yelling something; the car pulls off in a cloud of dust and we are off to Americus for lunch.

"Now," Billy says, "do you see why I hired an agent?"

"You better love me!" Tandy Rice had exclaimed over the phone a few days before. He said he had persuaded his new client to let me hang around with him if it turned out that we got along. "And I can't imagine anybody not getting along with Roy Blount," Tandy had cried in his Mod-Southern-evangelist-gone-more-than-about-halfway-worldly voice. "Unless they run over your damn dog with their car!"

That is the way the President's brother's agent talks. He is thirty-eight, dresses sharp, moves fast, has a bright toothy smile and an intermittently hard cast of eye.

"I'm just a little country booker," Tandy may tell you, but in the eight years since he bought Top Billing, Inc., the Nash-ville-based booking-and-management firm has gone from a single telephone line to twelve, any one of which is likely to be answered by someone crying, *"Hi!* How you *doing!"* Top Billing handled Dolly Parton's bookings before she shifted her business to Los Angeles and still books Tom T. Hall and Jerry Clower. "What happened, I read that the William Morris Agency had signed not Gerald Ford but the entire Ford fam-ily," Tandy says. "And the William Morris Agency is my competitor. And I'm probably the most competitive man that ever lived. Son, I'll tackle a buzz saw. We went after Billy with letters, Mailgrams, and phone calls."

Tandy went down to Plains and shook hands on the deal with Billy. "He gives his word, it's bond," Tandy says. "He's the kind of guy, to paraphrase Jerry Clower, if he says a piss-ant will move a bale of hay, I'll start clearing a space." A more formal agreement was worked out between Tandy and Billy's three Americus lawyers, of whom Tandy says respectfully, "They're fat. And they like it."

One day, first in Tandy's offices and then in a Nashville bank lobby, I watched Billy meet, pose for pictures with, and equably insult nearly everybody in Nashville who owned a set of dress clothes.

"She's a lawyer now," Tandy said, introducing someone.

"Oh, I don't like women lawyers," Billy said. "Tandy done introduced me to thirty lawyers. Anybody knows that many lawyers can't be honest."

Tandy beamed.

"That's quat a sports coat," Billy told a man who had been waiting in line for twenty minutes.

"I only paid fifteen dollars for it," the man said.

"You both got screwed," said Billy.

"The wit and wisdom!" said Tandy. Later, surveying the bank lobby chock-full of politicians waiting for a shake and a photo, Tandy cried, "This man.... It's a dern phenomenon, that's what it is." From time to time, Tandy counsels with Billy about avoiding impolitic statements. Billy nods and goes out to make more of them.

"He's the biggest celebrity in the world today!" says Tandy. "And I hope you're laughing with me, not at me, because I can just about defend that statement." A group in North Carolina wrote in, Tandy says, listing the people they would most like to have address them. In reverse order, those people were the Six Million Dollar Man, Wonder Woman, the Fonz, and Billy.

Billy generally begins his speeches by throwing the floor open to questions. "Why is Pabst your favorite beer?" a banquet-goer asked in Tifton, Georgia. Aha, I thought. But Billy told the banquet the same thing he had told me:

"Pabst is my favorite beer because Robert, who drives their beer truck, is my favorite beer-truck driver."

Ever since then, I have been trying to imagine a commercial with the real Billy Carter in it. He is standing knee-deep in a mucky fishpond, perhaps, and he is holding up a can of Blue Ribbon and saying, "I'd recommend Robert to anybody." Or he is hiding from tourists behind a pile of peanuts and grumbling, "Well, I'm allergic to peanuts"—which happens to be the truth—"but if I wadn't, hell, I'd as soon eat Planter's [or whatever the brand is] as any others, I imagine. As long as they got 'em from our warehouse."

"How come you had your picture in *Time* drinking Budweiser?" somebody else in the Tifton audience asked him.

"The day that was taken, it was a hundred and ten degrees," Billy said. "If they'd handed me a milk, I would've drunk it."

"How about Coors?"

"Coors is like marijuana. If you could buy it in Georgia, you wouldn't want it."

As a matter of fact, I can't remember hearing Billy say anything favorable from a podium about anybody or anything except Roy Acuff, Mel Tillis, Blue Ribbon/Robert, and the Israeli army. This last came when he was asked what he would do about Idi Amin. He replied, "I would send one company of the Israeli army over there and clean up the whole mess."

At the end of some remarks in Nashville, he was presented with a fine big jug of Jack Daniel's—a Tennessee-distilled whiskey of which the state is extremely proud—and a beautiful handmade dulcimer. Billy's response to these gifts was the most sublimely ungracious acceptance from a dais I have ever witnessed.

"Thank y'all very much and that's another vicious rumor, that Jack Daniel's is my drink," he said. Then, looking blatantly like a man who didn't know what in the hell he was going to do with a beautiful handmade dulcimer, he dabbed bemusedly at one of the instrument's strings: *plank*. Tandy looked uneasy.

"I ain't the Carter that won't tell a lie," Billy frequently says, but he doesn't tell polite lies. "I'll lie like hell in a minute, but I ain't humble worth a damn."

Here is a representative sampling of Q's and A's:

"How is Miss Lillian?"

"My mother very seldom speaks to me unless she wants something."

"How do you get along with your brother?"

"We get along fine as hell as long as he's in Washington and I'm in Plains."

"Did you ever lust for a woman besides Mrs. Carter?"

"You know I said I'd answer every question." Pause. "You must think I'm a damn fool."

"Were you accused of cheating in the Plains mayor's race?"

"Ma'am, the accusation wasn't exactly that. The accusation was that I was doing it like hell and lost."

"What has all this fame done for your sex life?"

"Nothing. It's still once a week."

"Are you smarter than your brother?"

"I know I'm smarter than Jimmy. I *think* I'm smarter than Gloria."

"Did you really sell beer on Sunday?"

"Sunday used to be my best day. It is against the law in Georgia. I got caught. I didn't know how to plead lazy, so my lawyer said plead *nolo contendere.* I said, 'John, I better plead just as guilty as hell, because that's what I am.' He said it wouldn't cost me a thing. Cost five hundred dollars. I'll never plead again."

"What do people think of you back in Plains?"

"They took a poll to see who was the biggest son of a bitch in Plains and I won hands down. And you'd be surprised some of the son of a bitches running against me."

"Are you for legalized gambling?"

"No. If they do that, I'll have to pay a tax on it, too."

"On the serious side, would you speculate on your brother's energy policy?"

"I'm kind of against it. I've got seven cars."

"What do you talk to your brother about?"

"Well, he's got this blind trust, and it's got so blind now. . . . I used to talk to him about peanuts. Can't do that now. We can talk about the fishpond, but if we start charging people to fish, we can't talk about that. I guess we'll start talking about nut grass, except they got some stuff now that they say will do away with nut grass."

YES, BUT HOW MUCH
OF THAT IS CALCULATED?

I feel sure of my ground when I say that Nashville writer John Egerton was mistaken when he wrote in *The New York Times* that Billy has retained not only a booking agent but also gag writers. Conceivably, that notion arose while Billy was addressing a tourism association in Nashville. He was following his usual format, which is to stand squarely behind the lectern, take a swallow from a can of beer, field a shouted question, squint, lean into the microphone, toss off an irresponsible answer, sip again, and giggle deeply. After some twenty minutes of this, someone cried: "Who writes your speeches?"

Billy looked over at the press table, where I was feverishly taking notes. As though offering the audience a chance to see his writer at work, he said, "Right there; Mr. Roy Blount does."

I, of course, felt honored.

DID BILLY EVER OWN A GOAT?

I'm glad you asked that question. Billy says, "I had the smartest goat I ever saw. It'd sit up here in the front seat and people would think it was one of the kids. It wasn't housebroken, but anything it did on the floor it would either drink or eat, so it didn't have to be housebroken. I'd take it down to the gas station and it'd eat all the cigarette butts. I hated to get rid of it, but I came to find out it had been stolen. It was a hot goat. So I took it into Atlanta and left it in Charles Kirbo's law office."

IS BILLY A REAL REDNECK
OR A BUSINESSMAN?

You're assuming that the two categories are mutually exclusive. I'll say this: Until recently, Billy had a '49 Studebaker in his front yard. It had a piece of angle iron for a front bumper, there was hardly any paint on it, and it took ten quarts of oil to get it started. Sybil made him haul it off.

"Do you know how much value there is in a 1949 Studebaker that *runs?*" Billy demanded as we drove to Americus for lunch. Nobody responded. "Okay, when I have my party with the five thousand dollars I get from selling my Studebaker, I'm not going to invite y'all."

"I just didn't want it in my front yard," said Sybil.

"When it was there, we didn't have all those tour buses turning around in the front yard," Billy said.

People might say that Billy doesn't dress like a businessman. He wears jeans and boots and a wide belt with a big buckle. In Nashville, he stood in the doorway of his hotel room dressed in coat, vest, trousers, tie, off-white shirt, and everything else required of a man about to address a big banquet. He grimaced and said, "I'd rather eat shit than wear a suit."

On the other hand, when Billy ran the warehouse he would get to work at 5:30 A.M., and he seems to have whealt and dealt peanuts pretty ambitiously for somebody who wasn't entirely violating any laws.

DOES BILLY RESENT HIS BIG BROTHER?

Well, once during the campaign, Billy kicked a dog all the way through a press conference Jimmy was holding. But that was because Jimmy was holding it on the scales outside the warehouse and a long line of peanut-laden trucks was backed up, waiting to weigh in.

It is generally assumed that a certain gap exists between Billy and Jimmy, dating back to Jimmy's being away during most of Billy's boyhood and then returning and presuming to act paternally toward him after their father died. But rather than repress the tension between them, the brothers tend, publicly, to acknowledge it slyly. I remember when, deep into the vote-counting night, after Jimmy had been projected as President, someone asked Billy on television what he was going to do now and he said, "Stay up all night and when he gets here, still call him Jimmy."

And when he did get there, Jimmy said, "The first thing I want to do is thank Mr. Carter for waiting up all night to meet me. Everybody's got to call him Mr. Carter till dinnertime."

Part of the impetus behind Billy's flowering as a public figure was his unspoken message that "I, the President's brother, ain't only the President's brother. In fact, I grew up more original and more like Daddy and deeper-rooted and more independent and sounder and wilder and a *hell* of a lot more normal than he did." Like any entertainer or politician of interest, Billy is insecure enough about that proposition to need to keep proving it but secure enough about it to be convincing.

It is true that Billy sleeps badly, smokes and drinks more than is healthy, shows a lot of aggression and has apparently been known to get a chip on his shoulder.

He may resent something. He may resent that people tend to assume that a man from South Georgia is quaint, for one thing. And he may resent that his father died when he was fourteen or that he is going to die himself sometime. In Nashville, the night of his fortieth birthday, a lady asked him what his greatest goal in life was and he said, "Ma'am, it's to live to be forty-one. And I think I'm over the hump."

HOW COME BILLY POPPED UP
OUT OF NOWHERE ALL OF A SUDDEN?

"There's a vicious rumor," Billy says, "that I was hid from the Baptists during the '66 governor's campaign." It does seem strange that Billy was so little heard of even in Georgia until national reporters started going to Plains. But according to Atlanta newsmen who covered Carter campaigns from the first, Billy was never covered up. He just didn't strike Georgia reporters as too remarkable. Most people who run for anything in Georgia have a brother or two along Billy's lines.

"He was not perceived as a wit or a talent," says one Atlanta newsman with asperity. "He was no dunce, and beneath the surface he was sensitive. But I always viewed Billy as an ill-tempered, bad sort. During the governor's campaign in '70, he would get really upset and offer to punch people out if they wrote badly about Jimmy. After Jimmy was elected, Billy invited me to come down and go bird hunting with him. If I'd promise to walk ahead of him the whole time."

WHAT DOES BILLY DO FOR
ENTERTAINMENT WHEN HE'S NOT
BEING A CELEBRITY?

"Running dogs, drinking liquor, and eating turkey nuts" are things Billy's friend Dr. Paul Broun says they enjoy doing together. Turkey nuts are turkey gonads. "You fry 'em," says Dr. Broun. "I never cleaned a turkey to get any myself, but a dog trainer in Leesburg, Georgia, gave us a big hog-nut and turkey-nut dinner. Turkey nuts are . . . bigger than a pecan."

Billy also derives pleasure from driving around drinking beer with friends like Bud Duvall, who superintends the gas station for him, and Tommy B. They'll stop in at the Plains Country Club, which is a small cinder-block building with a pool table inside and a sign outside saying MEMBERSHIP FREE. Or they drop by the Americus Moose Club, where Billy still fits right in, though nobody else there is world-famous. Once a year, at the end of peanut season, he hosts a hat-burning. This custom began one night when Billy got to drinking and climbed on top of a car and burned up his hat. The only price of admission is to bring a hat and burn it.

Sometimes Randy Coleman from the office will drive him around. "The first time Randy drove me and Tommy, we got to fighting and I had my loaded .38 cocked and holding it to Tommy's head, and it scared Randy to death," Billy says.

He enjoys reading—"chemical magazines or something light. Or if there's nothing else, encyclopedias. Just to read." A mystery that I was unable to penetrate is exactly what *titles* he reads. When I pressed him on that point, he was evasive. When I pressed his friend Broun, he said, "Billy reads just anything he puts his hands on. It doesn't make a whole lot of difference to him what it is. He's a real rapid reader. He read one book in the time it took us to fly from Nashville to Columbus, Georgia." Broun couldn't recall the book's nature.

Billy entertained himself and others pretty well the night of the presidential election. "We had eighty people in the house and didn't know but four of 'em. One of 'em introduced me to one other, so then I knew five. Next morning, there were sixteen asleep on the floor. Sybil got dozens of bunches of flowers from people we never heard of the next day, thanking her for the hospitality. We drank up a whole lot of champagne and everything else in the house, and all the beer at the station, and then we took up a collection of three hundred and sixty dollars to buy more liquor and drank all that. Then a stewardess showed up with a case full of miniatures. We still kept running out.

"By that time, I was down at the depot and Sybil saw me on television and called down there and told me to stop drinking. I was supposed to be interviewed live. But then they had a delay of twenty-two minutes and, in that time, I started drinking again and drank nine beers, and then I disappeared. I don't know what became of me."

IS BILLY PREJUDICED?

"When did you get over being prejudiced?" I asked him the first time we talked. I assumed that he had gotten over it, since Miss Lillian and Jimmy said they had and since Billy had sued the members of the public-school board to try to require them to send their children to public schools instead of to private segregated schools. "I'm still prejudiced, I guess," he said. "It would still bother me for my daughter to marry a black man."

But the person he most enjoyed meeting during the campaign was the former Atlanta Hawks center Walt Bellamy, who is seven feet tall and black. (The two people he told Jimmy he wanted to meet were Bellamy and John Glenn; of the two, Bellamy was the one who sufficiently impressed him.) And Billy is friendly with Kenny, the traveling black American Express man whose stops include his gas station. "Kenny is going to ruin my redneck image," he says. To Billy's surprise, he trusted Bill Turner, the black pilot who for a while flew out of Peterson Field, the airstrip in Plains. "I'd never been in the air with a black pilot before. I didn't know what to think. But he's a good pilot. I'm particular who I let fly my kids, but he's real nice to them, makes sure they get to their next connection." And Billy sends his kids to integrated public schools because "I'd rather fight than quit."

As a matter of fact, Billy tends to make his school suit sound like a local political struggle more than a stand on principle, but Manuel Maloof, an Atlanta tavernkeeper and populist politician who is a friend of Billy's, says that Billy used to come into his place wearing a Wallace button and speak privately with feeling about the rightness of integrated schools.

Billy undoubtedly makes a point of avoiding anything resembling a lofty liberal pronouncement. After I got to know him better, though, he confided, "You're the first one I've ever told this. Why I left the city council. I ran in the first place to change the vote against me getting a beer license. I won and got the license and then I told everybody I was going to run again. So nobody else qualified against this black man. He was running for my post and everybody figured I'd beat him. Then, when it was too late for anybody else to qualify, I withdrew and he got on. It was a flimflam deal. I figured it was time the blacks got some representation."

Now, you could say that Billy was making a calculated effort to sell me a Billy Carter who is at once nationally unfashionable on the abstracts of race relations and locally progressive on the specifics. But I'm inclined to believe that that is about what he is. I am also inclined to believe that however rotten a mayoral candidate he is, Billy commands a political and imagistic deftness comparable to—of course less ambitious than, in some sense maybe purer than—his brother's. Of course, he might have wanted a black to get on the council just to get under people's skin.

I asked Billy why he said he would campaign for George Wallace.

"George Wallace broke the seal," he said, meaning that Wallace had proved, before Jimmy Carter, that a Southern presidential candidate could command electoral respect.

"But to a lot of people, Wallace represents white racism," I said.

"George Wallace is not a racist," Billy said. "He stands for the common man. He stands for the common man a hell of a lot more than Jimmy Carter or anybody else."

"The common man black or white?"

"Yeah," Billy said. "That's my opinion."

"How do you feel about capital punishment?"

"I think everybody who deserves it ought to get it."

Billy's least felicitous public remark to date was "I hate to say this, but we've all left a nigger in the woodpile somewhere." That is what he said at a press conference in Oakland when black politician Carter Gilmore asked him whether they were related. Nobody white has a call to be flippant about the ways in which black people got white names. But then again, it was not too tasteful a question. Gilmore had been straining to capitalize on his first name (he was running for the Oakland city council on the slogan "Let's elect another Carter") and he and Billy had been kidding each other freely on the topic of their ancestry before the press conference. I would say Billy's remark was more satirical, cutting both ways, than bigoted. And Billy never said nigger, or anything like it, when I was there, though several people did who were good-old-boying around with him.

The question of women's rights seems to rub Billy wrong. He gives female reporters an even harder time than he gives male ones, and with less humor: "You'd make a fine cook, ma'am, but I don't know about a reporter." He opposes the Equal Rights Amendment: "I've got a brother that's in favor of it, a sister-in-law that's behind it, and four daughters that I don't want drafted." I'd have to guess that Billy resists competitive women because women in more or less old-fashioned supportive roles are so important to him. Sybil says she married him when she was only sixteen because his father had died and he seemed to need somebody to take care of him.

But Billy seems to see Sybil as a partner as surely as Jimmy does Rosalynn and, by all accounts, is as true to her as he claims to be. And he enjoys pretty much the same give-and-take with her and with their daughters as he does with his friends who are men.

Here is how a discussion of the ERA went in the office one afternoon:

"I can't see it," said Randy. "They want to have just one bathroom."

"There are good things about it, though," said Sybil.

"A woman ought to be able to make the same money as a man. A woman ought to be able to borrow money."

"Yeah, but . . . they want to be in the same bathroom."

"I don't," said Sybil.

"She does want to, too," said Billy, "with Randy."

"One thing for sure, nobody would want to be in the same bathroom with you," Randy told Billy.

"Billy is noxious," explained Sybil.

"I never did say," said Billy, "that my shit don't stink."

WHAT IS THE KEY
TO BILLY'S APPEAL?

He is unsentimental about people but still appreciates them. I asked him whether he was as moved as I was when all those variegated Democrats stood with a white and a black Southerner and sang "We Shall Overcome" after Jimmy's acceptance. "I left just before that part," he said. "Daddy King— he and I are friends. But when he starts preaching, you have to ring the bell on him. Then, when you ring it, he preaches harder."

Another time, Billy started talking about Miss Julia Coleman, the Plains schoolteacher Jimmy invokes so reverently and quoted in his inaugural address. "She pulled me through school," Billy said. "I'd say, 'Miss Julia, you know I can't take this D or this F home.' She'd say, 'Well, how about a C?' I'd say, 'Naw, you know my parents, I need a B-plus or an A.' She'd say she couldn't do that. I'd say, 'Please, Miss Julia, just this one time.'

"She would write every week to every former student of hers who was in the service. When I was in the Far East, I'd get a letter two inches thick, handwritten, with three or four lines on a page. Because she was so nearsighted. I could have gotten another boy to sit in my chair and she wouldn't have known the difference.

"You know, when she had her funeral in Plains, I went. Only twenty-five people came to her funeral."

DOES BILLY HAVE A SERIOUS SIDE?

If pissed off counts, he does. Years back, at a high school basketball game in Unadilla, Georgia, Billy took on a man who he claims was six foot seven. "I jumped on his back and started biting him and he fell backward over on top of me. Then Sybil come up and hit him on the head with her high heel."

"Well, he was scrubbing your brand-new blazer on that concrete floor."

"When I got up, I spit out skin, backbone, T-shirt, and shirt. Later, people came around saying, 'Did you hear a man died in Unadilla of a human bite?' It scared me for a while."

Another time, he was in Atlanta with Tommy B. and another friend and was having a drink in the hotel bar, waiting for them to come down. They came in and took a table. Billy paid his bill at the bar and headed toward them, but the bouncer stopped him.

"He said those two men said I was queer and had been bothering them, following them around all night. Said he wasn't going to let me join them.

"I said, 'The hell you aren't,' and he got another man and they threw me out. So I went drinking somewhere else and when I got back to the hotel room, Tommy was sitting there, laughing, and I hit him, and he'd of gone thirteen stories if he hadn't fallen out of the chair before it got to the window."

Billy can go at it verbally, too. "We were at this party and one man started saying he wished he hadn't contributed five dollars to Jimmy's campaign, the way it was going. There's always one like that in each crowd. Finally, I said, 'Here's your five dollars, we don't want it,' and started in on him. Within two minutes, I had his wife crying, and in one more minute, I had him shut up. I'm a professional dozens player."

Aside from that, I can't say for sure about Billy's serious side. But he probably has one. Somebody once asked him why he didn't go to church. He said, "Well, maybe I'll talk about it later. It gets kind of deep."

DID BILLY EVER OWN A MONKEY?

I'm glad you asked that question. One time, he and his son Buddy went into Americus for groceries and Buddy saw a spider monkey in a pet store that he couldn't do without. He begged and pleaded. So they came home with the monkey and named him Tommy B., because his ears stuck out like Tommy B.'s, and the monkey would get on their pet rabbit's back and ride him around. The only way the rabbit could get the monkey off was by running under the bed and bumping him off.

Then, just before Christmas, the monkey got up onto the tree and started throwing all the ornaments off. Billy grabbed him and the monkey bit his hand down to the bone and held on. Billy was yelling and waving him around, trying to throw him up against the wall, and the children were yelling, "Don't kill Tommy B.! Don't kill Tommy B.!" So he had to hold still "and we prised that monkey out of his hand," Sybil says. "We gave him to a man who sprayed the house."

"The next time I saw that monkey," Billy says wistfully, "he was in the sheriff's office, riding on the back of a dog."

Jeane Dixon, the seeress, predicted in 1977 that "Billy Carter will become a popular television personality, much to the dismay of the White House. He will become the Martha Mitchell of the Carter administration, but he will always know what he is saying and where he is headed. In time, his

talents will be recognized and his wisdom better appreciated."
I don't usually set much stock by Mrs. Dixon's sooth, but I'll
tell you one thing: If any Secret Servicemen ever try to stick
a needle in Billy's ass, I will join the revolution that should
ensue.

More Carters

Freeman Carter, 28, Philadelphia, black fugitive. "Well I
ain't telling you the whole thing of it 'cause it's famly. Anyway nobody ever told me the *whole* thing of it. What I heard,
doctor looked at me when I arrived, you know, said '*Uh*-oh.'

"But evybody was real nice, you know the Carters, we was
ahead of most folks in the area. Yeah, when I was little, 'bout
two or three days old, they sent me on out to Wyomin', that
was cool, I could understand that.

"Didn't fit *in* Wyomin' was all. So I run off and come on
here to Philly. Kinda lost touch with most of the famly, you
know I didn't have no *addresses* for 'em and I wadn't but five.
Fell in with some arm robbery, man. Shot a man three times
and hit 'im wif a jack hannle, twice. And a great big old man,
too. And that was on the *way* to the liquor store. Got nine
years in the joint.

"Didn't fit in there either, too well. So I got me a job in the
prison bakery, man, baked myself into a twenty-foot pan of
cornbread they was making in there for the Cornbread Fest of
a nearby town, see, was the Cornbread Capital of the World
for that area. 'Cept I couldn't find no way to get out you know
until the *ceremony*, man, mayor getting ready to cut it you
know and I come busting out of there, people screaming and
crying and cornbread evywhere and I was *gone*, Jackson.

"I felt bad about the cornbread and all, it was a community
relations projeck, you know, but *what you want me to do?*
See, an nen I couldn't really help Jimmy much in the campaign, see, 'cause, you know, I was *wanted*.

"Ony thing of it is, I'd like to get somese endorsements. I'd endorse a little wine. . . .

"But thing is, lot of people be into things that ain't got *brands*, see what I'm saying?

"But that's cool, that's cool.

"I sing, man.

> *"I'm the ony person I know whooo's*
> *Fum Wyomin' and got the blues.*

"Yeah, heh. Yeah, said '*Uh*-oh.' "

Smack Dab in the Media

"But there was no norm, it was doubtful if there had been a true norm, in New York." —F. SCOTT FITZGERALD

"Djaseeda nooze?" —NORM

The other night I heard on the CBS-TV news that Pope John Paul II had told the United Nations, "Edwin Newman has a dignity that must be preserved if we are to have world peace." Well, I wouldn't want to do anything to impair Edwin Newman's dignity myself. As a writer he fails by just a bit—which is far worse than by a long shot—to be elegant enough to be the arbiter of English usage he comes on as. But whenever I see him on television, I think, "There's a man with a head on his shoulders."

Still, why would the Pope single him out? And why would *CBS* report it, since Newman is on NBC?

Then it came to me. The Pope must have said "every human." Well, it is getting harder and harder to draw a line between humanity and the media. An old boy in Manhattan the other day was telling me:

"No way you can't be aware of it, they had like a whole special on it the other night—the hat radios, the great-photos-from-Life vinyl siding, the flashing newsbriefs going round and round, even like at the Plaza now. Those stencils on Fifth Avenue saying, WATCH CHANNEL 5 and the bulletins creeping across Channel 5 saying USE FIFTH AVENUE. Those YOUR MESSAGE IN THIS SPACE stickers you see on people's foreheads, this new sausage they have out now that when you chew it at the right speed it plays easy-listening and commentary. The other day

Floyd Kalber ran right up to me in the street, wanted to know was there anything I needed to get across, or anything I needed gotten across to me. Any other time, hey, listen, but you know ever since I had the alternative dental work I get WBAI in my sinuses—reception, you wouldn't believe the reception. Right that instant some group was overthrowing the station again, live, I didn't want to miss it, I just said, 'Floyd, quickly. What you're looking for, we all need it: feedback. You and Tom and Jane and Gene and the guy, what's his name, who does the doctor—what you're doing morning after morning, we're *with* you.' Loved it. Thanked me personally from the whole 'Today' crowd. Gave me a MEDIA, WE NEDIA T-shirt to wear.

"Because, you know, a lot of people take it all for granted. There's a theory out now, I heard the other night, the media anymore is like plumbing to people. But, hey, they're doing these media-deprivation studies: people forget the names of *prod*ucts, they're dis*or*ientated, *list*less, loss of *app*etite, *hair* loses its sheen, extreme cases they even get these spontaneous involuntary hums. Pathetic.

"But you know it works both ways. One of the impacts of cable TV, they say, you know, people are forming 'Cable People' groups working to cut down on formula slickness in their own lives, and, on offshoot, they're promoting like just live people who are into things you'd never see on television. They just sit around on curbs and stoops and in parked cars, and I hear some of then are unreal. I mean, hey, guys in these sweaters and ties entirely out of soy products, and for two hours they rebut, like, Rosicrucianism. Beautiful!

"And there's this aspect of it. They're working toward—the *inside access* available to the media, you know, extending it to the consumer. I mean, you get these expectations raised, right? Maybe you want them to go to you on the convention floor. So a big thing along those lines is this Quick Cuts outfit. You've like done a scene at your place and it worked, you know, nothing sensational but you'll take it, and okay, okay, now it's time to pick up the Debby Boone concert. But, okay, hey, it's not televised. You've got to put on your parka and one of your gloves is missing you finally find it under something weird how the hell it's there you don't know don't care. Where your keys, make a long story they're in the freezing compartment, how the hell, oh yeah it's not even interesting, can't use the keys with thick gloves on, take them off, keys are freezing cold now, right, they been in the freezing compartment, right, you go out, triple-lock the door you've dropped a glove inside. Unlock unlock unlock open bend over pick up stand up shut lock lock lock you're finally out its all ice on the stoop you could break your neck, six blocks through slude and dog piles, wait a couple lights, jump out the way a couple people running down the street with a hatchet or something, blah blah stand in line buy a token the woman selling them has this, like, *hatred*, three cops all they got to do is stare at you make sure you don't defraud the turnstile, they don't like you a lot either, blah *blah* blah *blah*, is it this train, is it that stop, where's the shuttle, this stairway, that line, dedumde*dum*, announcement on the train 'MWORWORMBLOR145thStreetMMBLOR' but, okay, say the subway don't experience a delay and you get out the other end eventually, you still got, now, at the Garden, where's your ticket, which gate, which ramp, which level, which color code, which section, which aisle, which seat, it's got some guy's wet sheepskin coat on it that's passed out next to you going 'Uunngghhh.' And that's like just the *high*lights, right? When what you want is—you're not into these dragged-out transitions. You want to establish, you know, you're leaving your place, and then cut, boom, you want to, boom *be there man*, screaming at the music.

"The only trouble, this Quick Cut thing, what they do they chloroform you at your place and take you to the concert and wake you up. And they're still working bugs out. Listen they used to *hit* you, on the *head*, but that got sticky, but even now with the chloroform, and now they got the dosage right, I hear, I mean still they had this guy on the news, this guy woke up in a swingers' retreat he was supposed to wake up in the Cloisters. Guy forgot his entire past, they had to Quick Cut him back to his old high school and his aunt's house and things to get him straight. Had to go all the way back to Indianapolis. Another thing, it's one more hassle for everybody else, squeezing past all these guys carrying unconscious people through the street.

"Let's face it. Logistics. Always going to be with us. This other deal, I don't know, there's a story in *Time*, I guess, they were advertising it in between Tom Snyder last night, and this ad says what they're working on according to this story is *The New York Times* for the Individual.

"Yeah. Like, you're out really really late, right, next morning you get up, open your front door, and there's—like, your name is Phil DiLiberto—the *DiLiberto Times*:

YOU LOSE YOUR WALLET, $84;
AGREE TO WED POLICEWOMAN;
BATTERED CLERIC VOWS SUIT

REGRET FORSEEN

SERIES OF VERY BAD MOVES
LINKED TO GREEN PILL,
TEN DRAMBUIES

"See? I mean maybe you say who needs it, but, hey, don't blame the press. And there's other stories and, well, an editorial page you don't have to read that, but on the Op-Ed balanced viewpoints on what you've been doing, what you'd better get started doing, and there's like a 'Home' section geared to your own place, how it could be fixed up here and there, where the roaches may be hiding. Movie ads, only the ones you haven't been to yet. Sports, kind of nice a big three-column shot of you yelling remarks at Bob McAdoo, won't play any defense, and, hey, in the cultural section reviews of stuff you been putting out. I mean, they don't give you Mimi Sheraton for some zucchini you did in a wok, but it's a place young critics can get started: 'Your previous work in book-cases has shown a peculiar hesitancy, a sort of pedestrianism in imagined heavy traffic. It was as if you were so ridden by doubts as to where Phil DiLiberto was going in life to find and own so many books, and so haunted with fear that, once obtained, they might all shift suddenly some evening and come cascading down on you, that you were unable to take any real risks as to how the case might stand, itself. But now you have surprised us with this provocative new five-shelfer, which . . .'

"The only problem, as far as general availability, this personal *Times*, it's going to cost you they estimate like around $2.4 million a year, even if the newsstand price goes as high as a dollar and anybody besides you ever buys a copy. There's offsetting deals you can get, a group called Freebienetics is working on this. What it is, you subscribe and get *all* the press screenings, the bio folders, the review copies, the fights with Norman Mailer, and you know passes to everything, but that can only go so far. I mean Warners is not going to fly everybody in the country, like two hundred mill, to the Bahamas for a media preview of their latest big one. And say, well unless Warners goes and plows that into a documentary of the junket, see, figure everybody wants to see themselves in the documentary. But then everybody can't expect to get into the *documentary free*. Probably cost you a couple grand just to get into the documentary.

"Go back to the *DiLiberto Times*, a lot of people just want the reviews. You can plug into that. Say your plants are about to peak out and you want a notice. Or you explain something to your wife and you want to know how it went, whatever. And, for sure, you can clip out the blurbs and the service will like découpage them and you can hang them up. I hear now with some services you can specify if you want rave, mixed, whatever you want. But people know, I mean you get a lot more credibility out of a service that's got like objective standards. And listen it's a business for them, they're not going out of their way to pan like their clients. Hey, I can already hear people, friends of mine, you listen to them, their service hates *everything*, it's out to get them, it's twisted, got terrible taste, it resents them for some reason, blah blah. But let's face it, some people just can't explain things to their wives."

Now, Jimmy, he realizes how entangled we are in the media. Nobody wants to be an *object*, everybody wants to be part of the *perceiving apparatus*. The South has always been an object, or a mote, or a beam, in the national eye. And Presidents are supposed to stand up there as big old objects we can glare at.

Jimmy doesn't want to be an object; he wants to be a medium. In part he has attempted this by snythesizing, synthesizing: if 23 percent of the people are hollering for pizza, 17 percent for soup, 19 percent for ice cream and 36 percent for a burger, and 5 percent are undecided, he will deliver what *may be* one big soupy ice-cream pizza on a bun. This kind of middling puts people off, but it also makes them stop hollering for a minute and say, "What in the world is *this!*"

Jimmy will also go on TV and try to turn Americans' lack of confidence in their President, and his own temptation to lose confidence in himself, into *America's crisis of self-confidence*. You are not going to hear Jimmy Carter making Nixon's mistake, standing there flat-footed on camera and saying "I am not a crook." You are going to hear Jimmy saying, if an issue of Presidential crookedness should arise, "This motion of our national crookedness is dragging us down." Jimmy wants to be looking through that TV screen *at us*.

In this he is unlike old Billy, who says, "Y'all perceive me a fool?" Hell, Billy has internal voices that are way ahead of us. He's got one that comes from big brother Jimmy saying,

"Now, Billy, act right." He's got one that comes from his mother and daddy and friends saying, "Oh, fuck him." To the nation Billy says, "Perceive away."

More Carters

Reverend Dulcent Carter, 43, West Weaver, Indiana. "I believe if there is any way wherein that I perhaps share a leadership quality with that of my relative in the Highest Office, it is in the area of achieving consensus. I am, I believe I can say, a man who can pull a broad spectrum of people's thinking together on an issue. When, for example, I learned on arrival at this pulpit that my predecessor here at First Church, Dr. M. Elmond Whisnant, was suspected of walking out of Wednesday Night Family Fellowship Supper every week with there packed in between his skin and sport shirt sometimes as many as five dozen of Mrs. Hoopy's, our cook here for many years, so wonderful light but butter-rich rolls, I was able to reach and ease and settle and reconcile I would say at least 85 percent of the hearts of our congregation with this way of looking at it: It was sure a shame if he was doing it, and if he wasn't, well, it was sure a shame that anyone would think that he was."

Later Billy

Western Civilization. . . . I thought I could handle it. I tried, did all the work. . . . Western Civilization.
  —TONY MESSINA, retired Coast Guardsman who entered college at forty-four and fulfilled his lifelong ambition by making the football team, then became ineligible by flunking Western Civ.

Since I visited him in '77, Billy has come under several clouds. What has he done wrong, though? He has gone out of the way to be openly unbecoming to his brother's office, and charged as much for it as he could, sure. But apparently without winding up with any money to show for it—grant him that—and without ever saying what the people paying him wanted him to say. "I actually tried Piggy's Pizza down South," he said in Boston. "And I liked it, my wife liked it, my six kids liked it, my maid liked it, my dog liked it . . . "

"Okay, Billy, that's enough," interjected the president of Piggy's Pizza.

"Well, my cat didn't like it," Billy added.

Billy took himself a leak on an airport runway in the presence of an Arab diplomat. Whom did that injure? I call it an open-and-shut case of not standing on ceremony. If it sounds heinous, it is only because you so seldom see the word "urinate" in *The New York Times*. What did you want him to do? Squirm and fidget? *Billy's* not a diplomat.

As for the peanut-warehouse funds, Billy's books seem to have held up under scrutiny. And you have to give him credit (even if not as much as Bert Lance did): he didn't let somebody like Robert Vesco or Howard Hughes use him. He let the media use him. The media use people the way stripminers use land.

For a while Billy went right along with just about every opportunity for foolishness that America afforded him. Just having a big time, and in the process gigging American Celebrity and the American image of the Cracker. But that is a harder career than people realize. He started out as a folk hero, but now that he has appeared shakily in a TV tribute to Elizabeth Taylor, and had a doomed beer first-named after him, and modeled a beercan-tab costume, and gone off to an alcoholics' hospital (not, apparently, under duress, like Mrs. Mitchell, who incidentally was a kind of Southern woman I want to stay a long way from), and gotten involved with Libyans, people think he is about what you would expect from a Cracker. A lot of Southerners act ashamed of him, and I have a hard time arguing with them.

I do, though, and sometimes win. I even get carried away and start claiming Billy as my Adam Clayton Powell or Muhammad Ali. About the kind of excuse for an Adam Clayton Powell or Muhammad Ali that a Cracker would have, you may be saying. For one thing Billy can't legislate or box. For another thing, he hasn't got any high purpose. But I think he's more interestingly irritating than the public has perceived him to be. When I was with him, he didn't give a shit, in the best tradition of that phrase. Later, he let the bottle get him down and the media eat him up, but most recently he has dried out and ceased to be quoted so often; and he still doesn't give a shit.

Let me say this: I know a lot of people who, if *they* had been the President's brother, or even if they hadn't, would've acted worse, and did.

The man consorts with Libyans. Well, Billy must surely have brought Libya more bad publicity than anybody else ever has. To tell you the truth, I didn't realize Libya had such a deplorable regime until Billy gave the media an opportunity to point it out. I am not sure now that it is any more deplorable than some of the regimes Jimmy (Russia, Iran) and Israel

(South Africa, Paraguay) deal with. Crazier maybe, but more deplorable?

What did Billy know about Libya, as a regime? I am remind-ed of the old boy at the end of the bar who told the bartender to send a couple of drinks to the two ladies at the other end. "Well, they're Lesbians," said the bartender.

"That's all right."

A little later he wanted to buy them another round. "Well, there ain't no point to it, I'm telling you they're Lesbians," said the bartender.

"I don't care, that's all right."

So the bartender set them up again and a little later the old boy made his way over to the two women, smiled, and said, "Well, how're things in Beirut?"

What seems to have happened is that Billy came to feel that *certain particular old Libyans* were all right with him. I guess he was geopolitically naive to let himself be used for Libyan public relations (and so were the Libyans to use him, as it turned out). But put yourself in Billy's shoes. With a chance to be convivial with some people he liked and had given him an $8,000 saddle (for what an $8,000 saddle is worth), he could have taken the geopolitically knowing option, or he could have taken the spontaneously neighborly option, which he did. One great thing about Billy is that he has shown what happens when a regular decent disreputable down-home old boy, who is honor bound to speak his mind and be himself for whatever his mind and self may be worth, goes public and in-ternational. He gets into a world of trouble, which he never made, although he did have a hand in it. If that isn't geopoli-tics all over, I don't know what is.

SOMETHING MUST BE DONE ABOUT BILLY'S RAFFISHNESS proclaimed a headline—in the New York *Post!* How vastly would the *Post* be ennobled if it could *rise* to raffishness. "He's not up to your standards," presidential image-builder Gerald Rafshoon admonished the producer of "Face the Nation" when that program lined Billy up to appear. Oh, go away, Rafshoon. If only the President had more raffishness and less Rafshoonishness.

Okay, but how can you defend what Billy said about the Jews? I am willing to grant that "There's a hell of a lot more Arabians than there is Jews" is not, on the face of it, morally telling. Except insofar as it tells against, or *mostly* against, the geopolitical thinking of the ordinary unregenerate old down-home boy or girl immemorial—who is the person that we eventually have to come down to in geopolitics. "There's a hell of a lot more Arabians than there is Jews" is a thought we should transcend but not repress.

Here's a stark contrast in Southern communications: William Styron gets millions of dollars and critical esteem for writing page after page of presumptuously empathic bad prose about a concentration camp victim, and Billy Carter gets nothing but abuse for an authentic and not unrepresentative whiff of himself. Is it any wonder that so much bad country music comes out of the South? Nobody will import the real stuff.

There is an official morality in the media. Amendable, and also defensible, and in many ways elevating. But often cheap. And essentially more moral and tighter-assed than life. There are things the media can't report—they are *inaccrochable*, or "unhangable," as Gertrude Stein said about some of Hemingway's short stories because they were too sexually explicit for the time. To report something in a major newspaper or magazine is in a sense to endorse it. To bring it into the parlor. A minor folk hero of a black athlete recently told George Kimball of the Boston *Phoenix*, drolly but with some feeling, "There is no such thing as an ugly white woman." How can the media get a handle on something like that? It's serenely sexist and *double-edgedly* racist. It seems to confirm too many prejudices at once. There is no telling how loathsome a tangle of bigots is out there waiting to perceive that quote as *pervasively* illuminating, and no telling how prudish a clot of abstract arbiters is waiting to perceive it as too dark for words. The media honorably dread gratifying the tangle and cravenly dread offending the clot.

What if Muhammad Ali had said "There's a lot more Arabians than there is Jews"? A certain leeway is allowed proven frank colorful black folk heroes whose temporal power is not great enough for their blind spots to be generally oppressive. The media used to allow Billy some of that leeway, or thought they were allowing it. Everybody who knew Billy used to give him that kind of leeway, because he was doughty and small-time enough to demand it. But when he went national, he couldn't rely on his listeners' knowing where he was coming from. Unlike Jimmy, he didn't allow for the lurking assumption in the national media that rednecks are by nature oppressors and therefore don't deserve leeway, and are showing their true character—*which the culture has to smash*—when they say something illiberal. Rednecks are the only minority in the culture who have to be liberal (in other words, not quite themselves) to be nationally admissible. When Prime Minister Begin is reactionary, Mary McGrory writes, "As a Jew in this century, he's entitled." Only rednecks and Republicans have to be liberal, or *very* moderate, in order to get media sympathy. And Republicans have the consolation of money.

Any tendentiousness of Billy's quote about the Arabians is nicely undercut by the term "Arabians," which can't have gladdened Arabs' hearts. Rednecks are literary, as opposed to forensic, enough to like saying things for the way they sound. But I realize it doesn't really seem savory in the national forum for a redneck to be saying anything at all about Jews. Maybe I have no business going into all this myself. But it makes a Cracker feel good just to get to where he can *read* about Jews and keep his bearings. And now here I am writing about them!

I may not be entitled. But Norman Podhoretz feels entitled to write, with easy obtuse humor, about "good ol' boys." In

Breaking Ranks, he says, "According to my wife, Midge Decter, who worked on the editorial staff of *Harper's* under Willie Morris of Yazoo City, Mississippi . . . and got to know dozens of 'good ol' boys' [I'll bet Richard Nixon used to speak of having gotten to know "dozens of Jewboys"] who came around in search of assignments, they would have been altogether unstoppable [!] if not [whew] for the fact that 'they always needed a beer.' " Did she ever consider that they might just always need a beer when they're in New York? " 'The first one of these good ol' boys who comes along and can manage without a beer,' she said one evening after a day in the office in the company of a troupe [!] of good ol' boys who couldn't, 'is liable to end up running the country.' " For his own part, Podhoretz notes that these *Harper's* good old boys were forever bragging about how they had fought the oil interests back in Texas. He found that naive. What would really be courageous, he says, is to defend the oil interests in New York. In other words, politics is ideas. I find that naive.

Let me say that I do not take Podhoretz as an exemplar of Jewish thought. I don't take anybody as an exemplar of Jewish thought, and I wish people would stop taking individuals, or even troupes, as exemplars of good ol' boy thought.

Billy never set himself up as a commentator on subjects more global than beer-drinking ("I never chug. It always comes out my nose"). But just because he tried to broaden his horizons and bring a little Libyan business to Georgia, people set up to bring the Holocaust down on him, to corner him into making a pious disavowal.

Billy wouldn't be pushed that far out of character. What he would do was allow the impression to be given that he had told the American Jewish community it could "kiss [his] ass." More precisely, when a reporter persisted, at a party, in asking him what he had to say to people who were accusing him of objective anti-Semitism, Billy answered, "The way I feel right now, they can kiss my ass."

Well. Give the man credit. If you seek to shun or revile

someone, or you suspect him of plotting to overthrow God's America and kidnap Christian babies for purposes of ritual murder, you don't tell him to kiss your ass. That is something you say, sociably or defiantly, but not repressively, to someone on your own level or a little higher. What would really be invidious would be for Billy to single out a given ethnic group to be polite to. I would have thought that Billy's remark might make the Jewish community feel like one of the boys. I know I would be flattered half to death if I were to find myself, a stolid grit, accused convolutedly of intellectual viciousness in *Commentary*. What is disgusting about Billy's being willing to tell given Jews—presented to him secondhand in the form of outraged moral abstractions—the same thing he would be pleased to tell them, or General Westmoreland or Billy Graham, face to face if provoked?

I remember reading, in *Armies of the Night*, Norman Mailer's confession that, while waiting forty minutes for the Reverend Ralph Abernathy to show up for his own press conference, he (Mailer referring to himself in the third person) "had become aware after a while of a curious emotion in himself, for he had not ever felt it consciously before—it was a simple emotion and very unpleasant to him—he was getting tired of Negroes and their rights." That passage must have refreshed many a reader, black and white.

I say that partly, of course, as one who is all but inured to being refreshed, so to speak, with regard to his own heritage. But I also say that as a damn *reader*. I mean everybody gets tired after a while of giving due to martyrs. I grew up with Jesus as my martyr and I got tired of *that*. Never got legitimately tired of Jesus—I just got tired of being nice to him in my mind. I know, in my soul, that Jesus got tired of it too.

Incidentally, Mailer in *Miami and the Siege of Chicago* gets up before a revolutionary audience and says, "You may wonder why I am speaking to you in this Southern accent which is fake and phony. It is because I want to make a presentation to you." He goes on, I have to admit, to say some interesting things about "shit" and "glory." But how would it sound if I got up before a revolutionary audience and said, "You may wonder why I am speaking to you in this Jewish accent . . ."?

The wave of knee-jerk reaction which followed Billy's remarks caused William Raspberry, who is black, to write in the Washington *Post:* "Many of the Jews who shout anti-Semitism every time they see their interests in jeopardy don't really believe the charge. . . . They simply understand that American politicians are so sensitive to the allegation of anti-Semitism, and so sensitive to organized Jewish pressure, that they use it as a device for influencing policy and muting criticism. (Ironically, you cannot even acknowledge the fact of that influence without being accused of anti-Semitism.)"

Billy accused "Jewish media" of "tearing up Arab countries full time." Well, that smacked of dumb-assedness to be sure. But nobody has really given this matter of Jews and the media the rigorous and mostly grateful consideration it deserves.

Recently on the "Today" show David Steinberg, the comedian, made a remark that reminded me a lot of the kind of joke Billy makes at his best. Gene Shalit asked Steinberg if he had any fears.

"I'm afraid of *everything*," Steinberg replied. "I'm afraid of pork."

"Pork?" asked Shalit.

"Yes, I'm afraid eating pork makes you stupid."

Both Steinberg and Shalit broke up. Hey, so did I. And I *love* pork.

Now, I won't say that "I'm afraid eating pork makes you stupid" is a cabalistic remark, but it *is* ethnic. It is almost the history of Jewish humor. Pork is Gentile meat and Jews have traditionally had to survive (with reason to be afraid of everything) by outsmarting Gentiles. And this is a joke that everybody in America who is not stupid appreciates.

Whereas Southerners have had to survive by outdumbing, sort of, Northerners. Watch "Hee-Haw" (a widely popular show that is too ethnic for the networks) sometime. Southern apparent obtuseness and its subtleties is Billy's basic joke. But that basic joke, *from its own viewpoint,* doesn't work on network TV. It only works in the form of things like "The Beverly Hillbillies," an atrocity that would never have been perpetrated as late as the sixties on any other ethnic group. Would you call a television program "The Bel Air Bagel-Eaters"?

The Jewish influence on media morality has been great and preponderantly beneficent. Hey, what if the Jewish influence on the media sense of humor were supplanted by Eastern Wasp influence?

"Do you have any fears?"

"No, because of a good neighborhood and excellent police protection."

"Do you sniff at anything?"

"I sniff at *everything.* I sniff at pork."

"Pork?"

"Yes, I feel pork makes one greasy."

(Everybody breaks up.)

I don't see how there can be much doubt that Jews have brought into American media—and American currents of thought, standards of argument and politics—powerful Old World, Old Testament, soulful, nervous influences, praise the Lord. The price we have to pay for these liberating influences is, for instance, *Commentary.* (If there were serious journals for which I could write heavy essays entitled "A Southern Methodist at Harvard," I might still unhappily be one.) I have always thought of the Judaic as a prince among ethnoses because it is so far from being parochial compared to other ethnoses, *and* has kreplach. But, to the extent that persons purporting to represent "the Jewish community" want to suppress or make capital out of Billy Carter, or to the extent that they insist on his brother's denouncing him or describing him as anti-Semitic, they deserve a short answer.

Praise be to the greatly-influenced-by-Jews ACLU for defending the American Nazis' right to march in Skokie, Illinois. But there ought to be more room in public American debate for even *credible* disagreement with what are considered to be Jewish positions. Granted that no member of the United Nations here on earth has any business denouncing Israel for racism, why is the *idea* that "Zionism is a form of racism" off limits? Zionism *is* a pretty aggressive form of ethnicism, at any rate.

Nothing *shameful* in that.

I for one would like to see Billy be able to work through some of his feelings in public.

The way Richard Pryor has. There's somebody who is dirty-mouthed, intemperate, ethnocentric, and obstreperous, and valuable to listen to. He lets those internal voices come *out*. He's one of the few people in the American public who are as funny as American life.

I honor Billy because he is not the kind of person people say "I tho-o-oo*ught* I detected an accent" to, any more than Richard Pryor is the kind of person people call a credit to his race. Billy's not defensive—he doesn't censor and corrupt his natural way of talking, the way Jimmy has done and the way Lyndon Johnson did in public. If only Lyndon Johnson had ever said "I'm the leader of the Free World, and you ask me a chicken shit question like that" *on* camera instead of off!

Billy talks the way he thinks, and the way America talks in beer joints. It's too bad so much of his shit gets taken out of context. I have stood right there and heard him say funny things and seen even Southern newspersons quote them dumbly so that they sound dumb. For instance, when he said "Coors is like marijuana. If you could buy it in Georgia, you wouldn't want it," he was quoted in Nashville as saying, "Coors is like marijuana." Unfortunately Billy is no writer, singer, politician, actor, or boxer. He just gives quotes. Which means he has no way of knowing what he is going to say in the paper.

Anyway, I have just about given up on halfway wishing that Billy would go ahead and move Jimmy aside and be President himself. Billy might have done some good things in the job, like round up a couple of TV cameras and go down to Congress and buttonhole an actual oil lobbyist personally and ask him to justify himself—old lobbyist blushing and blinking and flinching and trying to sidle off the screen and talking technicalities and Billy shrugging all that off and asking simple-minded questions like "How *come* y'all got to be so protected when you're making more and more while the small farmer's got to be so regulated while he's making less and less?" Billy might have been a redneck domestic Andrew Young, kept people off balance, held to his own instinctive non-governmental frame of reference. That's how Jimmy got elected in the first place, wasn't it?

Trouble is, my image of Billy as an anti-lobbyist is a liberal fantasy. On the "Today" show in late 1979 he defended OPEC for charging so much for oil. If NBC had a monopoly on television programs, he said, it would charge what the traffic would bear. When he was asked if he had an oil deal with the Libyans, he said, "I'd love to have an an oil deal with *anybody*. But I don't." Billy has a better handle on mortal man than Jimmy or I do.

But I still like to think that Jimmy could get away with more progressive things if he were a better old boy. He probably wishes he were one.

> I got the redneck White House blues.
> I thought he'd give a lift to us Yahoos.
> He's got 98 advisers
> and none of them chews.
> I got the redneck White House blues.

The first Cracker President should have been a mixture of Jimmy and Billy, a cobbler of Billy's basic blackberries oozing up into and through Jimmy's cut-to-specifications crust. Billy's hoo-Lord-what-the-hell-get-out-the-way attitude heaving up under Jimmy's prudent righteousness—or Jimmy's idealism heaving up under Billy's sense of human limitations—and forming a nice-and-awful compound like life in Georgia, like life—I wouldn't be surprised—in other areas of the country that haven't been over-mediaized. That Cracker President would have had a richer voice, and a less dismissable smile.

P.S. Late note, August 1, 1980: I haven't changed my mind on any of this. Personally I hand it to Billy for being the only American in years to rip off an oil-producing country. If the nation can't tell the difference between Watergate and "Billygate," then it probably deserves Ronald Regan.

More Carters

Sister Muriel Oriola Carter, 50, Far Caverns, Georgia, who speaks in tongues. "I'm not saying it's Jesus; it's not all necessarily the Lord. It could be my momma way back off up in there deep down inside of my sinus—*and* God cherubim seraphim owls powers roots imps dominions. Jigljigljiglj. WOMPH. *Wee sleekit.* I'm the Church of *Poly*glossolalia. *Woo* nawny nawny nawny, h'*Wew* nawny nawnym'narsenal. *Weeee*-geriblerablet.

"*Nawnk nawnk* Molybd'num. K'cockerophylogeno-rogero-bomplet. Arbiofi. Toombes. Geriblet. Hootin' Newton nicens tuckoo wotheth bloom me Belchum Yaw Yaw.

"It goes way back. It comes way out. The *door*'s on the tip of your tongue. Alveralvry. Phlempopocantata-p'tetre-p'tetl. Jimmy ain't opened it. Jimmy ain't opened it. *Yet*. Not in his *public* utterance. Geriblerablet. Wooo, m'wooom: *sleekit*.

"I tell you this, Buddy-Roe. Women likes it, at certain times, and so does babies."

Smiles and Grins

*She's a real lady. I don't think I've ever seen her when she
wasn't breathing through her nose.* —Junior Samples

"As soon as Jimmy got home from school," Miss Lillian Carter has recalled, "his daddy put him right to work. When his
friends drove by and waved and laughed, he waved back and
grinned." Miss Lillian's own grin reminds you of Jimmy's,
only freer, far less toothy, more provoking, a little wicked, a
little complacent, a little loony, and then too you know it has
been directed with real, difficult feeling toward lepers in India
when she was bathing their sores.

I am even inclined sometimes to defend Jimmy's infamous
grin as the natural defense of a person who is trying to stay
composed, and think, and not offend, and not really pander,
while people are staring at him from no telling how many angles. Also the natural defense of someone who is trying to
smile and at the same time to grit his teeth against the internal voice that says, "Boy! Quit mediatin! Git down in there
and *rassle* with them congressmen. *Plow through* them quib-
blers! Kick some ass!"

You know he'd love to kick some. You know he'd love to
break out in a *wrath* when they snigger at him as though he's
a puny little unpopular kid.

People take such liberties with a modern President's face!
This from Liz Smith's gossip column:

"Do you wonder what sort of things preoccupy the leader of
the Western world? Well, for one, Jimmy Carter is hopping
mad at that friend of his sister Ruth Stapleton—I mean Dot-
son Rader. It seems Mr. President really didn't like it that

Rader, in *New York* magazine, likened his smile to 'the grin of a Florida land salesman working a room full of potential buyers.'

"Carter was mortally offended that Rader called his smile 'often defensive, a nervous reaction to tension like a facial tic.' Oh, Mr. President, touchy, touchy."

What do you mean, touchy, touchy? How would you like, in the first place, your sister hanging out with a guy who has written with a certain relish about male hustling, which, when you get right down to it, is trashier than presidential nervousness *or* Florida land sales. And then to have a guy like that (whose own smile, judging from the dust jacket of his recent bad novel, is a sort of flabbier Rex Reed-ish smirk) getting paid to pick your smile to pieces. Who could ever smile easily in public again, knowing what a jaded, surly squirming can-of-snakes tangle of self-appointed critics is out there scrutinizing your ingratiation-bent arrangement of lips and teeth condescendingly, as an object, with some distaste? How well would *your* smile pass muster if it had to stand accountable to every dogfighter, fence, writer-in-residence, human potentialist, geek, Elk, Rastafarian, PR guy, ophthalomologist, VFW bartender, Moonie, roadie, dean of nursing, Chamber head, and snot-nose child in this vast teeming sluggish soured spirally inflating nation of ours, in its capacity as, according to how you look at it, Presidential Rictus or First Beam of the Land?

Of course it doesn't exactly light up the damn room, does it.

I never cared for Jimmy's smile myself. During the campaign, I suspended judgment on it, because, for one thing, I liked it better than Hubert Humphrey's, and, for another thing, I was so gratified to see a Southern white guy bowling over all those severe Northern observers.

During the summer of the campaign, I happened to be at a picnic with Jack Newfield, the Northern muckraker, whose scourging of political trash I have long admired. "I love him!" Newfield said about Jimmy. Hearing that made me feel like a man who has taken his dubiously bred dog kind of apologetically to the national dog championships and suddenly hears the hardest judge of dogs in the country exclaiming, "*Hey*, that's a *good* dog you got there. My, I *like* that dog." I felt proud. I felt apprehensive. I felt that my dog was smiling at that judge in a way that I had maybe never appreciated, and that my dog was perhaps understandably liable to start showing a certain coolness toward me.

Newfield also said he assumed the South would vote overwhelmingly for Carter. Now, I am sensitive about the Southern vote. I can't help identifying with it to some extent. Which is like being identified with original sin. The Southern vote is crazy. Putting together a national Democratic candidacy that will work always requires doing something dumb to accommodate the Southern vote. It's like baking a good nourishing pie and then saying, "Well, it's nice, but we got to put some shit in it. If we don't, the South won't eat it." The great thing about Carter, of course, was that he appeared to be an almost shit-free pie that the South would have to eat anyway because he was *baked* in the South.

I hated to argue with this notion. But I had to say to Newfield, yeah, I guessed so, I guessed the South would vote for Jimmy all right, but I had detected a certain amount of sentiment in the South to the effect that if the North wanted to be bowled over by some Southerner, we could have sent up a better one than that. I felt bad about saying that, and in fact I just sort of mumbled it—as I would have mumbled any reservation I might have about my dog after the big judge had raved about him. But deep down in my heart, I felt he wasn't all that great a dog.

And as I say, I *had* detected sentiment in the South that we could have sent up a better man of the hour than that, any day of the week. To the extent that this sentiment implied, as it often did, that we could have sent up a *slicker* one than that, or a less nigger-ridden one, or a more aristocratic one, or one of these new plastic Southern Republican ones, I was glad to disassociate myself from it. But to the extent that this sentiment implied we could have sent a more resonant one, a lot funnier one, a generally more eloquent and hell-raising one, a more expansive one, I agreed with it. A better-mouthed one, we sure could have sent. I mean one who could roll flavorful Latinate terms, ruminative noises, glad snorts, and farm animals into his discourse a whole lot better. And, too, I mean one who could *smile* better.

I don't recall another President whose smile has been such an issue.

George Wallace, whose smile told you exactly who he was—a by God mean wily shifty redoubtable pissant original—said that Carter betrayed the voters with his "grins and smiles."

That silly, wrongheaded, affection-starved, embarrassing, childish, but finally in a way kind of likable figure Lester Maddox, with his gift for taking things personally, said, in a letter to Jimmy after the new President telephoned Lester in the hospital: "In my opinion, and I hope I'm wrong, you haven't sincerely listened to me or followed my advice or sincerely smiled at me since you were campaigning for governor in 1970."

An Alabama writer named Johnny Greene, in a *Harper's* article entitled "The Dixie Smile," interpreted Jimmy's grin as a Confederate aggression. But by completely messing up a great Kissing Jim Folsom anecdote, Greene also showed he was no judge of Southern jocularity. Marshall Frady, in his book *Wallace*, gets the story right:

While Folsom was in Oklahoma City, Averell Harriman, then governor of New York and aspirant for the Democratic presidential nomination, decided to drop by Folsom's hotel room to pay his respects, impelled no doubt by the fact that Folsom had just won re-election by a heavy margin. Folsom received him in his undershirt. After a short exchange of pleasantries, it suddenly occurred to Folsom that Harriman was cultivating him. With his huge arm wrapped around Harriman's dapper shoulder, Folsom advised him, with a benign little tilt of his head, "Now, don't piss on ole Jim's leg. You can't piss on ole Jim's leg."

Now that—especially when you consider that Harriman is reported to have exclaimed about Carter, "How can he be nominated? I don't even know him"—is a story that Southerners, black or white, drunk or sober, deserve to be proud of. (Incidentally, Harriman, according to *The New York Times*, arrived at a costume party the night before John Kennedy's inauguration "as an ambassador for every country and performed a Russian Cossack dance. His wife wore a space suit." Do you think Billy and Sybil Carter would behave like that?) There are a lot of people Averell Harriman never heard of. I have spent a lot more time with those people than I have with people who might belong to a crowd with which Averell Harriman is conversant. But I have met a random sampling of long-standingly rich residents of Eastern states, and I am going to say something now that may sound rude. I don't mean it to be rude—because most of those long-standingly rich people were perfectly nice. But most of them struck me as being extremely poor at *sounding people out*.

Here is another Folsom-Harriman story, told by Robert Sherrill in *Gothic Politics in the Deep South*:

At a between-campaigns political rally to which Averell Harriman had been invited, once again Folsom stretched out on the stage and went to sleep. When it came his turn to take the microphone, several aides tried to hoist the six-foot-eight-inch governor to his feet, without luck. Finally he became conscious enough to raise up on an elbow and say he felt too humble to follow such a great man, and fell back.

Folsom had his faults. But lack of spontaneous charm wasn't one of them. And yet what Johnny Greene wrote in *Harper's* was that (as people shouted, "Show 'um, Jim!") Folsom went up to Harriman at a political gathering in an Alabama hunting lodge, indicated for a moment that he was about to endorse Harriman for President, but then instead did what he had intended to do from the first, "which was, in full view of everyone, to urinate on Harriman's leg." Greene quotes Folsom as explaining that "everybody in the whole South always wanted to piss on the governor of New York, and I just done it."

Greene goes on to say:

I don't believe this story is true, though I know the sentiments expressed in it are. I have never seen a white Southerner fail to crack up over it, slap his kneecap or the shoulder of someone sitting nearby, and say: "Ole Jim, he really showed 'um that time, didn't he?"

When I heard the story repeated this summer by a liberal Alabama supporter of Jimmy Carter . . . , I realized it is no longer just a horrifying regional anecdote of misbehavior and crudeness. Twenty years after the Folsom-Harriman meeting, "showing 'um" is still the governing principle of Southern Democratic politics. The only changes within this historical precedent have come through the New South's "new respectability." "Showing 'um" no longer means a knee-jerk incontinence or a blatant stand in a schoolhouse door. It more readily manifests itself in the obfuscating smile of a Good Ole Boy who is touching on the one issue the defeated South has always immediately understood—being "born again."

What Greene has established here is that there are good old boys who have bad senses of humor and character, and they are the ones he knows. None of the ones I have spent much time with would have liked that story, or believed it. I disbelieve because I can't see anybody who can do a Cossack dance holding still long enough to be pissed on more than a couple of drops, and also because it's the only story I ever heard about Jim Folsom that wasn't funny. As for "showing 'um," well, I wouldn't deny that that can be a self-defeating activity, but then Greene's article strikes me as an attempt to show 'em back home. "Obfuscating smile," though, well, I can't argue with that. Jimmy does have a lot more obfuscating a smile than Folsom's must have been. But how many fine, open, unafraid, to-the-point smiles do you see on politicians on television these days?

"That born-again smile," M. F. K. Fisher, the food writer, was quoted as calling it. From her residence in France she agonized: "Should I come home or should I stay? It's hard to live in a country that has a President with that born-again smile. I feel fastidious about it. But I'm an American and don't want to be an expatriate. I'll go to my grave feeling split."

That last sentence has a ring to it.

> I'll go to my grave feeling split
> 'Tween I and you and we and they and it.
> Don't like how the President smiles,
> So I'm staying off thousands of miles.

But I am reluctant to call Jimmy's a *born-again* smile. I would be more inclined to call it a shit-eating grin. I guess you know what that is. If you have ever seen a dog eating some. A dog will do that—a dog is a noble animal in many ways, but it will eat shit sometimes, when it finds some appealing. I bet Lassie did it if they ever let her around any.

It is not exactly the same as "grinning like a mule eating briers." That is a kind of tough, perversely proud, indefatigable, and mysteriously, innerly motivated grin. But they are both fixed grins. And a shit-eating grin has this sort of mean shame in it. It has the courage, and pure pleasure, of mean shame.

You might say, well, now wait a minute. Everybody who is on television regularly has a shit-eating grin. (Except for the network news guys, who have this sort of *that's-the-way-the-shit-went-down*, *don't-look-at-me*, *well*, *ahem*, *I-guess-you-*

are-of-course-looking-*at-me, like-the-way-my-hair-does!*, *but-I-mean-none-of-this-shit-is-any-of-my-doing* look of gravity.)
And people on television don't have any shame.

But those aren't real shit-eating grins, *because* they don't show any shame. TV people have these sort of cosmeticized, sicklied-over, self-denying, *I'm-eating-chocolate-pudding-re-ally-and-you're-eating-it-too, and-so-are-my-guests-here-who-are-getting-ready-to-appear-at-the-Sahara* shit-eating grins.

Whereas a real shit-eating grin is by definition not quite a denial. It's the glaze that highlights what's going down underneath.

And white folks in the South have had to eat a lot of shit—well, nobody *has* to, but most people just about have to, so they do. Have to eat something, and history and economics and many other things will mix a lot of shit in with your daily bread. When I say white folks in the South have had to eat a lot of it, I mean the country has made a national moral issue of how they ought to have to. When I say you don't have to eat it, I mean you don't have to eat your daily bread. Saints don't. Heroes find ways for a while of avoiding it, or appearing to avoid it, while getting plenty of nourishment. Or maybe they have the voraciousness to eat a whole lot of it for the sake of the nourishment mixed in with it, until the shit starts backing up and then they fall.

Most people do eat it anyway, and call it Death or Tradition or Realism or What the Government's Doing to Us Now. Religion and fortitude and hot sauce and music and love and meanness and venery help us get it down.

People in the South know this. But they won't admit it. But they will grin about it.

I guess what bothers me about Jimmy's grin really is that it is sort of denatured. Which is partly the nature of a shit-eating grin, though—being denatured.

Oh, this is an intricate concept enough. Anyway, Jimmy's grin is brave; it is edited for television but not edited enough to look falsely affectionate—or not falsely affectionate enough to deceive anybody with shit for sense; it is troubling, if you dwell on it, and I guess that's good. It isn't the most honest shit-eating grin I've ever seen, by a long shot, but you probably can't get elected nationally if you have an honest one.

Lyndon Johnson could probably marshal an honest one in private, but on TV he had one that said, "Who me?" George McGovern, when he was running for President, had sort of a sick one that said, "Oh this stuff tastes *awful*." We don't need a man leading us who has as weak a palate as all that. Nixon smiled like he *liked* it. We don't need that either, couldn't stand that any longer. Gene McCarthy looked like shit wouldn't melt in his mouth. He wouldn't take enough of it to get nominated, even. Jack Kennedy got his ashes hauled so often he was always feeling too good, except for his back, for the shit to show in his grin. Or he burnt it off or something. Bobby Kennedy had this really fierce, but vulnerable, shit-eating grin; he is my candidate. Gerald Ford, I don't know, who gives a shit?

Anyway, a President has to eat a tremendous lot of it. More and more, it looks like that is what we elect him for; that is his job. Somebody has got to digest all the exhaust, bad faith, and guilt that is building up, and maybe if anybody can do it, it's a Cracker.

Not Jimmy, though. I don't know whether you have noticed, but by the time of the Iran crisis, that old peculiar grin of his was gone. The pressures of his office and his jogging and his sufferance of all those wild redneck Iranians had given him a more truly hurt-looking austerity. He looked like he could reach a little deeper and come up with some real country music.

More Carters

Chinquapin Carter, 40, Cope, Alabama, whose profession is visions. "Wull *yeah* it's a good living. It *deserves* to be, don't it? Where you going to get that kind of work done today? What does a lawyer do for people, and he gets a *gooood* dollar. He'll probly make better'n I do.

"I might of studied for a lawyer if I knew what I know now.

"How I usually work it, well, people get word to me, you know, and I pull on this whole chicken skin on over my head and look out thoo his little leg holes and move into their attic for a week, ten days, and have the visions that's backed up in there awaiting the adept. Certain number of fat oxens eating certain number of skinny oxens, or young people getting preternaturally wrinkled, or gret huge certain-colored birds across the Milky Way, whatever.

"Haven't been to the White House yet, no. I'd be tickled to—I think I could clear up some things been *bothering* people.

"So, anyway, I'll have a vision for you, give you an idea. Couldn't have a full one on this short of a notice but let's see, well, there's a bear with a flaming head and feet running thoo a bus station, only the bus station is, it's sort of got a funny *tone* to it, it makes this kinda hum, kinda *wooooooonnnn* . . . "

Whiskey and Blood

The entire value of my book, if it has any, will consist of my having known how to walk straight ahead on a hair, balanced above the two abysses of lyricism and vulgarity (which I seek to fuse . . .).
— FLAUBERT

One big reason I wanted to write this book was to find out what Billy Joe Shaver said to the woman who wanted his fingers.

Billy Joe Shaver has been in a creative decline here lately, partly because he is bad to get in fistfights. You'll go into some place in Austin where people on the music scene hang out and there will be some big old boy sitting there pissed off with his shirt hanging on to him by threads and his eye swelling, and you'll ask him what happened and he'll say, "Well, hell, I don't know. Me and Billy Joe was drinking and changing a tire and the next thing I knew . . ." But Billy Joe Shaver has written some of the greatest songs of country music. Lyrics in them like:

> The Devil made me do it the first time,
> The second time I done it on my own . . .

And:

> I just thought I'd mention
> My grandma's old-age pension
> Is the reason why I'm standing here today.
> I've got a good Christian raisin'
> And an eighth-grade education,
> Ain't no sense in y'all treatin' me this way.

Don't you think Jimmy Carter would like to be able to represent himself that sympathetically? Billy Joe Shaver takes *the way people put things* and puts it to music. In a country music fan magazine, I read that when he was eleven he caught his right hand in some mill machinery and had to rip his fingers off to keep from losing his whole arm. And then:

"As he held back the spurting blood in his mangled hand, a Negro woman picked up his severed fingers and said, 'Can I have these?' "

That was the end of the story, as told in this country music magazine. It was one of those stories where you wanted to know what happened next. But I didn't know Billy Joe from a bale of hay, personally, and I couldn't just call up his record company and ask for his agent's phone number and then call his agent and ask for Billy Joe's phone number (and all along I'd have to be explaining, "I want to know what he told the woman who asked for his fingers," and they'd be saying, "Say what? What woman?" and I'd be trying to explain) and then call Billy Joe and ask him, "Billy Joe, just out of curiosity. You don't know me from a bale of hay, but you remember that time the woman asked for your fingers?"

"Yeah."

"What did you tell her?"

"Who'd you say this was?"

I couldn't even afford all those long distance calls unless I could write them off as a business expense.

And I like country music. My parents never did, and I didn't used to, but ever since I moved North I've been listening to it the way James Baldwin listened to Bessie Smith records in Paris, to remember his native tongue. My friend Ann Lewis, who grew up in South Carolina, conveyed some of country music's appeal in a letter she wrote me once:

While I was going to school, I worked several nights a week at the telephone office, Central. There was a woman named Mrs. Fields who had just gotten a telephone and liked it. She would call up whoever was working at night and ask if they wanted to hear something pretty. And then she would play and her little girl Neecie would sing "I wish I had never met Sunshine and Sunshine had never met me," or "Seven years with the wrong woman is more than any man can stand," or, great favorite, "Wreck on the Highway":

> When whiskey and blood ran together
> I didn't hear nobody pray.

One time the Briarhoppers, a singing group from Charlotte, had a flat tire in front of our house, and they came in and sang for Nannie, our great-aunt who had broken her hip and was in bed for ten years. There was a Baptist preacher's wife named Mrs. Cave who used to come in wearing a black cape and flap around the house and tell Nannie she could get up and walk if she wanted to. But the Briarhoppers did her a lot more good.

When the Carter phenomenon was new, people who had never had such experiences with country music were paying obeisances to it. In *New York* magazine, Northern political writer Richard Reeves wrote:

Something very big is happening in the country right now. In shorthand, the South is rising again and Jimmy Carter just happens to be the symbol of that resurrection. A few years ago, I was drinking a night away with Gene Roberts, a North Carolinian who was then a colleague on *The New York Times.* . . . He . . . put on some records— Johnny Cash records. "C'mon, I don't understand that crap," I said. "Anyone who doesn't understand Johnny Cash doesn't understand America," he said. My friends, it's time to start learning what Johnny Cash is all about.

In *New Times* magazine, Northern political writer Robert Sam Anson wrote:

Outside, the [Grand Ole Opry] parking lot is jammed with . . . cars from every state in the nation. Inside the packed house, the audience, well-scrubbed and white, sits attentively, almost reverentially, as one "beloved" performer after another struts his stuff. Backstage,

C. W. McCall, a former Omaha adman now on his way to country immortality, explains the appeal: "It's honest," he says. "Telling a story in no uncertain terms so people can understand it . . . sort of like Jimmy Carter."

Now I know how my colleagues and I all went wrong. Instead of listening to Hubert Humphrey, we should have been hearing Johnny Cash.

. . . If there were a chance to get back to what we once were, if there could be change, if there were hope left for this country, any hope at all, it was here . . . in Dixie.

Remember when Northern political writers were writing things like that about the South and country music and Jimmy Carter? (Since then, Anson has written that what he wrote then was "absolute crap.") They could have found a lot better people to cite than gimmicky C. W. McCall and embourgeoised Johnny Cash, but for those of us who came of age at a time when the working national-media assumption was that everybody white down South was a turd, it was almost too much. Well, it *was* too much. But it *was also* kind of gratifying.

It was also peculiar. It was sort of like—well, this actually happened in Plains: Say you're heading off up the road toward Sunday school on Sunday morning, dressed up in scratchy clothes, and it is sho-befo-God hot, and deep down inside you have a whole lot of mixed emotions about heading toward Sunday school—you hope you don't get cornered by old Miz Wingo, pore old soul, she just don't know any better, she'll start telling you how she was at your wedding when she wasn't any more at your wedding than the man in the moon, but she'll tell you all about how your wedding was anyway, twenty years ago or whenever it was, and she'll just go on and on and there won't be any way to tactfully get out of listening to her because you've been listening to her tell you about your wedding for the last eight or ten years and you can't suddenly reach out and grab her by the throat now and holler, "MIZ WINGO NOW GOT DAMN IT YOU WASN'T *AT* MY WEDDING!"

And, well, there's hard feelings at the church about nigras trying to get in and whether to build a new sanctuary, now that the Methodists have one (a new sanctuary) with a steeple six feet higher than yours, and there's accusations that the preacher is skimming nickels from the church Coke machine, and—well, for instance, I knew of a church once where the pastor at the age of about sixty-seven ran off for carnal reasons apparently with his secretary. "And to think," a lady of the congregation said, "I sat there and listened to that man's sermons for three solid years."

Say you have all these mixed but deep-dyed feelings about going to Sunday school this morning. But you're going anyway because, hell, you always go to Sunday school on Sunday morning if you're well enough to walk, and there's generally some part of it that makes you feel closer to the Almighty, or anyway it's a rest from stringing telephone wires or snapping beans—but *anyway* you *do always do it* on Sunday morning and you always figured everybody did except those that were content to be looked on as heathens.

And this really happened in Plains, Georgia, after Jimmy arose: TV crews were going up to people who were going to Sunday school on Sunday morning, and these slick-haired interviewers were asking the people in tones of amazement what they were doing.

"Going to Sunday school."

"And you do this every Sunday?"

"Well, yes. I can't rightly do it on Tuesday."

"And then what do you do, after Sunday school?"

"Church."

"And then what?"

"Fry up a chicken. Get irritated by the children. Have Sunday dinner."

And then the TV crews were cutting away back to New York or wherever the hell television comes from and talking about how this stuff actually goes on in Plains, it's a custom, a folkway.

Well. So country music, which is getting ruined anyway by the Los Angeles influence or something (the same thing has happened to it that has happened to work clothes: gone from well-worn blue dungaree overalls to funny-colored wearproof polyester jump suits), was being poked and prodded at and trotted forth and applied to national affairs by people who acted like they never heard of it before, hadn't anybody ever called them up and sung it to them over the phone or played it for their broken-hipped old great-aunt. I figured I was a lot better person to write about country music.

After all, when I am driving down the road feeling sad and see something on the roadside that strikes a chord, I am not moved to sociological observations. I am not moved to tears either. I don't make a note of some good material to take up with my therapist. I don't have no therapist. I pull out my imaginary guitar and warm up my imaginary voice and strike up a song:

"Fill Wanted," says the sign on the side of the road.
"Fill Wanted," bring in another load.
"Fill Wanted," and that's what I need too.
I need some fill to fill the hole I'm filled with without you.

The other night a bunch of us were sitting around in a Manhattan drinkery drinking and talking about country music. We were making up song titles, like "Hard Liquor, Loud Music, and Your Soft Eyes (Will See Me Through the Night)" and "I'll Never Get Over Women (or Out from Under You)" and "My Company's Sending Me to Memory School (and All I Want to Do Is Forget)." We were rejoicing in recently recorded songs, like "It Was Always So Easy to Find an Unhappy Woman (Till I Started Looking for Mine)," sung by Moe Bandy, and "My Head Hurts, My Feet Stink, and I Don't Love Jesus," by Jimmy Buffett. We were telling about how Dolly Parton had responded to a question that was passed up to her during a concert in Memphis—she didn't read the question aloud, she just said, "About like cantaloupes, and wouldn't your mother be proud of you."

Suddenly June Jenkins, who is from Fort Worth originally, hollered out:

"Country music is terrible! It reminds me too much of what I got away from. Y'all are just pretending to love it to make fun of it."

I brooded over that for a while. Thinking yeah, but naw, but then too what you have to consider is, the virtues of country music's defects are better than some other musics' pure virtues, even if the defects of its virtues are worse than other musics' pure defects. And then there are country music's pure virtues, which are honeyed things, and its pure defects, which are such terrible things you can't help but take your hat off to them, and . . .

And what I want more than anything else in the world, except inner peace and the ability to eat as much ribs and peach ice cream and not get fat as I could when I was twelve or thirteen, *is to be a country singer.* One of these country singers who appeal to the dope smokers and the fruit-jar drinkers and the buttermilk chuggers and the hard-eyed middle-aged men and the big old fat women and the little young women that might if things get going good take off their halters and just be jumping around to your music there in their shorts. One of these crazier than hell but also plain as dirt and spiritually sound country singers. Though I wouldn't take acid and sing "Will the Circle Be Unbroken," as I have heard that certain ones have been known to.

I'd be singing country music that *was* country music, shit-kicking nasal *wang-ang-ang-ang-ang-ang* dog-loving truck-driving train-whistling daddy-remembering heart-grinding country, but somehow it'd evoke or incorporate rock and roll, Randy Newman, Kurt Weill, white gospel, black gospel, hokum, Stephen Foster, blues, Western swing, and ragtime—it would range from "So fine so fine so fine" to "*Yee*-hiiiiighhh!" to "Preh-eh-eh-eh-cious bluh-uh-uh-uhddd" before you had time to sit back and swallow good.

Why does anybody from Georgia want to be *President*? Why doesn't Jimmy want to be a country singer? I think I'd sing about myself in the third person, as though I had died. Call myself Buddy Roe Bear and His Ruined Choir, who would be two laid-back semi-depraved-looking youngish women going "So fine so fine so fine," and I'd develop my own legend, like Walt Whitman only sadder. Lapsing into the past tense for one thing.

> His *life* was a *mix*ture of *great* rights and *wrongs*.
> He wrote *bad* checks, his *ma*ma and *beautiful songs*.
> He *lived* in the *pines* with the *great* speckled *bird*.
> He *wrote* ev'ry *tune* and he *earned* every *word*.
> If you *say* that he's *ly*ing, he'll *call* you a *liar*.
> He's *gonna* go *off* now and *practice* his *choir*.

Lord, Lord, if I wouldn't have fun it would be my own damn fault. Singing love songs, like:

> She said she thought she might adore me.
> I thought she *would* do something for me,
> But now I'm feeling twice as gloomy—
> All she did was something to me.
> > Oh the last thing I needed
> > To be was bereft.
> > As soon as I was feelin right she left.

And:

> Here I am a-comin atchew,
> I don't know no one to match you,
> I am swoopin down to snatch you,
>> Where'd you go?
>
> So fired up I'm getting reckless,
> You to me are wholly speckless,
> I'd buy you a diamond necklace,
>> Where'd you go?
>
> You are my supreme objective,
> You are it from my perspective,
> I'm on you like six detectives,
>> Where'd you go?
>
> Baby, I just don't know.
> You were here just a minute ago.
> Or anyway I thought so.
>> Where'd you go?

And here's another one that goes back, like everything else,
to a person's high school years:

Scrunch Song

> Oh we scrunched down on the couch,
> Her father was a grouch,
> But we scrunched down on the couch
> Until she hollered, "Ouch,
> Let's get down on the floor."
> So we scrunched down some more
> On the floor.
>
> Oh we scrunched down in the car,
> In fact went pretty far
> In that dark unmoving car.

We scrunched down on the beach—
Didn't need to beseech
Her to scrunch down on the beach.
We scrunched down in the yard,
It wasn't very hard
To scrunch down in the yard.

Oh we scrunched down on the couch
Until she hollered, "Ouch,
Let's get down on the floor."
So we scrunched down some more
On the floor.

And:

Lean on Me

Oh I don't make advances
Except toward folks I fancies,
So come on now and trust me,
Sugar plum.

You can *lean* on me.
You can *lean* on me.
You can lean a little harder.
You
  can
    let
      me
        see
          your
            garter.
Come on now and trust me,
Little one.

I am pretty well adjusted,
I won't ever get you busted.

I speak Spanish—Como esta usted?
I'm a man who *can* be trusted.
Come on now and trust me,
Honey bun.

You can *lean* on me.
You can *lean* on me.
You can lean a little harder.
You
  can
    let
      me
        see
          your
            garter.
Come on now and trust me,
Little one.
And if you do you'll be
The
  only
    one.

And (excuse me, I know I'm running long here, but I don't get many opportunities—being, as I say, no singer—to put my sounds before the *public*. I'll be *god damned* if I'm going to err on the side of leaving too many out).

Laughing,
Laughing,
Senses all aflame.

Nobody . . . sounds . . . the same.

She wasn't riding six white horses,
But she tapped primary sources,
The girl who bust out laughing when she came.

Laughing,
Laughing,
Nobody sounds the same.

Nobody . . . knows . . . your name.

But I know, and you, who you ah,
The girl who bust out hoo-hah,
The girl who bust out laughing when she came.

Laughing,
Laughing,
Without a sense of shame

Nobody . . . sounds . . . the same.

So let's toast her and let's treat her,
Let's all go down and meet her,
The girl who bust out laughing when she came.

And some more reflective, personal songs, like:

The Lose-Your-Mind Blues

Don't know what to think
Or even what not to,
Don't know what I can't
Or even what I got to—
Can't make head
Or tails of my head—
I got the lose-your-mind blues.

The lose your mind's
A bad kind
Because you got to use your mind
To find it.
Once you forget
Where your head was at
It's hard . . . to . . . be . . . reminded.

Can't make head
Or tails of my head,
I got the . . .

Some say out of mind
Is outasight
But I'd take mine
Right back tonight—
I got the . . .

Is what I just thought
What I really thought
Or just what I ought
To be thinkin?
All I ever wind up
Makin my mind up
Is to think I'll do some drinkin . . .

And some sophisticated songs:

Bored

Oh I'm having an affair
With a lady millionaire
And my *chargée d'affaires*
Is a girl with curly hair
Who wears no underwear
But I'm bored.

Oh I'm heavily in debt
And I'm not approaching yet
The place I meant to get
As a master of vignette
But I'm bored.

If I want to I can wail
Or sit here drinking ale
Or open up my mail

Or go my lawyer's bail
But I'm bored.

I've got a cowboy hat
And a perfect Persian cat
But what the use is that
Until you come I'm flat
As a board.

I'm still looking foard
To you of course, but *Lord*,
Until you arrive . . .
I'm turning thirty-five,
Sitting getting older,
Waiting and accumulating
In my heart's manila folder
Clippings from the papers, near and far away,
And all they ever say
Is I'm bored.

And some social comment songs, like:

It's a Coldhearted World

Everything real is vinyl,
Everything vinyl is real.
Everything temporary's final,
Everything final will heal.
Every little bend is straightened,
Everything straight is curled—
When the mannikins have nipples
It's a coldhearted world.

These things belong to people, they're taking them away,
When the mannikins have nipples it's a coldhearted world.

There's no sense going forward,
No way of going back,
We don't know which way's toward,
Don't know where's the track.

Every little bend is straightened,
Everything straight is curled—
When babydolls got vaginas
It's a coldhearted world.

The movies show folks fucking,
Fucking don't move folks.
They tell you keep on trucking,
But the wheels ain't got no spokes.
Every little bend is straightened,
Everything straight is curled—
When pinup girls got pubic hair
It's a coldhearted world.

These things belong to people, they're taking them away,
When pinup girls got pubic hair, it's a coldhearted world.

I wouldn't sound anything like Bob Dylan, though. I hate to pick on a man when he is down, except that come to think of it I don't hate to pick on a man who is down after making a terrible five-and-a-half-hour movie about himself and his wife and girlfriends starring himself and his wife and girlfriends, but I never could open up to Bob Dylan. "Something's happening and you don't know what it is, do you, Mr. Jones?"— do you call that a grown-up sentiment? Bob Dylan says things like "autymobile" in his songs. That's a "Beverly Hillbillies" word. He also has words like "cosmic." Bob Dylan sounds like he has become this man of the people for the purpose of being better than people who aren't of the people, but not for the purpose of feeling out anything in common with any people except disgruntled well-off Eastern white kids who are pissed off because the world, which their daddies are running, is going to hell and they have got too much free time.

I'd like to sing a woman's song every now and then, if I could think of a way to do it without looking silly:

> I've given my hair more body,
> And given my body less hair.
> Now you git
> th' bene*fit* of the doubt—
> Take me out somewhere.

But mostly I would treat women as people to get embroiled with in more intellectually relaxed and terrifying ways, like this:

At This Intersection

> I'm comin on in my jalopy,
> Ain't no way no one can stop me
> Till I see that highway sign
> Where I lost you who were mine:
>
> 6 Killed at This Intersection.
> You were the object of my affection.
> 6 Killed at This Intersection,
> And number 6 was you.
>
> 50, 60, 65,
> In a 30, here I drive,
> Just you wait up there in heaven,
> Pretty soon now there'll be 7:
>
> 7 Killed at This Intersection.
> Now my life has got direction.
> 7 Killed at This Intersection
> And I'll be seeing you.

And like this:

Odi et Amo

I hate . . . tiny flying bugs
And little slippry rugs
And people going on and on
And on on the telephone
But most of all I hate you.

I hate TV commentators
And supermart tomaters
And people going yodel eedel ady o
Yodel eedel ady on the radio
But most of all I hate you.

I hate sitting in the rain
And all forms of pain
And people going honky honky honk
On their horns when I'm happy in a honky-tonk
But most of all I hate you.

Hate your lips, hate your eyes,
Hate your smile, hate your size,
Hate everything about you.

But I'll be through
In an hour or two
And then to be candid
I won't be able to stand it,
How much that I don't hate you—

Won't hate your lips, won't hate your eyes,
Won't hate your calves, won't hate your thighs—
Oh then I'll be fit to be
Tied—
How did I git to be—

> Why'd
> I ever fall in
>   love with a girl I
>   hate as much as I hate you.

I know! I know! I know! This is getting embarrassing! You didn't come here for this! But I can't help it, I got to sing my songs:

Girl with a Big Gold Tooth

I've known fat girls, I've known skinny girls,
I've known girls with evocative names:
  Maryjo Marimba, Loretta Louche,
  Harriet Zwischen and Dinah Eine Kleine Heinie Manush.
And I've known girls whose hair was red
And when they scooted down in bed
It rose around their head
Like flames.
But all I ever wanted in the world, to tell you the truth,
Was to have an experience with a girl with a big gold tooth.

Oh, a big gold tooth, a big gold tooth,
Ask your orthodontist for a big . . . gold . . . tooth.

Here is one—please, please, I'm *singing*—I wrote for my wife:

Always Telephone

> l find myself a thousand miles
> From you my dear tonight.
> I can't touch your pretty skin
> And you know that ain't right.
> The only way that I can hook
> Us up before next week

Is hold a clammy vinyl thing
Next to my ear and cheek.

Oh . . . I . . . can always telephone
But I can't tell it much.
That telephone connection
Don't put us two in touch.
That telephone receiver
In my hand is hard and cold.
I can't telephone
And tell what I want told.

What I want told begins with "Mm"
And ends with "My oh my."
What's in between won't go by phone
And I know you know why.
What's in between is just between
You and me and how.
That's why I'm wishing you weren't there
Or I weren't here right now.

This is the kind of song I wrote—listen, just turn on to the
next chapter if you want to, this *means something to me—before* I met my wife:

Oh I've Broken

One was Elaine,
Who she maintained I caused consid'rable pain—
Caused her so much she went away on the train
And married a telephone lineman named Wayne.

Oh I've broken a whole lot of hearts,
Sure as old crushed grapes make wine.
Oh I've broken a whole lot of hearts,
And several of them were mine.

That one's got several more women and several more
verses, but I can't get them in because—*help me, Jesus!*—here
comes another whole song:

Also the Birmingham Blues

I'm all weighed down with woes and abuses,
It's got me singing two different blueses—
Singing the Mobile and also the Birmingham blues.
   Bad news.
Singing the Mobile and also the Birmingham blues.

My Mobile gal is crazy—
She'll drive me insane—
But every time I go to take the Birmingham train
I think: I got a crazy gal in Birmingham too!

Oo-oo.

It ain't any wonder I'm drinkin booze
And singin the Mobile
And also the Birmingham blues.

A man in Mobile says he
Gonna shoot me if I stay.
But if I go I'm prob'ly gonna get shot anyway.
'Cause there's a man lookin for me up in Birmingham too.

Oo-oo.

It ain't any wonder I'm a man who's
Singing the Mobile and also the Birmingham blues.

Ain't got no credit.
Ain't got no shoes.
Ain't got no way to take a Mobile Bay cruise.
But I owe a thousand dollars in Birmingham too.

Oo-oo.

It ain't any wonder my soul is colored bruise—
I got the one hand
And also the other hand blues.

Woes and abuses.
Two different blueses.
I got the Mobile and also the Birmingham blues.

"How 'bout Tuscaloosa,"
I heard somebody cry.
But that ain't no good either, and here's the reason why:
I got plenty trouble in Tuscaloosa too.

Oo-oo.

A gal there who's a momma wants to sue me. And I'd lose.
I got the Mobile
And also the Birmingham—
I got the Tuscaloosa
And Anniston and Selma—
Got the tween here and Birmingham,
And also the Birmingham—
The all over Alabama blues.

You know what? Maybe this *isn't* so embarrassing. Maybe some of these songs are pretty god damn *good*. Maybe you ought to be thankful I'm here before you with some of these songs. You could be reading worse. You could be *watching television*. Hell, this song here is very damn nearly a standard:

> ### I'm Just a Bug
> ### (on the Windshield of Life)
>
> He drove up in his big new car
> And gave a little toot on his horn,
> And drove off with the prettiest little girl

That ever was born.
He's in the driver's seat now,
Beside him sits my wife.
And I'm just a bug on the windshield of life.

Now they're driving down the road
And never think a thing of me.
Two in the front seat's company,
You know what they say about three.
Now my wife looks over at him,
Her words cut like a knife:
"Old Arnie's just a bug on
The windshield of life."

The Lord above looked down on me
And said, "I tell you, boy.
Where you are there's just misery,
There is no earthly joy.
You and him and your wife are all
In a world of sin and strife.
On down the road I'll cleanse you from
The windshield of life."

Hey, it's hard being on the road. It isn't easy standing up before people with your songs even at *home*.

Of course, I wouldn't be alone on the road, because I'd have my wife along. In fact, I'd advertise her: "Hear his big hits! Meet his little Mrs.!" And I'd introduce her from the stage and break into several choruses of "She Ain't No Bigger Than a Minute (But She Can Go Like an Hour and a Half)."

Then too—hey, I don't acknowledge *limitations* when it comes to my songs—I'd want to sing us-rollicking-old-boys songs: ones which linked me with Willie Nelson and Waylon Jennings, of course, like Billy Joe Shaver's "Willie the Wandering Gypsy and Me" and David Allen Coe's "Willie and Waylon and Me" and Willie and Waylon's song which has the line about being "with Willie and Waylon and the boys." Actually, I don't like Waylon's tone lately. He's taken on this surly-martyr tone which seems to be saying, "If you don't watch out I'm going to come down off this cross and kick your ass." I don't care for that, that's the worst of two worlds. But I'd include him in for old times' sake.

And Willie Nelson. I admire Willie Nelson more than I do Ray Charles and J. Robert Oppenheimer. Willie wrote "Family Bible," which is about as solid a traditional old work as you can get, and he also performs in tennis shoes and a beard and long hair and a sweatband, with people passing him up joints *and* whiskey from the crowd. Good old boys who have some hippie in them, and hippies who have some good old boy in them, and good old boys who don't, and hippies who don't, all feel good about him, with reason. And old folks and young folks and Democrats and Republicans, or anyway just about every kind of Democrat. He answers my desire for white Southern role models who *include folks in,* who aren't *scared,* who *integrate.* When Willie sang, in "Devil in a Sleeping Bag," the words "Rita Coolidge, Rita Coolidge cleft for me," he integrated the rock of ages and fleshly desire in a way I realized I had been waiting for all my life. A country singer who will integrate is like a beautiful woman who can cook, likes working the crossword with you, and enjoys you when you are drunk and smell bad. Or like Jimmy Carter when he had Daddy King up there leading the nation in "We Shall Overcome." Almost too good to be true.

Only I think Willie is true. I came up to Willie once and asked him, "How does it feel to be replacing Jesus in country music? I mean you're being mentioned so often in the lyrics."

And he grinned like a tired but shaded dog and said, "It's embarrassing, isn't it?" In a way that suggested he knew he never *would* replace Jesus in anything actually; and even though it was embarrassing, he kind of enjoyed it; and even if he didn't enjoy it he didn't give a shit as long as he was singing and writing good; and somehow or another it was something that I, whom he didn't know from Adam until that moment, was joining him in the temporary mystery of.

Willie broke away from the hackneyed big-business Nashville ways of doing country music, and they started calling him an outlaw and a revolutionary. And just as that outlaw stuff was getting boring, he recorded an album of church songs. And then an album of old-fashioned Lefty Frizzell honky-tonk songs, respectfully but freshly rendered. And then when other big-time country singers were agonizing over whether they should go pop or not, had gone pop or not, or *could* go pop or not (I shouldn't say I don't like old Waylon's tone—after all, he was the one who said, "I couldn't go pop with a mouthful of firecrackers"), Willie went pop. By singing an album entitled *Stardust*, with songs on it like "Stardust" and "All of Me" and "Unchained Melody" and "On the Sunny Side of the Street." And these songs sounded like themselves and also like Willie Nelson. I tell you what, if Jimmy Carter could stay one jump ahead of everybody the way Willie Nelson has, he not only would have gone over big as President, he'd be receiving a big hand at the Enthusiastically Empowered World Council of Folks All Over the World to Cut Out All This War and Terrorism Shit and Settle Down to Enabling Everybody to Build the Nice House and Cook the Healthy Supper of His or Her Choice *right now*.

Well, I don't mean to go overboard on the subject of Willie Nelson. But Willie Nelson has come on up out of his origins carrying them along with him and going where he wants to with them. And you can hear it in his voice. You can hear in his voice that he talks like regular people *and* has got a lot of sense (and incidentally you can hear behind his voice not only his great guitar but his sister Bobby's great piano-playing, which I don't think receives enough credit), common *and* private sense, more sense than Waylon sounds like he has got, for instance. More sense than Jimmy Carter *sounds* like *he* has got, although he knows about more subjects than Willie does. When you can get mentality, as well as music, into your voice as well as your lyrics, and you still sound like a plain person, you are doing something.

Willie gets his life into his music too. His friends, and his wife's name and everything, and it's not embarrassing. Those would be things I'd like to get into my songs. Every song wouldn't necessarily be something I had lived out, or would feel obliged to keep on living out, but I would try to maintain some consistency, I would draw some lines about what I would say and then do or vice versa. I was at a party in Los Angeles once and a famous country singer was there who had just recorded a touching ballad about how much he loved his wife and wouldn't do nothing to harm their marriage if somebody was to take and hold a gun to his head, and I looked over at the cloakroom as I left the party and there was this same country singer, drunk and trying to pick up the hat-check girl. "What's your sign?" he was asking her.

Now a country singer hasn't got any business asking a girl what her sign is. He is supposed to be telling her Hey, good-looking, what does she have cooking. But she responded what her sign was, in a kind of jaded manner, and the singer said, "Well that goes exactly right with mine. I'm a Libra."

"When's your birthday?" I asked this country singer.

"January fifth," or something like that, he said.

"You're not a Libra," I exclaimed.

"Shhhhhhhh," he told me.

Now a man who will lie about being married, or owing money, or being likely to come back in town any time soon, or having entirely gotten over his virus, is one thing. But a man who will lie about his sign is a poor excuse for a country singer.

"The only thing worse," a friend of mine told me when I told him this story, "is somebody who actually knows what his sign is." But I'm not ashamed of it, I got a song out of it.

Sign Song

Oh she was a Virgo and I was a Libra,
We might's well've been a raccoon and a zebra—
We just weren't written in the stars.
Oh passion dimmed our minds,
We forgot to check our signs—
Oh Lord please Libra-rate me from behind these cold iron bars—
We just weren't written in the stars.

Oh I was a Libra and she was a Virgo,
And Lord I was sorry to have to see her go—
We just weren't written in the stars.

Well, I know you probably don't have time, right now, to
hear every song I've written. Like "The Sweet Little Agnes
Fordyce Stubblefield Rag" and:

> Ev'ry door I come to says
> "Use Another Door."
> Ev'rywhere I turn you
> Ain't there no more.
>
> In case of illness notify
> The one who broke my heart.
> She'd love to hear I'm coming
> All the way apart.

But I just want you to know that I have every kind of coun-
try song. Middle-of-the-night-drinking songs, like "There Are
No More Tomorrows, Yesterday Must've Been Three Months
Ago, and This Sure Don't Seem Like Today."

Songs inspired by my love of animals, like "You Know How
a Dog's Leg (Twitches When You Scratch Him on the Stom-
ach, Well, That Is How My Heart Is Doing Darling over
You)."

Songs that don't quite make sense, though they sound thoroughly felt, like "I'd Give My Right Arm (to Hold You in My Arms Again)," and songs that you can't tell whether they make any sense or not until you think about them for a couple of months, like "If You Were Me, You'd Leave You Alone."

Songs that bring together concepts old and new in unexpected rhymes, like "Jesus" / "autokinesis." Songs of an almost Zen-like inscrutability, like "The So Damn Bad, Can't Bring Myself to Sing About 'Em Blues."

And you know "Gentle on My Mind"? Those words about the rivers and the back roads that go on and on and on until you think they'll never turn the corner? Well, I have a song along those lines that just won't let up:

Underneath her *sweat* shirt by the *mole* beneath her *rib* cage
   in the *magic* of the *moon*light on the *porch* swing on
   the *front* porch of the *house* of her Aunt *Hel*en in
   Man*a*ssas Springs Vir*gin*ia where her *Un*cle Ed's a
   *law*yer I was *try*ing to be*stow* a little *kiss,*
When she *said* you better *quit* it or my *un*cle will come *run*ning
   from his *stud*y by the *par*lor where he's *work*ing on a
   brief beneath the *lamp*light on his *desk* top by his *files* which are
   ex*ten*sive, running *nine*ty miles an *hour* yelling
   "*All* right now just *what* the hell is *this!*"

I've *got* the songs. The only thing is, I'm not musical, in person. It's not in my heritage to be too *thoroughly* musical. Country music's not any more musical than it has to be. But I'm not even that musical. I can dance with both feet, for instance, but not with more than one at a time. I wouldn't be surprised if that lends a little poignancy to my dancing once I get going, but that doesn't qualify me for professional work in music. I mean there's a sense in which, if I'm dancing, it must mean something. It's like seeing an old fat dog running—if he's running, he must be after something awful good. But once I was in Spanish Fort, Texas, at a middle-of-the-night dance following a coon hunt, and an about fifty-year-old woman who looked like she deserved to have had more exotic sensations in her life than she looked like she had had, came up to me and said would I dance with her, she wanted to know how somebody from New York danced. I tried to explain to her I just was living in New York, I wasn't from New York, but she kept after me, so I danced with her and after about five minutes she said, "I danced better than that already *earlier tonight.*" I've got it in me, but when I'm dancing or singing I'm like Jimmy when he's making a speech. I'm thinking *about* my feet and voice instead of *on* them.

So all I can do is write songs about my dreams—like my Hank Williams song. Semi-necrological songs about and references to Hank Williams constitute a major theme in country music. There's "Hank Williams, You Wrote My Life" and "Do You Think Hank Done It This Way?" and "If You Don't Like Hank Williams You Can Kiss My Ass," and any number of songs by Hank Williams Jr. about his daddy ("They say old Hank was a mighty big drinker. I don't know"). I call my Hank Williams song "Why Ain't I Half as Good as Old Hank (Since I'm Feeling All Dead Anyway)?":

> If old Hank Williams had had my luck
> He'd've died in the back of a pickup truck
> Instead of that Cadillac limousine.
> He's a legend and I'm selling sewing machines.

And I'll go on trying to *delve into* country music. I have met with Billy Joe Shaver, for instance, and he said actually he wasn't asked for his fingers until he reached the doctor's office. And he told the woman, yeah, he guessed so, and she took them. And that was the last he saw of her or them. Then when he got to the hospital somebody asked him where the fingers were, maybe they could be sewed back on. He said well, he'd given them away.

"It's not important," he told me. "The kids like it." Then

he showed me how he could hold the stubs to his nostrils so it looked like his fingers were way up his nose. I could see how kids would like that. I liked it.

Why did he guess the Negro woman wanted his fingers? I asked him.

"I don't know, to keep 'em in a bottle, I guess," he said. "You know how they are."

How *they* are, hell. Those fingers are liable to be worth a lot of money someday, if folks' values swing back to the down-to-earth. What would you give to have Hank Williams' fingers in a bottle?

Or a man in the White House who, when it comes time to express to the nation how it feels to be in there, will go on TV and favor us with a song:

> I got the redneck White House blues.
> When I'm just about to register my views
> Another lobby lights up
>   and blows out my fuse.
> I got the redneck White House blues.

If there ever was a time for sincerely mournful every-way-I-turn music to issue from the White House, now is it. I mean, Jimmy releases long-imprisoned Puerto Rican nationalists out of the kindness of his heart and they immediately announce that they won't rule out using bombs. He sells kerosene back to Iran (whose leader called him "the vilest person on earth"), even though he knows it won't be good politics for him at home, because the Iranians say they have to have it to heat their homes. Then the Iranians announce that they'll probably sell it again at a higher price—because it's bad politics for them at home to admit they are accepting help from America. They're worrying about politics at home even though they can apparently shoot all the citizens they want. And then they seize our embassy because we are trying to ease the Shah's gallstones and cancer.

Country music is about how life is difficult, and limited, but lively. About how life don't really respond to programs, but life without programs (and I don't mean TV) is nothing at all. (Donna Fargo put the problem of being and nothingness more succinctly than Sartre when she sang, "This awareness of nothing / Is driving me straight up the wall.")

Jimmy doesn't seem to have the consolations of that music. He wants to make life finer than it is in that music. He's moved on up to classical music, more seriously than John F. Kennedy did. But Kennedy said "Life is unfair" and parents to this day are quoting him to their children. Jimmy Carter said it, talking about abortion—coming out for Motherhood, sort of—and it didn't go over worth a damn. So he didn't try it when the Shah came looking for a hospital or the Iranians for kerosene. Kennedy was lyrical and vulgar and knew where to draw the line. And he could use his roots.

I can't see that Jimmy is reaching way back down very deep into the tough part of his. Oh, he likes Willie Nelson. He plays Willie Nelson so loud in the White House that Rosalynn keeps turning it down. But, hell, everybody likes Willie Nelson.

More Carters

Jesse Suede Carter, 31, Nashville, Tennessee, contemporary country singer. "People want to go into 'Are you country? Are you pop?'—I'm an entertainer. I'm an artist. That's all. In the South any more, they're selling boiled peanuts and roach clips in the same stores. It's not the bib-overall music today, it's white shoes it's plaid pants it's blue leather jacket, it's whatever you like to wear and got $7.99 for an album. Today's country-oriented artist don't have to call her 'Sweet Mama' or 'Pretty Baby' in the lyrics, we can come right out and call her 'Sexy Lady' like the rest of music. Five years ago I couldn't have recorded 'My Mind Between Your Thighs.'

"Sometimes I'm egotistical. Sometimes I cry out in pain. Okay? There's a mystical streak in me, but it don't run my life. My people got a thing in negotiation—I'm about this far from going on Merv, going on 'Password Plus,' *co-hosting* Dinah. It's between me and Lani Cartlidge for the Arthur Treacher's Fish and Chips jingle. It's a big world out there. I'm an enormous talent. The thing is happening. People want to put you in a category—I go, 'Whoa!' "

And Even More Carters

"Limber Kimber Lee" Carter, 19, who performs a "topless, tapless, semi-bottomless" dance with a trained badger in a roadhouse near the University of Wisconsin and is now developing a new "Lust in Her Art" routine in a frank attempt to capitalize on her distant kinship with the Chief Executive.

"Oooh, right, right. I get all the little numbers about am I really Jimmy's great-great-cousin. 'You don't have a Georgia accent, Kimber Lee! You're not a Babtist, Kimber Lee! You *sure* don't mooove jerky, Kimber Lee! You promise you're related?'

"So, then, in the act, I go—I pop the badger into this like little peanut costume? and, b'dum, and one and two and, b'dum*bump:* show 'em my teeth."

I May Have Sung
with Jerry Jeff

The Medical Council are conducting an enquiry into the bed-side manner of a certain doctor. According to Mrs. Gail Webb of St. Mary's, Fromer, the doctor "came into my bedroom, sat on the end of the bed, then lay down and went fast asleep. After about two hours he woke up and said it was time I had my injection. Then he went back to sleep again. When my husband came home the doctor asked if he could stay the night. He said that he was fed up with doctoring and wanted to be a singer."
—Dublin (Ireland) EVENING PRESS

I can't really demand that Jimmy be a true-country-music President. For one thing, black voters tend to turn up their noses at country music—although it started out very close to the blues. I do think, however, that I can ask Jimmy to go a little further toward getting unconscious on stage. That's what Jerry Jeff Walker gets. When you're unconscious on stage, you don't argue with your internal voices, you don't even *hear* no internal voices. You *are* the voices.

"Jerry Jeff is a saint," says Pete Axthelm, who has spent time with Willie Nelson, who is considered to be pretty strong himself in the category Jerry Jeff is a saint in: out all night and running wild.

I was saying to this guy with a lizard foot around his neck in Tucson, whose name I never did catch, "You know I don't believe I saw Jerry Jeff do anything *obnoxious* all night."

"I don't wonder," this guy said. Who this guy was and why he was with us, I don't know. I know why Ape was there. I was the one who brought Ape along, from Phoenix, because I thought Jerry Jeff was passed out in the van behind us and it was up to me to get him to Tucson, and I didn't know what direction Tucson was. Only it turned out it was worse than that, Jerry Jeff wasn't even in the van. And then Ape started acting strangely. But I don't know who this other guy in Tucson, the one with the lizard foot, was. He was short, but he wasn't a midget. I know he wasn't a midget because I had been hoping I would meet Jerry Jeff's midget friend Thunder Fart, who says things like "Never marry a tall blond woman" and who used to work in a bear suit, turning somersaults, as the NBC bear, in Olympics promotions. Why NBC wants a midget bear I don't know; a big outfit like that could afford any size of bear *suit*; but the point is that the whole time I was with Jerry Jeff I kept looking for a midget and none ever showed up to my knowledge, though a lot of other people did. But this guy in Tucson was short, and he was wearing a lizard foot around his neck on a silver chain.

"I don't wonder," he said. "You spent at least an hour standing there on stage with that buffalo head on backwards."

"I did?" I said, surprised.

"Well, if you're that sensitive about it," this guy said, "maybe it was me."

That reminds me of the time Jerry Jeff called my home in Massachusetts to report that he was going to be appearing not too far away, in Hartford, the coming weekend.

My wife and I weren't home; our friend Rose answered the phone. "Where exactly in Hartford are you going to be?" she asked, taking the message.

"I don't know," said Jerry Jeff. "Where exactly am I now?"

Since there are no telephones in drunk tanks or on the ground beneath motorcycle boots, Jerry Jeff was presumably in neither of those places, although it was in a drunk tank that he met the man who inspired him to write his most famous song, "Mr. Bojangles," and it was when he was being stomped by a motorcycle gang that he made what may be his most famous remark: "Y'all don't fight as good as rodeo cowboys." Nor was he likely to be in the White House. In '78 he showed up there at Jimmy Carter's invitation, but after cooling his heels for two hours (some graver presidential crisis than Jerry Jeff's presence having, almost unimaginably, arisen) he walked out, saying, "I guess the President and I aren't going to get together, because I'm not hanging around this place any longer and I hear he don't hang out in any bars."

Jerry Jeff just might have been, strangely enough, in repose: abed, in what his wife Susan called "the Howard Hughes room" of their ranch house outside Austin, Texas. There, before his marriage broke up, he would sometimes lie in the company of his baby girl Jessie, with several vials of a restorative ginseng-and-bee-saliva solution handy, an oxygen mask on his face, and, preferably, Monday Night Football on television.

Not that Jerry Jeff had become, by common standards, domestic. After Susan and the baby came home from the hospital, he absented himself to a friend's house for a while, saying that he didn't feel quite right at home. When he did show up to take on paternity, he stayed just long enough to voice some firm opinions as to how a baby should be held and what a baby ought to listen to, and then he went off again on his motorcycle to get some formula and was gone for three days.

But I remember how Susan smiled as she and I watched him one night in New York, working well with his band. He had been up drinking for thirty-six hours, but his set so far was tight, the crowd was loving it, he had a faraway yet engaged, suffering yet grinning look on his beaked, heavy-lidded face; his potbelly was thrusting in tempo; he was strumming his knuckles bloody on his electric guitar strings; he was what he most likes to be, which is "unconscious on stage."

It was a different time, in Tucson, when I was unconscious on stage with him. First let me just say that one balmy night on the isle of Kauai Jerry Jeff came out of a bar and couldn't get in his rental car, so he started banging away at it with a heavy wooden chair which came to hand. Then an outraged Kauaian appeared. It turned out Jerry Jeff had the wrong car.

Jerry Jeff usually has the wrong something. One time his friend Bud Shrake's straitlaced father-in-law, who didn't approve of his marriage, came for dinner. Bud's wife Doatsie wanted things to be right. She told Bud, "Just keep Jerry Jeff away."

But just as Doatsie's father was loosening up a little, here came Jerry Jeff bursting through the front door pursued by Billy Joe Shaver, who was yelling, "You one-song son of a bitch." Bud tried to make polite introductions as the pair chased each other around the house. Billy Joe said, "Nice to meet you," and then, catching sight of Jerry Jeff behind a couch, took off his hat and jammed it onto Doatsie's father's head down beyond the ears and resumed the chase.

"Bud god damn it get them out!" Doatsie was yelling. Finally Bud thought he had them out, but then, as Doatsie yelled *"Bud god damn it"* again, he realized he just had Billy Joe out. He ran back inside to get Jerry Jeff. Jerry Jeff was hunkered down beside Doatsie's father. "No, you and Billy Joe go on without me," said Jerry Jeff. "Me and this man have a lot to talk about."

"Billy Joe grew up a lot poorer than Jerry Jeff, just desperate poor. Townes Van Zandt has been through long periods where he slept in a Dempster Dumpster," says a friend of all three. "They get on Jerry Jeff sometimes, telling him he's not crazy, he's not entitled to sing country, he hasn't ever been through enough. That probably works on him, that probably pushes him on a little bit. But he's not crazy. He knows what he's doing."

In a sense. In New Orleans there is a man who passes himself off as Jerry Jeff. Jerry Jeff says he hopes their paths never cross, because "I'm liable to jump on him and beat the shit out of me." Once he called up Shrake and said, "I'm coming over with a friend." On the way Jerry Jeff ran off the road in his jeep. (Jerry Jeff has wrecked three different cars between his house and Shrake's.) Jerry Jeff showed up saying, "I think my friend's dead."

But there was nobody in the wreckage.

"We still don't know who the friend was," says Shrake. Jerry Jeff is as mystified as anybody.

Before hooking up with Jerry Jeff in Phoenix, I had never been on the road with a band of Texas country-rockers. I figured that when they weren't country-rocking on stage they were whooping and yelling and fighting and riding down Main Street shooting holes in the watering trough. It turns out that Jerry Jeff's band—Bobby Rambo, Ron Cobb, Tomas Ramirez, Reese Wynans, Leo LeBlanc, Fred Krc—don't look like cowboys at all. They look like young hippie musicians, except for pedal steel player LeBlanc, who looks like a cross between a *Bürgermeister* and an elf and wears a porkpie hat with a feather in it. They do find time to whoop, but they also talk a lot about sound systems: monitors, tri-amps, dynamics, twin reverbs, things like that.

And the sound the night I met them in the Celebrity Theatre had not been right. The crowd had seemed satisfied, but the crowd had also seemed stoned, and what Jerry Jeff said between songs had been mostly inaudible. The current Jerry Jeff show's audio is a complicated fabric: the voluminous folds of the electric instruments, the stitching of Jerry Jeff's between-song mumbles, the burlap of his low notes, the vinyl of his high notes, and what critic Robert Palmer has called, approvingly, "the frayed living-room rug of his middle range."

Jerry Jeff and his band have never yet rehearsed. Sometimes a couple of sidemen will grab a moment in between songs to coordinate licks in advance: "There goes the band, arranging again," Jerry Jeff will tell the crowd with asperity. But they never know what songs are going to be played, they just wait until he gets going on one (he doesn't like to count off) and then come in gamely behind him. But the new band takes rock sound more seriously than did the Gonzos, who at least when they were with Jerry Jeff were more into country fury. The heart of the act, when the act works, is still Jerry Jeff's earnest or jocular and often slurred but still edgily intended words, the ungainly semi-grace of his physical dips and didos, and his imperious, clowning, vexed, meditative, pained, wasted, whoopty-dooing point of view. But the band's dynamics compensate for the limitations and occasional strayings of Jerry Jeff's abused vocal equipment, and those dynamics need to be miked right.

The theater management blamed the muddiness of the evening on Jerry Jeff, and he blamed it on them. "I ate, I slept, I did *everything*," Jerry Jeff griped. Slowing down long enough to go to bed and have a meal during the twenty-four hours before a show is Jerry Jeff's idea of monkish propriety. He was damned if he would persist in self-denial if its upshot was going to be a show in which he didn't get unconscious.

So for the next twenty-eight hours or so we worked ourselves into a waking dream state. The first thing we did was stay up all night in Jerry Jeff's motel room debating the following topics: whether Jerry Jeff was going to tour England and Japan and Australia, whether Jerry Jeff was going to appear in New York if he couldn't get on "Saturday Night Live," and whether Jerry Jeff was going to sell his Jaguar and his Mercedes.

A motel security man was on hand, presumably to protect the motel from Jerry Jeff, but he was ignored. So was nearly everyone else except Jerry Jeff. The debaters included Jerry Jeff's then-manager, Michael Brovsky, and his colleague Witt Stewart. The part about the Mercedes and the Jaguar went on for at least four hours, and the only conclusion I derived from it was that the difference between an average country person and a country music star is that the latter has more and fancier cars that won't crank. Jerry Jeff kept complaining about how many vehicles he had—something like twelve, of which only the pickup worked—and, oh, I don't know.

Then a question like whether to go to Japan would arise and Jerry Jeff would consider all the pros—"at least if the band got lost I'd be able to find them in a crowd"—and the cons—"Raw fish! Raw fish!"—and just as it seemed after an hour or two that Brovsky and Stewart had talked him into it, he would announce, with Churchillian resolve, "I still won't go." He didn't care that people adored him in Australia: "I hate adoration! One guy said I was one of the smartest guys he knew and then he jumped right in the middle of my guitar!"

Well, how about buying an airplane, Brovsky suggested. "All right," said Jerry Jeff, "and if it'll make it to, say, Texarkana we'll go for Ireland!"

Apparently this is pretty much the way Jerry Jeff works out his business affairs. As he debated, Jerry Jeff blew snot on the floor. I have never been around anyone with such a facility for clearing his nose. A couple of nights later as Shrake, Pete Gent, Jerry Jeff, and I leaned against something in Wimberly, Texas, Shrake brought the matter of phlegm up to Jerry Jeff. (Shrake says he once watched Jerry Jeff blow it on the walls of the New York offices of a major record company. Shrake asked someone there why they let Jerry Jeff get away with such a thing. "He sells records" was the answer.) Jerry Jeff actually looked almost chastened. "I have a lot of mucus," he said. "It's a mannerism. One of those mannerisms people have. I started doing it in motels, on rugs, where it doesn't make any difference. But in people's houses, they can't handle it. I'm trying to wipe it on my leg now."

Mostly, that night in Phoenix, Jerry Jeff complained. The band, the road crew, the security man one by one went off to bed. And the sun rose and the last of the scotch went down. And those of us who were left wandered out into the dry Arizona daylight and leaned against some of those little trees they have in Arizona, and Jerry Jeff said to Brovsky, "My wife Susan, who's so pretty, who's so smart, who's only done one thing wrong and that was when she married me, wants to know what I'm going to *do!* And I can't look foolish in her eyes." ("A marriage is what it is," says Jerry Jeff. "It's not *supposed* to be anything.")

And somebody found in the room the following note:

Dear Jerry Jeff Walker,
Message from your friendly security creature.
I watched you for a few hours and this is what I think.
Your warmth, benevolence and brilliance can radiate through an almost lethal dose of ethanol and I hope that there's someone or some people you know/love who rediscover Jerry Jeff Walker every day—people who ask why it is that your mother cries all the time.

That is surely among the most tender messages ever left by a motel security man. And sure enough, the most striking complaint Jerry Jeff had made all night was: *"Every time I talk to my mother, all she does is cry!"*

Jerry Jeff doesn't talk readily about his childhood or his parents. He does refute the argument, sometimes advanced by Texas peers, that being from Oneonta, New York, he lacks a country-Western background: "I did all the same things you guys did. Listened to the Everly Brothers, learned to play ball, jack off, and drive a car, and left.

"My parents were good people, they paid the bills and did what you have to do. My father worked bars, sold liquor. They were dance champions, traveling around, following music, but when they were nineteen they had me, and quit. They sacrificed. When I got old enough I said, 'Thank you, goodbye.' My father said if I didn't stop staying out late I'd have to move out. I told him, 'It doesn't make any difference to me. I'll move out. I don't even want to stay in town.' I didn't want to be sacrificed for. I wish they'd gone on riding motorcycles."

Jerry Jeff says he doesn't know what his father is doing now, but he recalls playing golf with him. "Don't hit into that water," his father warned him. With that, Jerry Jeff hit into it.

"I said, 'I didn't even see that water. You gave me a negative attitude.' " His father would say he'd never amount to
anything. His mother would grieve. His grandfather, who had
a square-dance band, is the one Jerry Jeff speaks of most com-
fortably. "He'd be lying there, and take off his shoe and attach
the ground wire to his toe and we'd listen to the ball game on
the radio."

Sometimes Jerry Jeff will say to someone slightly his senior,
"You're older than I am, but I've been up more hours." Maybe
he is trying to go directly from teen age to old age. But he and
his mother still break each other's hearts. When a story in
New Times portrayed Jerry Jeff primarily as a man who pisses
in beer pitchers and falls into drum sets while performing, his
mother somehow saw it in Oneonta and called him up crying.

"I told her, 'Whatever I do . . . I do what I do . . . but . . . just
don't let it hurt *you*.' " That conversation still weighs on his
mind.

After a good night of arguing Jerry Jeff seemed to feel refreshed, and we set out for Tucson at 10 A.M. Since Tucson is
only about a hundred and fifty miles from Phoenix, and the
show in Tucson wasn't until 8:30 P.M., we seemed to have a
good shot at getting there on time.

But drinking with no sleep eventually puts you on a plane
where life is simple and hard. You are doing well to focus on
more than about one and a half things at once, so life is simple. You feel as though all your body cavities have been
stuffed with oily rags, so life is hard. Most of America's great
music has sprung from conditions that were simple and hard.
Even so, you wouldn't think it would be part of the American
dream to recapitulate painful conditions, but it is; and after
you're on that plane for a while you begin to glide.

We took off in two or three carloads. The one I was in, with
Jerry Jeff and several band members, stopped in certain bars
before we got out of Phoenix, and in one of them Jerry Jeff
met a guy named Ape and another guy and decided to go to

another bar with them. Jerry Jeff got in Ape's friend's van and headed off, and I jumped in with Ape, who was following them in our rent-a-car. Then I got a good look at Ape. He was a monumental person in a black leather jacket with a lot of long black hair growing out of various parts of his face and head. "You can call me Ape, or the Ape Man," he said. "No other names."

Well, when we got to this other bar, Jerry Jeff was passed out cold in the van. Shaking him and yelling at him didn't come anywhere near waking him up. Ape and the other guy and I went into the bar for a while and then we decided for some reason to take Jerry Jeff's remains over to still another bar. Not until we reached this bar did Ape's friend, who followed us in the van, inform us that Jerry Jeff was no longer in the van.

Now, I had no idea where Jerry Jeff was. Maybe he had gone to join his friend who disappeared in the jeep wreck. I also had no idea where the rest of the band was or where I was. Ape decided something fishy was going on. He jerked his friend, the van driver, around a little and then Ape and I went to another bar and visited the homes of a couple of Ape's friends, one of whom kept flicking, no doubt quite innocently, a big knife open and shut. I think we made a lot of phone calls too. And then we returned to the bar where we'd left the band members and I sheepishly advised them that we had lost Jerry Jeff. *"Don't worry about it!"* they chorused. *"He does this all the time!"*

By now we were running a little late. I thought we ought to stop by the bar in whose parking lot I had last seen Jerry Jeff. As it happened, we discovered him in that bar, having a reasonably good time drinking with some people who were maybe going to drive him to Tucson.

The next thing I knew, Ape was driving the band guys away at a tremendous rate of speed and Jerry Jeff and I and some other people were in another car Tucson-bound vaguely. On the way we drank a good deal from a bottle in which Jerry Jeff had mixed scotch and ginger ale. None of us knew exactly where the auditorium was. At one point we saw a sign to El Paso. I remember spending what seemed like an hour getting advice in a gas station. Jerry Jeff was not real alert in the back seat.

But we were *up*, we were *up*, we were hurtling through the Arizona night heedless, unafraid, amusing, incredibly drunk, and functioning, functioning, sort of. Suddenly against all odds we hit Tucson and Jerry Jeff lurched to attention and croaked out directions that had just occurred to him and the *next* thing I knew we were on stage. The *right* stage.

We didn't get arrested trying to get on stage, the way Jerry Jeff did once in Chattanooga, when he showed up drunk and late and the police wouldn't believe he was Jerry Jeff because someone, trying to cover for him, had announced that Jerry Jeff wasn't going to make it because he'd been in a car wreck. Willie Nelson had to play the whole show that night, and Jerry Jeff emerged from the drunk tank the next morning, according to his friend Gary Cartwright, "looking like all the other drunks," and complaining, "They arrested me going on *stage!* I thought the stage was a sanctuary!"

No, we made it on stage in Tucson, and out there in front of us was a big young drunk yelling audience. Jerry Jeff is ambivalent about his audiences. "Sometimes they get too drunk," he says. And recently they are too young. And they've probably never been sufficiently discriminating. Once, years ago, he had been playing in New York for several nights when a rave review of "Mr. Bojangles" came out in the *Times*. That night he hit the first few notes of that song and immediately the crowd went wild. "They never did that before," he says. "They had to be *told* it was a great song." He moved from those first notes into a different song altogether, refused to play "Bojangles" all night, and the crowd nearly rushed the stage in their anger. Now, his band says, he wishes that his audiences would shut up and listen, the way Willie's do, when he shifts from one of his hard-driving rousers to a tender ballad. Once before a performance, he accidentally took some synthetic marijuana (something he eschews even in natural form because it makes him sleepy). "Great," said the promoter afterwards. For once Jerry Jeff was taken aback. "But I was hopping like a kangaroo!" he said. "That's what they like," said the promoter.

In Tucson, Jerry Jeff was geared for that kind of audience. He played "Redneck Mother." He played "London Homesick Blues." He played "Hill Country Rain," with those words that come to mind whenever I think about Jerry Jeff:

> I've got a feeling,
> Something that I can't explain . . .

He played "Pissing in the Wind" twice. The crowd seemed to be having the best time anybody had had in Tucson in years.

That was my impression at least. I was unconscious on stage. Jerry Jeff believes I *performed* in this state, coming in on "There Ain't No Instant Replays in the Football Game of Life," but since I can't sing and don't know the words to that song, I wonder. What I may well have done was pretty strongly hum along; I remember a certain amount of consternation and murmurs of *"What mike is he on?"* arising among the band.

As for Jerry Jeff, he played his electric guitar for the folks so hard that his untaped broken right hand (he fractured it punching a hurricane-glass window after "seeing too many rainbows" in Hawaii) got all ripped up. The review in the Tucson *Citizen* the next morning carried this headline: JERRY JEFF'S SOT IMAGE EXPOSED BY PERFECT SHOW. "Jerry Jeff Walker," the review said in part, "scrounged up his grungiest denims, staggered in through the side door an hour late, and generally worked hard at maintaining his 'image' for some 1500 at the Tucson Community Center Music Hall last night.

"By 8:30 P.M. with no signs of life coming from the stage, rumors began to buzz: 'Jerry Jeff's . . . drunk somewhere, you

know how he is!' It looked like many fans were going to
leave.

"At 9 P.M. his band started up. Bobby Randall (Rambo) took
the lead. . . . 'He's somewhere between here and Phoenix,'
Randall assured the crowd. Excitement and speculation built.

". . . Guess who wandered in from the side exit? The crowd
went wild. J.J. staggered; he kept his back to the audience.
Buzz, buzz, buzz. . . . 'Boy is he blitzed . . . really stoned.'

"Jerry Jeff Walker was a fraud last night. Stoned? Yes, stone-
cold sober. It was an act; it was part of the image; it was all
for a good time. Everybody got his money's worth." (This last
sentence particularly amused the troupe the next day, inas-
much as the promoter had left without paying them.)

"A more perfectly staged and timed show has rarely been
seen by these eyes.

"Walker had his voice tuned down to its gravelliest. . . . In
his studied uncoordination, he bumbled and mumbled. . . . He
played the part to the hilt. He kept a benign, stupid grin on
his face from start to finish, oozing the charm usually reserved for the truly besotted."

Well, that review tickled Jerry Jeff and his troupers no end.
The show had not, in fact, been what you could call musically
tight, and it had been truly besotted. But there was something
fitting about the review anyway. Some insoluble compound of
Jerry Jeff and his image had come through the wreckage.

I'll admit, I'm glad Jerry Jeff isn't in the White House. I'm
glad he's not in mine, either. But if Jerry Jeff were President,
he would *go with it*. If he took a rescue mission to Iran, he
would fuck it up, but in a way that might throw the Ayatollah off stride. Deep down inside, the Ayatollah probably
thinks everybody in America is like Cyrus Vance.

And Jerry Jeff would keep going if he lost *all* his helicopters,
and his map. The more helicopters he lost the better he
would feel. Out there in the desert with nothing, not even his
name, to call his own, except, such as they are, his voice and
his direction. Two things Jimmy doesn't seem to own.

More Carters

Knowland Boyd "Whiff" Carter, 28, New Era, Alabama, who has had a funny look in his eyes since he went off to college. "Hey, Jimmy: get on to the next *level*, man. I'd like to talk with the man; he ought to get on with the next *level*.

"Somebody says to you . . . something. You don't go: 'I wonder what he meant by that.' Naw. *He don't know*. What he meant. He may know what he *meant* to *mean*. But that don't mean that *that* is what he *means*, man. You just got to go *on*.

"Somebody goes: 'Naw, that ain't the train of thought.' Hey, what is it the train *of*, then? I'm *on* it, man. It's *moving*.

"If cats would eat cheese, they wouldn't have to eat mice."

Drugs in the White House

I've enjoyed some of the finest marijuana and cocaine available over the past decade, but nothing really compares with the rush from social change.
— KEITH STROUP, National Organization for Reform of Marijuana Laws

I have never used drugs in the White House myself. In fact, I have never used any anywhere except once under strict laboratory supervision. I'll never forget it, it was just me and five mice. The mice got pretty shaky there for a while, but everyone said I held up very well. Of course, I was so much larger than the mice, I felt an obligation. The mice seemed to settle down when they saw how I was taking it—I yelled "Hoo wooo!" once, but in a level tone.

"Here, have a little more," said one of the scientists. "Boy!" exclaimed another one. "I bet you drink your coffee black and your whiskey straight and will bite right into a whole raw onion just pulled up out of the garden, a little soil adhering to it even." "My granddaddy," I observed, "*Noah C.* Blount, would eat live oysters right off the jetty." A person from Georgia needs no drugs; I had Lester Maddox for my governor.

That administration was high times in some ways. I was working for the Atlanta *Journal* at the time, and one day I paid a call on Dr. J. I. Visor, the free-lance language consultant. Governor Maddox had just proposed staging, on Christmas Day 1968, a nationwide "demonstration for God and Liberty."

The affair, as the governor outlined it from his mansion steps, was to entail singing, marching, praying, bands, and floats; and "Georgia will be the national headquarters for this greatest of all American demonstrations that may well become known as America's multi-million-dollar demonstration."

It was to be "our answer," he added, "to the enemies of God and Liberty who would push back God and enslave our people."

It seemed like a heck of an idea, but it never came off, perhaps because of the difficulties Dr. Visor ran into with it.

"The only religious writing I had done before," Visor told me, "was in the area of bumper stickers." He showed me a white one, with tiny gold letters, reading: GOD IS DEAD. IF YOU CAN READ THAT, YOU ARE TOO CLOSE. IF YOU BELIEVE IT, I DON'T EVEN WANT YOU ON THE SAME ROAD WITH ME.

"God and Liberty Day, of course," Visor said, "is something bigger. And I am handling all the cheers."

"The cheers?"

"The cheers, and the big picture. I have the big picture roughed out already. On the one hand, you have God. And Liberty. On the other hand, you have things trying to push them back."

"What things?"

"All right," said Visor, "an example. The governor also announced that he was going to ride through the streets of Atlanta on Christmas Day looking for 'some child without a coat.' If he found one, he was going to get out and help him. That is the simple, efficient, godly, libertarian way.

"Now, set against that way is the welfarism and socialism way, which is big and confusing and costs a lot of money. It is always nagging at a person, no matter how hard he boosts God and Liberty. It denies a person his basic freedom to choose whom he wants to help and how he wants to help him, and what day he wants to help him on. And under welfarism, the giver doesn't get any cute grateful smile which will kinda chirk up his godliness."

"I see," I said. "How about the cheers?"

In reply, he sprang behind his desk, pulled out a sign reading "Smash Violence," and began to wave it and shout:

> "A-singin and a-prayin and a-beatin the band,
> Let's clamp Liberty down on the land.
> You can stop Communism, you can stop sin,
> You can stop alligators, you can stop men,
> You can stop a miniskirt, you can stop mod,
> You can stop drinkin, but you can't stop God!
> A-weepin and a-wailin and a-gnashin of teeth,
> Christmas tree, mistletoe, and holly wreath.
> Let's get to treadin where we ought to trod!
> Liberty, Liberty, God God God!"

He paused to catch his breath. "How does it sound?" he asked.

"Well," I said, "I don't know how well the Episcopalians are going to like it."

"Um," he said. "We'll work it out. The float people, I understand, were planning on ice carvings. Then they remembered the graven-image angle. So they're moving over to papier-mâché."

Lester Maddox always had some kind of visionary project in the works. Once he announced that he was going to form a Watchdog Committee, which would consist of a thousand grass-roots watchdogs who would report to him about immorality and corruption throughout the state. This caused a brief cacophonous outcry, but then, for a couple of weeks, there was hardly any public discussion of the committee—because everyone was busy writing the governor to apply for a job on it.

I managed to obtain copies of some of those applications, or something a lot like copies of them. Here are some excerpts, in which the applicants stated their qualifications and pin-pointed the corruption to which they had access:

I take pen in hand that I watch out for things and theys something fishy about my milkman, just come up every morning, don't look at anybody in the eye one way or another, leaves the milk. Turns off and jumps in the truck. I won't drink it. I won't touch it. What you think *in* the milk of a man like that!?!?!?

There's a woman down here name Peavle, or Peavy, she's got a suit in on a piece of land down here about four mile? Well her cousin A. L. Griffus use to work for the man is clerk of the Court of Ordinary over at B——— County whos the uncle, Uncle Vaughn, of the man down here, Hommem, Hommus, something, which voted I heard for the present mayor, but been working against him on the council. Well who you think I hear going to try that suit? Humh? *Who you think!*

I look in the Bible, and deep in my heart and got some 12-power binoculars my Daddy brought home from the Navy . . .

Want to help you do a good job of governor, and I got me a dog, got him from a man in 1949 I guess it was. He's half chow dog half close-hair setter, mean as a snake. He'd bark at anybody was to come up, even Mama. I paid $15 for him in 1949 and he's grow a lot.

There are fairies in the bottom of my garden. Miss A.O.

You know I'm a man 73, I always worked hard, tried to do right, listen to the preacher. Well I was in Piedmont Park here Sunday night, looked in a car there was young people—smoking—in there. I said you all now just go on home, tell me your names and howd you get them Cigarets and matches. I went on down the path come on a man, it was MY SUNDAY SCHOOL TEACHER. Smoking a big old cigar. I said now just come on out of here, we'll go home and find out what's causing you to do this thing . . .

. . . man teaching my boy Physics don't know enough to get in out of a shower of rain . . .

Governor I been thinking all along I knew what it was. What was the types and groups destroying our Wonderful and Very Fine State. But I come to find out it ain't them its THE GREEKS THE INDINS THE SOCAL AGRIVATERS. I grieve to tell you we gotem down here in my county, running the newspaper, all the write-ups. The sports. Don't print no baseball pictures but the GREEKS THE INDUNS THE SOCAL ...

During the week before I came up with those documents, the *Journal* editorial department had received only one drunken phone call—and that was from a man trying to reach an advice columnist—and not a single postcard written in blood or quoting more than three chapters of Scripture. Hardly a one of our young women reporters had been made to cry or swear over the telephone. Just as many people predicted, the governor's watchdog idea was usurping one of the most venerable functions of the press.

I feel I deserve a certain amount of credit for the style of Lester's governorship. At his inauguration, he gave a "moderate" address. Here was a man who had made a name for himself by selling pick handles and by writing—in newspaper ads for his restaurant, the Pickrick—some of the most hallucinatory prose since Thomas De Quincey. Now he was writing in a style which in later years we have come to associate with Jimmy Carter. It didn't sit right with me. I wrote this column in the *Journal*:

Lester Maddox has been kidnapped, and replaced by someone with no prose style.
Doubt it if you will, but first read this:
"The Georgia in which we live today is a vibrant, moving state whose future will be limited only by the failures of today."
And now think back to this:

God have mercy upon the souls of men in high public office who gave our citizens the right to protect the purity of their pets and livestock, yet are cruel and un-American enough to force parents to accept conditions that will bring crime, injury and racial amalgamation into the lives of their children and grandchildren. . . . Drumstick and Thigh 25¢.

Can the same man have authored both?

Surely not. Dean Rusk, maybe, wrote the former. Richard Nixon. Herbert Hoover. General Westmoreland. The president of the U.S. Jaycees. Patrick Nugent.

Not the Pickrick man.

Not the man who wrote:

ATTENTION

NAACP, SOCIALISTS, COMMUNISTS, power-mad politicians, deceivers and other left wingers. Is it not true that our own Federal Government, that threatens to occupy the South, does not dare to send negro troops to be stationed in Iceland? . . . Breast and Wing 50¢.

And yet we are told that the speech from which that no-doubt-already-forgotten opening quotation was taken is a speech by Lester Maddox. No, I say; I won't believe it.

Peruse these remarks from a text supposedly delivered by Governor Maddox at a meeting of the Georgia Press Association. Is the following a Pickrickian sentence?

"Several state departments and programs are now being reorganized and revitalized to better fulfill the needs of Georgia people."

More inspired passages have been handed down by lieutenants in the Adjutant General Corps.

And while, to be sure, the old Pickrick man may from time to time have let a little slack get into his editorial "we" ("FOR YEARS We have been called rabble-rousers, hate-mongers, racist, alarmist, demagog, etc. . . ."), he would never have given his readers such a sentence as this:

"Third, we have not overlooked those less fortunate Georgians who are confined in prison, in a mental institution, a turburcular [sic] hospital or who is without a job."

Or such a distinction as this:

"This view has no basis either in fact or in truth."

No, the so-called Lester Maddox who delivered that speech is an impostor. Note how, according to this GPA address text, he slips up and begins to refer to himself in the third person:

"This is an independent Governor.

"He wears no man's yoke.

"He dances to no special fiddler."

No, but he used to. He used to dance to a fiddler who could strike up cadences like these:

YOU WHITE RACE MIXERS OF HOPE; PARTNERS FOR PROGRESS; COUNCIL ON HUMAN RELATIONS; SOUTHERN REGIONAL COUNCIL, etc., plus the leftwing PUBLISHERS; EDITORS; PUBLIC OFFICIALS; MORAL LEADERS; CHAMBER OF COMMERCE OFFICIALS AND COMMUNISTS WHO HAVE BEEN WORKING TOGETHER AND FOR THE SAME CAUSE, should all line up together and "beat your chests" and boast of your success. You have inspired, supported and encouraged the lawless agitators until death, bloodshed, rape, robbery and property destruction has invaded Florida, Georgia, Alabama, Mississippi, the Carolinas, New York, California, Pennsylvania, Illinois, Washington, Ohio, Louisiana and many other states. . . . Thigh alone 15¢.

Well, right after I wrote that column, I had occasion to write this one:

Governor Maddox has appeared lately to have lost faith in his speechwriters. In preparation of his remarks before the Christian Crusade last weekend, for instance, he reportedly turned down flatly a script submitted by the men who had prepared his moderate inaugural address.

Then he overrode a second script, we are told, which was mostly his own work but "edited" by the writers. Six of the final version's nine pages were entirely the governor's, and they were the real stuff—they might have been restaurant ads.

It might be timely, then, and of some interest to students of the literary process, to take a look at present-day Georgia gubernatorial speechwriting in the works.

The scene is a small, dusty workshop somewhere along the corridors of the Capitol. Three small, gray-looking workers, Happy, Sleepy, and Grumpy, sit on brand-new stools, at brand-new writing desks, scratching with quills on foolscap.

On each desk are a copy each of *The WCTU Yearbook, Your Money and God, Patriotic Utterances of Many Lands, Pluck and Luck, The Egg and I,* and *Special Offer: The Collected Speeches, Papers and Novels of George, Lurleen and Lew Wallace.*

The silence is broken only by the sound of the scratching—until a bold, diminutive figure in glasses bursts in, waving a handful of script.

GOVERNOR: YOU'VE GOT ME COMING OUT FOR THE FIRE ANTS!

HAPPY: Ants, ants, let's see . . . "A lot of ants thought they came to a picnic at voting time last November, but they got stepped on."

SLEEPY: Mmmmmm-f.

GRUMPY: Oh, for . . .

GOVERNOR: Fire ants! Fire ants! Here it is right here: ". . . this administration, the administration of a great, a fearless, an impartial all-out Georgian, stands foursquare for religion, economy in government, and the fire ants"! What are you trying. . . ?

SLEEPY: Zzmfmzzmfmzzmfmzzm.

HAPPY: That's *"fine arts"*! "Fine arts"! You're addressing the Independent Christian-American Artists, and you're coming out for the fine arts. Lord, Lord.

GOVERNOR: Oh, well, anyway I don't like it. I'm taking it out and putting in [he reads]: "Since 1954 all the Supreme Court has been doing is abetting and encouraging bums. Now, I know there are several fine colored people living in the slums, and I think that's fine, but . . ."

SLEEPY: S-ssssssssssss.

GRUMPY: YOU CAN'T SAY THAT!

GOVERNOR: Well, why?

GRUMPY: It's despicable.

GOVERNOR: Hmmm. "Des . . ." I like that. [Marks on script and reads] ". . . and I think that's fine. But it's despicable the way the forces of socialism . . ."

Well, you seldom really know what impact you are having as a columnist, but to the extent that Lester Maddox did any-

thing flat and forgettable as governor, it wasn't my fault. Lester Maddox was probably the silliest person ever to head an
American state, and a lot of seriously nasty people liked him.
But he used to say that he got elected "with the help of my
family, my God and a station wagon," and he never appointed
the station wagon, nor any member of his family, to any state
job. Like Jimmy Carter, he was an honest, earnest, prudish,
come-from-nowhere politician; and a person-to-person, per-
son-to-media, as opposed to an organizational, politician. And
when Lester said something embarrassing, it had a real, personal feel to it, like a good country song. I remember when
Lester's son got arrested for burglary. Lester talked about how
it broke his heart to see the police car driving away "and his
little old head bobbing around in there."

I used to get stimulating mail at the *Journal* during the
Maddox administration. There was a letter from a state senator, W. Armstrong Smith. He wrote:

"I believe Lester Maddox should be rated with the Old Testament prophets Amos, Isaiah, and Jeremiah, who warned the
political leaders in their time that the mistakes they were
making in the nation would eventually lead to its complete
disintegration.

"Fortunately, Georgia has been spared and perhaps the reason is that the governor has publicly stated that any disorders
will be treated with firmness."

Unfortunately for Senator Smith's argument, nobody at the
time was getting up a Bible that needed a Book of Lester, and
too few of the downcast peoples of the world were able to appreciate the character of a man who would come out—*publicly*—against disorder.

I found more edifying a letter that arrived, unsigned, in the
same mail. This letter, it said, was inspired by a column of
mine which had reminisced about the (by then demolished)
Kimball House Hotel. The Kimball House was always having
bricks fall off of it onto passersby, and was fervently believed

by people in my high school to harbor whores. The Kimball House, as opposed to all the sharp and futuristic things that were being erected in Atlanta in the late sixties, was the kind of thing, I had written, with which I associated downtown Atlanta in my formative years.

I had been trying, in conjuring up the Kimball House, to account for the seedy tint to my urbanity; but this letter from an anonymous resident of Dublin, Georgia, put the old times in a different light:

"Do you remember or have you heard of the old Folsom Hotel. As I recall, it had a porch on the second floor, across the front.

"Well, my parents brought us children to Atlanta on an excursion via train. They parked us on this porch, went out and bought us bananas, big blue plums and other goodies while they went out over the city.

"Bananas and these big blue plums were a treat to us as the little town in which we lived had none. We traveled from Lavonia, Georgia, to Atlanta, and at that time, it was a long trip."

Oh drugs may be fine, but to my mind they don't compare with the further reaches of rhetoric, on the one hand, or, on the other, with a person's first banana or blue plum.

There is something to be said for not getting your first banana or blue plum until you are old enough to relish it consciously. Georgia was so late getting a taste of it that you would think the presidency would have been enough of a rush for the Carter administration without drugs. But then I don't guess you would want to eat bananas and blue plums day in and day out for four years.

But cocaine? Well, I don't think there is such a thing as a good old boy who is constantly wired. If the Carter administration were habitually coked up, national policy would be like Hollywood movies of recent years, and whatever you think of Jimmy's national policy, it hasn't been that bad. I do think, however, that a good old boy under, say fifty who gets ahold of a little cocaine might not want it to go to waste.

Oh, you might say that no good old boy should be attracted to any mood-alterer that "is now socially acceptable in Philadelphia," as the chief of that city's narcotics unit has said of cocaine. I wouldn't like to hear that the Carter people had taken to eating scrapple.

But how would you like to live under an administration, every member of which was completely above suspicion of ever having used an illegal substance?

Anyway, Valium, according to doctors testifying before a Senate subcommittee in 1979, is a much more serious threat to the nation's health than is cocaine. And yet on the same day that Liz Smith, the gossip columnist, noted that the investigation into whether Jordan had sniffed cocaine at Studio 54 "is a grungy story that seems to have brought out the worst in everybody," she also noted that *Starting Over*, a movie, "has got to be one of the most beguiling comedies in years, full of laughs and heart-tugging warmth and modern verities. (When one character asks a group of onlookers in a crowded Bloomingdale's, 'Does anybody have a Valium?'—every single person offers one in the emergency.)"

I don't think I *would* take any drugs right *in* the White House. Oh, maybe if someone there were to offer me a little toot, I'd accept it, but just for politeness and so I could run out and sell the story for a tremendous amount of money to the *National Enquirer*, and that would make me feel bad the next morning.

For the record, I would like to state that I know of only one instance of drug use in the White House. "When I met the President," a friend of mine told me, "I had no feeling at all in my gums." It was in the White House that this meeting occurred, and it was in a White House restroom that the gums were numbed. But no member of the government was in any way implicated, and there is no reason to believe that the President was aware that he was shaking the hand of a drugged person.

During the time when all the allegations against Jordan were hitting the papers, and Jordan was responding with his own recollections, I saw this headline in the Boston *Globe:*

KRAFT RECALLS MOZZARELLA

"Oh my Lord," I thought to myself, "Tim Kraft, the White House aide, is confessing that he has snorted Italian cheese." But what had happened was, Kraft Inc. had recalled 36,492 packages of mozzarella cheese because the cheese might contain small aluminum fragments. The corporation didn't know how the fragments could have gotten there; it had the grace not to blame the White House.

Once I was part of a group of several people that fortuitously included Tim Kraft, and we went to Studio 54. None of us used any drugs that I noticed except whiskey, but Studio 54 gave me the creeps so bad that I left after fifteen minutes. I had never been there before, I wouldn't have gone then if it hadn't been for the whiskey, and I will not go again. The question isn't whether Hamilton Jordan ever used any cocaine in Studio 54, but whether he ever stayed there longer than fifteen minutes.

Which leads us into the whole question of heterosexism and dancing.

More Carters

S. Ted Carter, 64, "early retired" personnel coordinator in Realville, Ohio. "Well gee whiz Iy don't know what to say as far as Mother and Iy. We're regular folks here, we have a cat. Does the cat have a name, Mother? Iy guess not. Iy'm around the house days, now. We make the decorated lifelike Vienna sausage novelties acourse, dye them the different colors and put on the feelers and, or the little outfits—we have oh, gee, several hundred of those in the freezer. And serve them acourse when we have the Wiltses over for Wednesday brunch—we thought, by golly, why doesn't anybody ever have Wednesday brunch? When you're retired, why you can. So we do with the Wiltses.

"Is that their name, Mother? No, Iy guess not."

Heterosexism and Dancing

What's so special about these Georgians—they don't wear queer clothes, they don't wear masks, they're not hermaphrodites.
— ALICE ROOSEVELT LONGWORTH

In Nashville just before he died I visited Allen Tate, the distinguished Southern poet and critic, whose notions included *tension* (the truth is established by bias, counterposing, suspension), "the fallacy of communication" (if you think you have signified anything by just opening your mouth and *disclosing*, you have another think coming), and the trashiness of modern Northern-industrial-dominated life. Notions such as these, with which I was imbued by the Vanderbilt English Department in the early sixties, when I should have been doing more to help desegregate luncheonettes, have meant a lot to my sensibility, such as it is.

Tate's poetry, Edmund Wilson observed, is "stony, nodulous and tight." To love much of it, you have to be receptive to an attitude of "Thank God I've kept my sense of loss." Some of it, however, is great country music:

> Far off a precise whistle is escheat
> To the dark.

And some of it great sportswriting:

> The going years, caught in an accurate glow,
> Reverse like balls englished upon green baize.

Anybody who can english a ball on a page, my hat is off to. And there curled on a narrow bed Tate was in the flesh, almost weightless, half-blind, nearly eighty, emphysemic and rigged up so he could push a lever and take bottled oxygen, as he needed it, directly into his nose through a tube.

He still had that great strange node of a head I had seen in photographs, and it was fine to see him carrying right on in vigorous conversation as though he was paying no mind to how little corporeality he had left. I asked him whether he had found himself stereotyped, down through the years, as a white Southerner. He said he sure had. Even in Paris in the twenties in Gertrude Stein's *salon.*

He remembered giving a lecture once in New York and pointing out that literary historians were like the old lady in the Faulkner story "A Rose for Miss Emily"—they were sleeping with their loved one's corpse. "And this symposium was *scandalized.* They said that kind of thing went on only in the South! Well, that same week in the paper there was a story about a woman in New York who had been sleeping with her dead lover."

Tate—who wrote a great poem about a lynching—shook his head over "Northern propaganda" which tried to make out that the darker side of the human condition was manifest only in Dixie. I was thinking amen almost wholeheartedly to that, when Tate went on to say he didn't respect W. H. Auden much as a poet because he was homosexual. "Now they're demanding their *rights!"* he cried. "The next thing you know *whores* will be demanding rights!"

Tate added that the trouble with homosexual poetry is, there are no women in it. There may be a sense in which that is so. And maybe the trouble with whores, although I believe they already have rights, is there is not enough woman in them. And let me just mention that I like plenty of women in my writing, as many as three or four in one sentence. I'll tell you something I'd like to get into poetry: the back of a woman's neck.

> The way you hold your head up,
> Dear, keeps me afloat.
> The smooth back of your neck there
> Gives me a lump in my throat.

That's just personal, and probably sexist. But I'm not going to lie and say, "What I like about a woman is the way she shoots her cuffs," or "What I like about a *person* is the back of her neck."

Still, I had to wonder why, if Tate could accommodate the notion of women sleeping with dead men, he couldn't accommodate the notion of live men sleeping with each other. And wouldn't you think a poet could disapprove of something without coming out against rights? Why is it that whenever people start demanding rights, *anywhere in the free world*, a clear plurality of my people gets so pissed off? Why is it that when I visit a distinguished poet of my people, he has to devote some of his last breath to assailing a minority? "That is the kind of distinguished poet," I can hear crisp Northern voices snapping, "your people would have."

"I don't *understand* homosexuals," Tate exclaimed. "How do people *get* that way?" This damn thing of people being homosexual just stuck in his craw. It looked like he never would get over it. *He didn't want there to be people he didn't understand.* And when he said understand, he *meant* understand.

In the background, from somewhere else in Tate's house, I kept hearing something incongruous. What it was, I realized as I left, was Tate's two young children, in the next room, plinking out on a piano the *Close Encounters* intergalactic communication music:

> Ba-*bah* bahh, bah *baaaaaahm*
> Ba-*bah* bahh, bah *baaaaaahm*.

. . .

I'll say this. If any outer-space people ever descended unto Tate and asked about homosexuality on earth, I know he gave them an honest answer. He didn't say, "Oh, I can give you the psychology on that." He said he was *mystified*.

I lay no claims, myself, to an understanding of anybody's sexuality except, of course, the President's, but I am tempted to envy those homosexuals who write. I don't like the idea, from either end, of what would appear to be implied when some gay men are said to be "good with their fists"; and I don't especially want to have to cut my hair short and grow it on my chest, either. But the *license*.

One form of freedom is being able to say *anything* in a certain tone of voice. Here, in *The Village Voice*, is Arthur Bell, sympathetically, on "the life of the gay outlaw":

"What they look for is Mother with a big penis to share the dream."

If you can get away with an image like that, you can get away with anything. Hippogriffs, flies with fawns' eyes, stones that have long telephone conversations. It's almost as good as being South American. What if you could be a Cracker with that kind of literary abandon? "What they want is Mammy with a big sweet-potato pie to (sort of) share the dream." "What they want is a mammary with a big fishing pole to share the bream." If I wrote something like that, people would think I was putting the Cracker outlaw down.

I'm not dumb. I know it is firmly established that we all have some gaiety deep down inside. Listen here: we all have a *bunch* of things down inside. I asked a psychiatrist friend of mine once whether it was true, as I had heard, that you can't hypnotize a person to do anything the person doesn't really want to do. "That is true," he said. "But everybody wants to do everything." For all I know, a caveman would couple with whatever he could get a good grip on. ("Since You Lost Your Love Handles / I Feel You Slipping Away.") I can sit here and deny until I am blue in the face that I have any gaiety to speak of, and everybody will just say, "Uh-huh, that's the tip-off. He's got a *lot.*" But a great many people get away with denying that they have any redneck in them. (You think a caveman didn't have any of that?) And—how can I put this?—there are writers who parade an innocence which I think it would not be unfair to call an at least partly homocentric lack of common sense.

Gore Vidal can say in a national magazine that when supposedly straight guys go together for days at a time, they of course roll out the other side of their bisexuality. In fact, when supposedly straight guys go off to hunting lodges together for days at a time, they by and large drink beer, shoot at inoffensive animals, and talk about pussy. Nobody would print it if I wanted to announce that when Eastern intellectuals go off to symposia together for days at a time, they of course cook chitlins, dip snuff, and tell jokes like, "Did you hear the one about a black person's idea of a holiday weekend?"

"No, what is a black person's idea of a holiday weekend?"

"Forty hours of fucking and eight hours of changing tires."

Vidal is a great critic, but he is at his worst, if not *anybody*'s worst, at sexual fantasy (a Breckenridge who is both Myra and Myron, and either way an asshole) and identification. He writes in the *New York Review of Books* that he can't understand why a wife should be at pains to keep her husband's ardor up over the years. "As far as I know no one in tribal lore has ever asked the simple question: Why bother? Why not move on?" Which is the equivalent, for appreciation of common human tribulation and entanglement, of "Why hasn't anyone suggested that they eat cake?" No wonder Vidal has never written a country song.

Arthur Bell can not only confer credence upon a quest for mutual revery with a well-hung mom, he can also write about how he tried to stop an inferably homophobic movie—*Cruising*—from being made in New York. Who would buy two thousand words from me about how I tried to obstruct the

filming of *Roots?* I wouldn't feel *entitled* to obstruct the filming of *Roots*, although it sure did present my people in a stupid light. I would be among the last to deny that my people
deserve intelligent opprobrium, and my objection to *Roots* is
not that it is at least as likely to inspire a misguided individual to murder redneck people as *Cruising* is to inspire one to
murder gay people. My objection to *Roots* is that slavery is
too important to be turned into schlock. And, incidentally,
that the supposedly sympathetic white characters in *Roots*
are as false as most of the unsympathetic ones are.

Now, I am not opposed to any form of liberation. I can't afford to be. If I were to say, "Well, I think this Scots Lib has
gone too far," people's reaction would be: "Because you're
Southern." (Either that or "Yeah, you're right, let's you and
me go roll a Scot.") And I would not only be giving a boost to
Scots Lib but setting back Cracker Lib. A Cracker Libber will
just be counterproductive if he takes to the streets with signs
that say PINEY WOODS PRIDE. In order not to have what several of
President Carter's pronouncements have been said to have—
"a boomerang effect"—we would have to go into the streets
carrying signs that say CRACKERS FOR RIGHTS FOR EVERYBODY ELSE.

So it may just be reverse ethnicism on my part, but I am inclined to favor every rights movement going. Years before it
was fashionable, I sent my shirts to a bisexual laundress and
they didn't feel funny when they came back. I have been
around gay couples who seemed a lot better matched than I
have been with several women.

But the demonstrations of Gay Pride that I have seen
looked to me like the work of FBI provocateurs. In Black Pride
marches, you didn't have people walking by dressed as Hattie
McDaniel, Butterfly McQueen, and the Zebra Killer. Back in
the sixties, I went to a Gay Lib parade in Greenwich Village.
A hairy-legged man in tight short-shorts went by carrying a
sign that said I AM YOUR WORST FEAR AND YOUR BEST FANTASY. Well,
he lied. He wasn't either one of them. And if he had been, he
would have let me down by being so out-and-out about it.

Nor was he doing much of a job, it seemed to me, of exorcising himself, if that was what he had in mind. He should have been carrying a sign that said I AM JUST ABOUT WHAT YOU EXPECTED IN A PARADE LIKE THIS: THE TYPE OF PERSON WHO GOES AROUND WITH HAIRY LEGS AND SHORT-SHORTS AND THINKS HE IS YOUR WORST FEAR AND YOUR BEST FANTASY.

In this parade there were men in harem pants and frilly dresses with signs commenting on the Vietnam War: GAY FEMMES SAY OUT NOW. What nation's army (I know, I know what they say about Frederick the Great's) is ever going to withdraw from anywhere at the behest of a man in harem pants?

In this procession, women in blue jeans strode along like artificial cowboys in town for trouble on Saturday night, with signs saying I'M PROUD OF BEING A DYKE and WE ARE LESBIANS AND WE ARE ALL BEAUTIFUL.

Men in high-heel shoes went by singing, "When the gays . . . go flaming in . . ." HOMOSEXUAL LOVE IS BEAUTIFUL said a sign carried by a heavily muscled bald man in earrings, walking with a small sandy man in a brown suit.

The last, and I thought most eloquent, person in the parade was a man whose only statement was to ride a bicycle with a white kitten in the basket. He pumped slowly, so as to keep the same pace as the walkers, but held the basket so level that the kitten slept. The parade disappeared up the street toward Sheridan Square, and the man next to me sighed. "See," he said, "that's where it's all leading."

Ten years later, in October '79, I read that fifty thousand homosexuals had gathered on the Mall below the Washington Monument to hear speakers denounce the "heterosexism" of mainstream Americans.

Nobody wants to *espouse* an ism any more, everybody just wants to find one for everybody else. Wants to accuse everybody else of a largely unconscious but institutionalized ism which is responsible for what is wrong, and which has been fettering the accusing party's consciousness until recently.

But all right, heterosexism it is—and just as I was getting it down pretty good.

No wonder the President doesn't have much panache. If an American white Southern straight Gentile man under sixty who grew up eating animals were ever to cut loose, in clear view of the nation, and do something that made him feel real good deep down, he would incur about forty-eight isms. Jimmy ran on all the things he wasn't. He wasn't a racist, an elitist, a sexist, a Washingtonian, a dimwit, a liar, a lawyer, a warmonger, a peacenik, a big spender, a Republican, an authoritarian, an idealogue, a paranoid, or a crook. He had found one last creditable ism: isn'tism. People in Georgia had said of him, "Well, there's not a whole lot *to* him." Jimmy turned that into a forte.

And he may have expected people to love him for it. Not just accept his bent toward extreme neutrality, but love him *for* it. That's where I think people who jump from being ashamed of their political, racial, or sexual orientation, on the one hand, to being ebullient about it, on the other, get carried away. A person's orientation doesn't make his or her shit bad; not in America. *But it doesn't make it good either.* I admired a black woman I saw once on the subway. She was wearing a button that said BEING BLACK OR PUERTO RICAN ISN'T ENOUGH.

Senator Sam Ervin Jr. was a fine figure of Southern White Pride until he started enjoying himself a little too much on TV. (Then he even started doing commercials. I swear, if Diogenes were alive today, he'd be doing lantern commercials.) When he was in his prime, Senator Ervin asked a member of the Nixon administration, a Mr. Sneed, how that administration could justify its having "impounded" funds that the Congress had allocated for social programs.

MR. SNEED: "Well, as I say, when we get down to, as I mention in my formal statement, situations in which all of the statutory justifications for impounding were stripped away and we have simply a question of whether there is any constitutional power of the President to impound and Congress has

said you must spend, it is our contention that he may refuse
to spend and that the collision in that case between the Congress and the President is a political question that is not justi-
ciable."

SENATOR ERVIN: "I am reminded of the story of the deacon
who desired to preach. The deacon went to the board of deacons and wanted to know why they fired him, and he asked
the chairman, 'Don't I argufy?' He said, 'Yes, you argufy, yes.'
He said, 'Don't I sputify?' The chairman said, 'Yes, you sure
do sputify.' He said, 'What's the trouble with my preaching?'
The chairman said, 'You don't show wherein.' "

Allen Tate would tell you that poetry has to show wherein.
So does politics. The way to show pride is to show something
other people will grant you reason to be proud of.

The Arthur Bell piece that had the image of beschlonged
maternity is mostly about finding a typical middle-American
gay person in Dayton, Ohio. When Bell finds him they have
this colloquy:

> I mention that the trend in New York is macho.
> "That's okay with me," he says. "I've got tons of Levi's and denim
> and checkered shirts."
> Does he consider himself masculine?
> "Yes."
> Does he consider himself feminine?
> He hesitates. "I can see myself enjoying things both ways. I enjoy
> the contrast. It's so beautiful to be a strong, virile, handsome kind of
> man who talks in a sensitive, romantic way and subscribes to cook-
> ing and needlepoint."

Bell finds such talk, and Dayton in general (where "even
the bellboys are giving"), a breath of fresh air. If a heterosex-
ual person were to talk about himself, herself, or any other
person in terms such as those, everyone within earshot would
be hooting and gasping for air.

By the way, *Levi's are work-clothes.* And I wouldn't be sur-prised if a greater percentage of people appreciated them for their function in Dayton than in Manhattan. When you get to loving your sensibility you stop being sensible, especially in the context of Dayton and especially if your sensibility is at the service of your sexuality and especially if your sensibility doesn't seem to incorporate the *vaguest notion* of what the inertia you are working against is like.

Growing up in the South, I got to where I couldn't stand people who were satisfied to think of themselves as dignified or sweet, who were proud of their mores, who had little ways that they thought were the most precious things in the world. I grew up wishing I could plant about half the adults I knew in the middle of Harlem at midnight naked. It wouldn't be fair, but it would be a step toward making them Americans.

"We are not all that civilized a people" was my feeling, growing up in the South. *"We are outlandish!"* Today, having moved North and traveled West, I would add: *"So is the rest of America."*

I am for gay public figures who work with that. Allen Gins-berg has. "America I am putting my queer shoulder to the wheel." Nothing shamefaced there, and nothing cultish.

You should have heard my internal voice that night when I visited Studio 54. *"Git the hell out of this place, boy!* Right now!"

I had, myself, long reviled the very notion of this place, where costumed residents of Queens, some of them nearly na-ked, stood outside pleading to be allowed in to view Halston and Liza Minnelli at play. I wouldn't know Halston from a sack of sand, but I knew I didn't want to view anybody who designed clothes. I had admired Liza Minnelli in *Cabaret,* but having seen her on television talking about how she was real-ly just a regular kinda kooky person at heart, I knew I didn't want to view her in person. Furthermore, I had read something about goings-on at Studio 54 that included the name Lala de la Lamour.

Now, I have no earthly idea, to this day, who Lala de la Lamour is. She may be eleven or sixty-three, or a man, for all I know. But it is just my luck that I would go into Studio 54 and she'd be there and she'd be like Mrs. Watts in *Wise Blood:* "Her grin was as curved and sharp as the blade of a sickle. It was plain that she was so well-adjusted that she didn't have to think any more. Her eyes took everything in whole, like quicksand," and I'd become infatuated with her—it wouldn't be anywhere *near* characteristic of me, I am just saying *"What if"*—and I'd go off to Antibes with her and run out of money inside of two days and become drunken and boring and she would treat me like shit and I would moon around for a while and overhear Halston murmuring, "Lala, *honestly,* who *is* he?" and I'd act like I was getting ready to hit Halston and that would really tear it and *tout le monde* would be wondering how anybody could have ever thought anybody from Georgia was chic, and I wouldn't have plane fare back and I'd have to work as a gigolo and finally I would put together a few hundred dollars hocking crazy old bony rich women's gold cigarette lighters I'd stolen from their purses and I'd crawl back to New York, take the bus up to Canaan, hitchhike the last few miles north, walk around to the back of the house and look at the compost heap, knock on the door, and my wife wouldn't have anything to do with me; who could blame her? And the kids wouldn't, either. And the dogs—not just Ned, who could be expected to side with whichever of his loved ones controlled the living room couch, but even *Peggy* would look at me sadly and decline to wag her tail. ("I am I because my little dog knows me"—Gertrude Stein.) And the cats, even. And the horse. And our friends the Swans, and Lee and Jim down at the store, and Addie at the post office, and my softball team.

And I'd drift back to Georgia and drink a lot without enjoying it, and get a job at the *Journal* writing obits, and I'd walk into the composing room and I'd see Wilcy—who when I told him back in '68 I was moving to New York looked at me as though I had said something filthy—and he'd give me a look that was only too keen to be gloating and he'd say:

"Um. Understand you um run off with a woman to France somewhere and left your wife and young ones and dogs and livestock and um softball team."

". . ." I would nod.

"And then when you come groveling back, um, they wouldn't take you in."

". . ." I wouldn't even have to nod.

"Um. Just curious—um what was that woman's *name?*"

And, spiritually dead, I would have to answer:

"Lala de la Lamour."

But I figured I had to go into Studio 54 once to prove I wasn't afraid of it. (I think that's what Hamilton Jordan probably had in mind. Hell, a person from the South ought not to be scared of decadence.) And the first thing I saw hit me like the shrunken man in the museum hits Hazel Motes in *Wise Blood*, the shrunken man about whom Sabbath Hawks later thinks, "There was something in him of everyone she had ever known, as if they had all been rolled into one person and killed and shrunk and dried."

It was a strange smooth two-backed beast: two expressionless bearded men of exactly the same stature hunching each other rhythmically at slight removes. Discoing with each other to beat the band. Both of them doing exactly the same thing. Two perfectly compensating dovetailed pistons, hyperkinetically yet nonchalantly canceling each other out.

I had always adhered to the old Cracker *koan*, "What is the sense of two men dancing?" But now I could see it: it was perfect, a closed system, perpetual motion, like two United Daughters of the Confederacy discussing history, or one movie critic writing about another one. That it gave me the creeps

was attributable, I guess, to heterosexism: I didn't *want* to be
turned on by that shit. It would make me doubt my motives
for either wearing or not wearing Levi's forever. But I was fas-
cinated.

The sound system was blaring "YMCA," by the Village
People. Now, there are many modes of androgyny for which I
have enthusiasm: the Tiresian, the Beerbohmian, the Billy-
jeanian, and others. The only one I can't stand is that which
puts together the most obnoxious of both sexes: the flouncy-
brutish. The Village People—dressed as Indian, Cowboy, Construction Worker, Policeman, etc.— are Barbiken dolls who
bump with no contact and grind with no grist. If the Beatles
or the Supremes or the Marx Brothers had ever dressed as the
Supreme Court, the Supreme Court would have been enhanced; if the Village People ever dressed as the Supreme
Court the legal system would be undermined. I had never
been able to comprehend why anybody would want to be both
swishy and muscle-bound; but now as I watched these two
men dance to this brain-squelching music, I could see. It was
what Yeats thought he was safe in yearning for because it
would never happen: "two natures blent into a sphere," leaving no nature at all.

Now this may be some kind of tacky Georgia notion. I
don't know. But my understanding is that loneliness abides,
neurosis builds, and generation occurs in the ineluctable
pockets of space between people, between sexes, between ethnoses, between people and other people's perception of them,
between people and their own perception of themselves, between the dancer and the dance.

For a gay person there might be a temptation to believe that
those lacunae disappear outside the closet. (And Jimmy may
have thought they would disappear outside Georgia.) Every
liberationist group has to get beyond the notion that pride of
group will bridge all a person's gaps, but blacks and women
have had reason, pre-Lib, to realize the pleasures and limitations of public wiggliness. Gay people, before they got into

Lib, were traditionally splendid at detachment, at *acerb* role-playing. In society, Lissome Movie-Stopping Me is not much of a role.

Okay, here it is, heterosexist case study: *I don't think Broadway chorus boys are a pretty sight, either.* Just *feverishly* grinning—worse than Jimmy used to—for one thing. And moving themselves any way they want to, twitching their hips the same way a girl would, if she had hardly any hips. *Dancing* is when people with something besides dancing in them dance. In Betty's Place, a restaurant in Dublin, Georgia, I saw a stout middle-aged woman in pants really dance— though only minimally; she was carrying a plate of catfish while she did it—to Charley Pride singing "Kiss an Angel Good Morning" (". . . and love her like the devil when you get back home") on the jukebox. To enjoy watching people strut their stuff, you have to be able to want to get into their stuff, one way or another.

But these two men dancing in Studio 54 looked like all strut and no stuff. I don't think Oscar Wilde and Noël Coward would have danced together like that. Noël Coward played a character based on Mountbatten in the movie *In Which We Serve,* and Oscar Wilde was a big hit in mining camps. They could *cut across lines* and yet keep a working sense of their peculiarity. I have always felt that homosexuals, like Southerners, are chosen people; it is our part to be out of whack, to hold back, to be unamalgamated. "In this country, I don't think you would ever have the Nazis," Art Rooney, the owner of the Pittsburgh Steelers, told me once. "The Jews, the Irish, Syrians, Italians, blacks. They wouldn't let them. It's not like there was all one kind of people, that could be fooled at once."

On the day of the Inauguration, the Washington *Post* published a tedious celebratory piece by Reynolds Price, the Southern novelist, in which he said the idea that the Southerner was peculiar was spread by Northeastern journalists who had "understandably stultified themselves on a diet of

Faulkner and Flannery O'Connor (writers whom some thoughtful Southerners see as sports to the region—homeless rhapsodists, fantasts, mesmerized haters)." That is a treasonous thing for a Southern writer to say. But that's the Carterian spirit for you.

In fact, Carter himself, in an interview with Harvey Shapiro in *The New York Times Book Review*, said that Faulkner, O'Connor, and other Southern grotesquists "have analyzed very carefully the buildup in the South of a special consciousness brought about by the self-condemnation resulting from slavery, the humiliation following the War Between the States and the hope, sometimes expressed timidly, for redemption. I think in many ways now that those former dark moods in the South of recrimination against self and others and alienation from the rest of the nation—I think they've been alleviated."

No, by heaven! That's Southern Chamber of Commerce Pride talking. Writers are *supposed* to be sports; and Southern writers have always had the advantage of being sports in a region of sports. *"The hope, sometimes expressed timidly, for redemption,"* is it? "Alleviated," is it? *Shit*, Jimmy.

Speaking of sports, the waiters at Studio 54 were striplings clad in basketball shorts, no shirts, only skins. The two-man dancing I saw was a little like basketball, but not enough. In basketball, one person is trying to outmove the other, get past him, take something away from him. No denying the homoerotic in basketball—here is Bill Russell on guarding Elgin Baylor: "We'd both take off and go up in the air together, with him wiggling around the way he always did. . . . We'd both laugh. . . . He had an instinctive awareness of the eccentricities of my game." But basketball has a point beyond sinuousness. "You know what I want them to be like?" asks Albert Murray, speaking of the new generation of blacks in *South to a Very Old Place.* "Our prizefighters. Our baseball players. Like our basketball players. You know what I mean?

"Then you'll see something. Then you'll see them riffing on history because they know history. Riffing on politics because they know politics. One of the main things that too many spokesmen seem to forget these days is the fact you really have to know a hell of a lot about the system in order to know whether you're operating within it or outside it. . . . The difference between riffing and shucking is knowing the goddam fundamentals. Man, when I see one of us up at Harvard or Yale I want to be able to feel like you used to feel seeing Sugar Ray in Madison Square Garden or Big Oscar there, or Willie Mays coming to bat in an All-Star game. You know what I mean?"

That's the way I feel reading Faulkner and Flannery O'Connor, and I sincerely want to work it out so that I can feel that way about the Carter administration. But I'll tell you what I am afraid happened. I am afraid Hamilton Jordan went in there to Studio 54 back before the election and saw them two scooters dancing. And it revealed to him how even rednecks could round themselves off.

More Carters

Barium Carter, 28, Poly, California, who is coming out, in principle, as of this interview. "Didn't say I was going to tell you what my p'effunce *is*, now. Told you what it is, you might just go 'Uuh!' No, now, yeh you might. Might be something you never *heard of*. You might've never *imagined anything like it.*

"Naw but just; it ain't the norm. But I got every right in the world to it, and I don't see where I should be denied, you know, like even vetina'y work or that. Because of it.

"I may have to go straight to Jimmy on this. I got to this Costanza I guess and she went, 'Uuh!' So that just shows you the mentality."

Redneck Androgyny

I still haven't gotten a good look at the President. All I can tell you about Jimmy Carter is that he comes up to my chin.
—Sergeant Margaret T. Hawthorne, White House guardswoman

Well, by now you probably have dismissed me and Allen Tate both as old boys with some kind of stony, nodulous, and tight sexual problem. As a Georgian, it's true, I probably am circumscribed. For instance, I am too courtly a gentleman for it to occur to me to tell a female subordinate, if by any chance I ever had one, that sexual favors were a condition of her employment—a practice which is all the rage now in the federal bureaucracy and America, if you believe the newspapers. And I'd be very reluctant to go into one of these orgy establishments, like Plato's Retreat.

> My darling's in a pile now
> Of six other guys.
> I've not for a while now
> Got a thing in edgewise.
>
> I'd like to withdraw from
> This nasty retreat,
> But all I can see now
> Is one of her feet.
>
> Back home she's regarded
> As perfectly sweet,
> But all I can see now
> Is one of her feet.

So I probably have no business touching on modern sexuality. Still, I am going to plow right ahead and tell you how it bears on the Carter administration.

Basketball, I have said, has a point beyond sinuosity. Also, Levi's have a point beyond "look." And style has a point beyond "style." Which is why it is imprecise to say the Carter administration has been more style than substance. What it's been is more "look" than leap.

I think it took so long for a Georgian to achieve national eligibility that this crowd of White House Georgians wanted to stay forever eligible. Politically bisexual: libervative, Demublican: coming on in all directions: running for President in place. If you can keep up a liquid-enough constituency and dip and bob on it fluidly enough, you can be as self-fulfilling an operation as those two men I saw dancing. You can be perpetually talking about, and proving, and coming just about up to, the limits of the office. Not even Gerald Ford ever did such a job of lowering everybody's expectations and then living up to them.

Did you really feel comfortable with all those Kennedys at the dedication of the JKF Library? Didn't Jimmy seem to be the only modern person there? Didn't you want to say, "Come on, Jackie, loosen up and smile when he kisses you, it don't mean anything, he's kissed everybody else"? Wasn't it embarrassing how she went kind of stiff on us?

Damn it, *Crackers* are supposed to be the embarrassing ones. Not sort of embarrassing, but good and embarrassing. Whereas the Cracker administration has tended more and more toward *abstract* embarrassment. There was that form Hamilton Jordan sent around through the administration so that the various superiors could rate the various subordinates as to such things as their savvy, and the form spelled it "savy." Then there was the time Jimmy went into Baltimore Manager Earl Weaver's office after the last game of the '79 World Series and said, "Sorry to hear about your mother,

Earl." Which was fine except that it was the other manager, Chuck Tanner of Pittsburgh, whose mother had just died.

Those aren't the ways Crackers are supposed to be embarrassing—by means of personnel forms and not getting people's mothers straight. That's not the kind of rip-roaring red-blooded embarrassment I was looking forward to. But who would have expected that the first Cracker President would be an androgynous figure, in the soft-focus neutral mode?

"Like a bridge over troubled water, I will lay me down" might be Jimmy Carter's theme song. Presumably that is because Jimmy came on with a sense of what the nation, at a moment in history, wanted. The nation, when it elected him, was vocally assertive, subvocally insecure, and above all tired of getting fucked. No one in such a state wants to hook up with a very stark example of either gender.

Maybe when you take the meanness and hambone out of a redneck, he loses all force and framework, becomes a wispy type that you wouldn't want to hang out with. But Jimmy is in every *passive* sense a liberal, in a way that newspapers and protesters seem to want a President to be. He is not functionally ethnocentric; he doesn't impose; he is tolerant, accommodating; he weighs all sides.

True, he fired Bella Abzug, after telling her committee that its confrontational tactics "sap our joint strength"; but after all, Bella Abzug had called him, again according to *Newsweek*, "a little f————." A person can only take so much. But Jimmy has the strongest wife in presidential history. And whereas other Democratic Presidents have screwed their United Nations representatives, Jimmy gave Andrew Young his head, and was screwed (politically) by him. In the process Young got a chance to be the most dashing UN representative we've had.

Jimmy's public image reflects a recognition on his part that the Civil Rights Movement unmanned Southern white men of his generation at the national level. It gave the national public a discreditable, unshakable image of Cracker masculinity (a mean and/or ludicrous deputy sheriff).

But who aspires to be virile any more? Aside from that guy in Dayton. Look at just about every rock-and-roll sensation today. What's gender any more?

Rock and roll is inherently androgynous. Aggressive thrust as serial orgasm. Elvis was a redneck, but he did look a lot like Katy Jurado. Proper country music is distinctly heterosexist, but rock and roll has had Mick Jagger.

Take Mick Jagger. The Rolling Stones make strong, if sometimes stupid ("Street Fighting Man"), music; "Far Away Eyes" is a good country song. But Mick Jagger has never made me want to holler, "Work on out!"

In 1968 I saw the Stones in concert, in Madison Square Garden, in the afternoon. They had been preceded into New York by stories comparing their hold on crowds to that of Hitler. They had been setting young folks on fire around the country, stirring them to jump from their seats and advance upon the stage orgiastically. The idea seemed to be that if Mick Jagger were only to take it upon himself some night to tell them to go get Mr. Nixon, or Mrs. Mitchell, the body politic would be turned inside out.

I had to take a matinee show because all the evening performances were sold out. But then the matinee show had a feature that the nighttime shows couldn't have had.

The Stones were lit, there in the great chamber of the Garden, by an awesome lot of whirling and flooding lights pouring down on them in lush columns and cones—and the flashing of cigarette lighters in the darkness beyond the confluence of beams made it appear as though sparks were shooting out from all that holy fire and briefly igniting members of the audience.

There was only one spotlight that I couldn't figure. It was a thick beam whose focus traveled, in the course of the show, very slowly and gradually over one section of seats. None of the enthusiasts thus illumined looked particularly interesting, much less charismatic enough to be lit up at the same time as the Stones. Only at length did I realize that this extra beam was a bit of the gradually setting sun, intruding through an opened door on the west side of the Garden.

The light, finally, I could figure. But I could never get a bearing on Jagger. He was undulant, all right, but anybody can undulate who is willing to be a blip of self-absorbed, undifferentiated id, flung impersonally about. I'd rather watch a dog kill a snake.

I'd a *lot* rather watch O. J. Simpson reach his leg out impossibly another three yards with three men hanging on to him and dig his foot in somehow and just pull himself on ahead. Or Tina Turner come at me with her hip bump-bump-bump, doing foxy-athletic things with her midsection that I couldn't have dared hope for and singing, "Uh think it's gonna WUK out fine." Or Charlie Chaplin walk-tumble down an up escalator. A performer's pelvis is like a President's smile: I want to know the *thrust* of it. I don't want it all over the lot.

Right after that concert, I figured the political implications of the Stones were limited. Twenty-five years before, people had been swooning for Sinatra, and so far the Mafia only ran Vegas and New Jersey.

But maybe I was wrong. Androgyny is big today. We aren't going to be able to stop androgyny. But we can drag our feet. You could make a case that my wife is better than I am at carpentry and pool. *But it pisses me off.*

In fact, I think androgyny is an area where Jimmy has shown commendable restraint. Amorphous as he is, he might have an iron grip on the American imagination right now if he had applied the lesson of rock and roll—which is to move from the groin. Even if he were more of an *old-fashioned* roller, he might have been more truly sympathetic toward, and therefore kept a tighter rein on, his brother and aides. He could have said: "Listen, you know I'd like to get drunk and pose for the cover of *Rolling Stone* in a derby and remark upon diplomat's wives at receptions and hit a little cocaine now and then too. But *we got to keep it in line.*"

But if Jimmy were a *now* kind of rocker he might be dancing with the Village People the way Betty Ford did with Tony Orlando.

Once a Cracker cuts loose on something—groin movement, or anything else—he goes all out. (Jimmy *moderates* to excess.) If the highest Cracker in the land had ever commenced to *dance* androgynously, he would have done it till hell wouldn't have it. Before long there wouldn't have been anything in this world to keep the whole country from just indiscriminately twitching and preening and hunching and flowing into a virilely jeaned, *soi-disant* beautiful, polymorphously perverse pulp.

Remember Jimmy in the Pirates' locker room after the '79 World Series, when he stood there blinking and looking like a small stick of wood (the only person in the United States who could be upstaged by Baseball Commissioner Bowie Kuhn, who was standing next to him), as the Series trophy was held up to the TV camera so that it completely covered Jimmy's face?

What if Jimmy had tried to turn this terrible moment to his advantage? Had peeked around the trophy and beamed and done a little shimmy? Said, "If you're wondering . . . if anyone out there is wondering whether I am . . . or not . . ." Paused suggestively. "Well, yes . . . I am." Paused again, lowered his eyes and done a little bump. "Well yes I am . . . the President."

No, Jimmy wouldn't do that. He wouldn't let me down that bad. It's not androgyny that he's gone all out with, it's something more complicated. What *is* it?

More Carters

L. Harwood Carter, 51, Grosse Pointe, Michigan. "My only reservation about the man—he *means* well—he's not forceful. I myself am. With Mrs. Carter, with my children, my associates, my household pets. The expression 'carve you a new asshole' is one I do not shrink from using. That expression is one I commend without reservation to the President himself. If the President would hold himself forcefully, if he would look at the labor union leader or the Jewish organization leader or the fault-finding commentator forcefully, and if he would put it to him. Bam. 'I'm going to carve you a new one.' No bones about it. In a forceful, clipped voice, much like my own. We would see a change."

Possumism

WOWP YOWP WOWP WHOOP OW.

    —Pogo, *at the dinner table. Grundoon the ground-chuck chile is biting on Pogo's tail, which is all Grundoon or we can see of Pogo because Albert has dumped potato salad all over him, because a bear dressed in a Santy Claus suit has dropped in and Albert is under the impression, for reasons too complex to go into here, that the bear is a Russian planning to put Pogo in a slave camp.*

Pogo, who was fuzzy, put upon, and a reconciler, ran for President out of Georgia long before Jimmy. Albert the Alligator was Billy, and Howland Owl, Brzezinski. . . . Maybe in the back of my mind that's what I was hoping for when Jimmy got in: a Pogo government. "Pogo" attacked McCarthyism, Birchism, and Agnew, and celebrated "*e pluribus unum.*" It was such a nice and rowdy strip, democratic, many-angled, and serene. Pogo will emerge unsoiled from the potato salad and go about his business, insofar as everybody will let him.

Oh, I remember one time Albert, Churchy, Pogo, and Porky—as pluralistic a group as you could hope to pile into one aged motor vehicle—are all piled into or onto one which has just one wheel but nonetheless is bearing them along like an avalanche. You can't ask for any more calamitous sound effects than "POCK DAM KABAM BAM! ROWR VROOM WHAP BOOMP! AH-ROOGIT!" and nobody knows where they are headed or who is driving, but they are all in this together, and "AH-ROOGIT" ought to be our national anthem.

From certain angles Jimmy looks a little like Pogo. So does Cyrus Vance. On the other hand, Pogo didn't look much like a possum. When you get down to the reality of a possum—which a lot of people might hold to be a Southern thing, but no, it's pervasive—you realize that it probably hasn't got any anthem.

It doesn't need one. It knows one big thing: how to hang in there with no show of dignity. Jimmy may turn out to have known how to play possum, when to fall and when to rise. He hasn't been as lovable as Pogo, but then Pogo isn't a realistic example of a possum. I wouldn't give Pogo more than about a 2 on "Ears."

"This possum's got *pretty* ears," said my fellow judge Louis Moore, and I had to agree with him. Just a gut reaction. That is what you go by, mostly, on show possums, though to be sure, the Beauregard, the world's most perfectly developed possum, was sitting up there on the stage for purposes of comparison. "You can just *tell* a good possum," says Basil Clark, president of the Possum Growers & Breeders Association of America, Inc.

In a person show, Clark would win best of breed by default: "There isn't but one Basil," says his wife Charlotte. He has a Coldstream Guards mustache, a bald head, a potbelly, and, usually, a doleful expression. He wears a cowboy hat, snakeskin boots, and a hand-tooled belt buckle with his name and a pair of possums on it. He says, "I was the only one who flunked sub-college English at Western Carolina College, but I am the only one from that class who ever got paid for saying anything." Talks on the possum is what he gets paid for. He says that a possum will fold the white part of its ear down in the winter to hold in the heat and stick it up in the summer to catch the sun. I don't know whether that is true or not, but I didn't need to know in order to judge possums. I gave this one a full 5 points on "Ears." Next category, "Feet and Tail."

There I was, at the annual PGBA International Possum Show at the Chilton County Fair, which takes place outside

Clanton, Alabama, which is near Thorsby and Jemison and between Montgomery and Birmingham. I was down on my hands and knees in the pine shavings, on the floor of the live-stock show building, trying to get a good view of a domesticated possum's feet. It was hard. This possum, nice as its ears were, was showing bad character.

(Note: Throughout this account, except where sources outside the PGBA are quoted directly, the animal will be referred to as a possum, not an opossum. "The *o* in 'possum' is invisible," says Basil Clark. "Like the *p* in 'swimming.' ")

"General Character, Size, and Balance" counts for 25 of the 100 points a possum can ideally score. "Feet and Tail" is 15. A possum—and this is something not everyone realizes—has an opposable thumb on its hind foot, as a monkey does on its paw. A possum also has twenty-one fingerprints—one for each of its toes and one for the tip of its tail. I didn't need to check this possum's prints, but I did need to get a good look at his feet in order to judge him properly. And his character was already down around 18 in my book because he kept scrabbling in the shavings trying to get away (his handler had him by the tail) and his feet stayed covered and moving. The assumption is that a possum that won't hold still for judging is showing bad character, though his balance may be fine.

I wasn't sure what a good-looking possum foot looked like anyway. I did know how the tail ought to look—clean. A possum's tail looks bad enough without being scruffy and stained; a conscientious possum owner will not only shampoo his possum's fur before a show, but will also take some kind of strong cleanser to its tail. The night before, Dr. Kent Johns, a leading owner in Clanton, had come to the back door of his house dangling a bubbly possum (shampoo was still foaming on it) by the tail and asked his wife for some Bon Ami. "Nobody uses Bon Ami any more," she said. She gave him some Comet.

"What should I look for in his feet?" I asked the man next to me on the floor.

"Well," he said, holding up one of the feet of the possum of the moment, "that's a good one there. See, shaped like that."

I realized I had just consulted the possum's handler, Jack Carlisle, who was biased. I put down 11 points for "Feet and Tail" and went on to "Head and Jaws."

When I first heard of the PGBA show I had no idea I would someday be a judge in it—or, for that matter, that my wife Joan, out of Cambridge, Mass., would be named Miss Possum International. It was in May that I saw a story in the Nashville *Tennessean*, under the headline "EAT MORE POSSUM" NO JOKING MATTER TO SOME.

Well, I had seen EAT MORE POSSUM bumper stickers and tags around the country, and as a boy I had often come upon a possum stretched out unconscious or dead on the sidewalk, and I knew that a possum had gotten into my mother's air conditioner in the middle of a recent Saturday night in Georgia. He made a noise like a burglar putting an aluminum ladder up against the side of the house, she said. Unless the burglar was out to steal the TV antenna, that would have been an odd tactic, since my mother lives in a one-story house, but you never can tell in the middle of Saturday night, and my mother was disconcerted. She had to call a policeman to coax the possum out. "I went off to teach Sunday school the next morning just knowing I was going to say 'possum' instead of 'Matthew' or 'Mark,' " she said.

So I had a natural interest in possums, and when I saw that headline in the *Tennessean*, the white parts of my ears pricked up. The story told how Basil Clark and Dr. Johns and some others down around Clanton were developing the notion that possums were animals whose time had come.

The story, by Wayne King, said that the PGBA had some 40,000 members, about 100 of them actual growers and breeders, and the rest, including former President Nixon, just people who were interested enough in possums to want an official bumper tag that said not only EAT MORE POSSUM but also MEMBER, PGBA.

There was also a quote from Curtis V. Smith, another owner and breeder and a member of the Alabama legislature: "We're just at the beginning of this thing. If it opens up as a supply of protein, it could be very valuable." Smith and Clark were said to envision possums as the answer to the world food problem. "You can communicate with people with the possum," said Smith. "You give them something to believe in. You give them something to eat."

I wanted to know more. I dialed Clanton information, called Clark, and asked him when the next possum show was. In the fall, he said. That gave me plenty of time for research. I didn't want to go into this thing cold. I noticed, though, that Clark wasn't falling all over himself in response to my query. "There . . . uh, really is a show, isn't there?" I asked.

There followed the quality of pause that might follow if one were to call up Bowie Kuhn and ask him whether there really was going to be a World Series.

I soon learned, if I hadn't known already, that not everyone holds possums in such esteem. When I asked a friend of mine, who is an authority on animals, whether he would be surprised to find that there was such a thing as a possum fancier, he said no. He said, "Anybody is fancier than a possum." Some of the things that supposedly scientific, objective men say about possums are even more slighting. In a reference volume entitled *The Animal Kingdom* (Frederick Drimmer, editor in chief) there appears a drawing of an irritable-looking animal sitting on a stump. This is the caption: "Ugly, stupid, and addicted to fainting spells."

"The common or Virginia opossum is considered unattractive, unlovable, and stupid. The familiar expression 'playing possum' comes from this animal's peculiar habit of falling into a coma when it is suddenly exposed to danger.

"Strange as it may seem," the book goes on condescendingly, "the American opossum was the first of the marsupials encountered by western civilization. It was discovered by the

Spanish explorer Pinzón in 1500. In fact, it was presented at
the court of Ferdinand and Isabella, where it created quite a
sensation.

"Knowing the opossum for the humble creature it is, we
find it hard to understand the amazement it produced among
the early Spaniards. They described this new kind of animal
as a frightful beast with a face like a fox, the tail of a monkey,
ears like a bat and human hands. Below, on the belly, they
said, it has a second belly hanging down like a great sack or
pouch in which the animal carries its young. To them it was
'the incredible mother.' " And they didn't even know what
kind of noise it could make in an air conditioner.

A more sympathetic portrait is contained in *The World of
the Opossum* by James F. Keefe. Even Keefe says that the possum "isn't an especially handsome animal"; "is so lethargic
... that it is sometimes hard to judge its reactions"; has a
brain case that holds only 21 beans, compared to 150 for a raccoon; and is not "very outstanding as a predator," being satisfied as a rule to prey upon persimmons, stink bugs, carrion, or
just about anything living that either doesn't move or doesn't
resist much.

Keefe confirms that "playing possum" is not a stratagem
but a swoon: "The animal can no more stop the involuntary
action than a sensitive plant can withhold the folding of its
leaves." When I was a boy and we found a possum stretched
out on the sidewalk, we would say loudly, "Well, I guess this
possum's dead. Might as well leave him alone," and hide behind a bush to wait for him to get up again. But it appeared
we could never fool him. In some cases, of course, the possum
might actually have been dead.

It must be conceded, however, that a possum's faint is ef-
fective, since most predators lose interest in prey when it goes
rigid. A possum in its trance will not respond though its toes
be twisted severely, its whiskers pulled, or even its eyeballs
touched. A dog will generally give a passed-out possum a couple of tosses, perhaps banging it up some (captured possums

are often found to have broken ribs), and then pass on to an edible that either struggles or is in a dish.

Keefe grants the possum a number of entirely good qualities. It hears and smells keenly and does not smell bad—no worse than faintly musky. It is a good swimmer. It is likely to hang by its tail only when someone poses it that way for a photograph, but it can use its tail for such purposes as gathering leaves for nesting. There is a great picture in Keefe's book of a possum wading placidly. The caption says, "Opossums seem to enjoy just ambling around in shallow water." The possum also has deceptive speed. That is not to say it is *fast*. But it can run.

The greatest testament to the possum is that it has survived since before the Ice Age and spread itself wider and wider, in spite of the many natural enemies before which it falls prostrate. The possum is beset by parasites, insecticides (even though it is an insecticide itself), foxes, bobcats, owls, man, and Chevrolets. The first Frenchman ever to meet a possum—La Salle in 1679—killed it with a stick. Then he killed the second one he met. He hung them both from his belt and walked back to camp. They appear, pendant, in the painting *La Salle at the Portage*, by Arthur Thomas, now hanging in the courthouse of St. Joseph County, Ind. I would like to think that after La Salle went to bed that night the possums came to and walked off with his belt, pants, and all. But about this possibility history is mute.

At any rate, in the last fifty years or so, while brainier species have been crowded into tighter and tighter enclaves or even threatened with extinction, the primitive American possum has waxed in number and extended its territory from the South well up into New England, over into the Southwest, most of the Midwest, and (because someone saw fit to transport a cadre to California) all up and down the West Coast. "This indicates success in meeting life's problems," notes Keefe.

One reason the possum has flourished is its adaptability to a wide range of climes, terrains, food sources, and other animals' burrows. It doesn't seem at home in snow but can contend with it (a man in southern Massachusetts reports he sees possums shuffling over ice and snow "like little old ladies in ratty fur coats"), though sometimes the white ear tips freeze and fall off. It can live alongside man much better than most wild animals, sometimes even finding its way into people's homes. A San Franciscan I know came upon a possum on his apartment terrace late one night when he had been drinking. "Shocked," he says, is not too strong a word to describe his immediate reaction. The possum, for its part, acted as if *it* had been drinking and was seeing something awful. If you think Jimmy Carter used to have a strange grin, you ought to see the grin of a surprised possum. The human visited by a possum may gasp or scream, the possum may faint or take on the air of a shanghai victim, but still he remains to be dealt with.

And if the possum is a female, she may have nine or ten young ones on her back. The possum's forte—one reason, I had read, why the PGBA envisions it as a prime source of protein for the world's hungry—is its quaintly managed reproductivity. Annually two litters, each of up to eleven living embryos, frogfaced and so small that twenty could fit into a teaspoon, leave the sow possum's womb, crawl hand over hand to her pouch, grow to the size of kittens, spend some time clinging here and there to her fur as she makes her rounds and then set out on their own.

Ferdinand and Isabella's court, then, had reason to be impressed. When you consider that in 1555 the Englishman Richard Eden described the possum as a "monstrous beaste with a snowte lyke a foxe, a tayle lyke a marmasette, eares lyke a batte, handes lyke a man, and feete lyke an ape"; that Captain John Smith once wrote, "An Opassum hath an head like a Swine, and a taile like a Rat, and is of the bignes of a Cat"; that Basil Clark has been quoted as saying that the possum, for all its nonaggressiveness, has a bite like an alligator's; that Clark has furthermore called the possum an evolutionary link one step up from the duckbilled platypus, between cold-blooded, egg-laying reptiles and higher warm-blooded, live-bearing mammals; and that "Yes I can" might be translated into Latin as *"Ita Possum"*—when all these things are considered, it is a wonder that possums aren't taken more seriously than they are.

As fall approached I called Basil Clark again. "When is the show going to be?" I asked.

"October 13," he said.

"I'm supposed to be in my ex-brother-in-law Johnny's wedding in Bryan, Texas, that day," I told him. Perhaps I assumed, in the arrogance of one who represents a national medium, that something like a possum show could be rescheduled for my convenience.

"Well . . ." said Clark.

"Are there going to be any other shows, other days?" I asked.

"Well," he said, "there might be some local ones. But this is the international one."

"Oh," I said. "Where will the possums be coming from?"

There was a pause, during which Clark seemed to be trying to think of some polite way to suggest that I must not know what "international" meant.

"*Everywhere,*" he said.

I had to miss my ex-brother-in-law Johnny's wedding.

The first possum my wife Joan ever saw, she ate part of. I had by then spoken not only with Clark but also with Dr. Johns, Congressman Smith, and another owner named Don McAfee, who had offered to provide a possum dinner the night before the show. As many possums as I had seen, I had never tasted one, so when Joan and I arrived in Clanton and walked into the back room of Barron's Restaurant, it was with fresh perspectives. There on the table, surrounded by sweet potatoes, was a fresh possum. It was a former show possum of

McAfee's that had lost a part of its tail somehow and thus become available for eating.

Since that night I have often been asked what possum tastes like. The question is vexing. It is as difficult to put a taste into words as it would be to manufacture ice cream the flavor of, say, a *New York Times* editorial. A man I know who ate dog in Vietnam told me what that tasted like: "Stringy, like pork, and strong, like beef." I was not satisfied. Flannery O'Connor once spoke with a man who had eaten owl. "What did it taste like?" she asked. " 'Bout like crow," he told her.

Let me begin by saying, then, what this baked possum looked like. A baked cat. I guess you could say it looked like many another baked small animal, but when I saw it, I thought, "That looks like a baked cat." I didn't *think* they would serve a representative of the national media baked cat.

There were two tables, set up in the shape of a "T" as for a modest banquet. Joan and I sat at the head table, whose remaining seat was empty, reserved for Basil Clark. At the other table were seated a small party of Clanton citizens. Smith and Dr. Johns had been unable to come, and Clark was late in arriving, but McAfee was there, a well-dressed real estate man of agreeable mien, and the three or four other PGBA members on hand seemed like nice folks.

So I assumed it was possum. Perhaps this was enough to explain why our hosts seemed to be holding back, as if waiting for some possibly untoward reaction. Perhaps other out-of-town guests had tasted possum in such a setting and bolted from the room. I noticed that McAfee ordered steak.

Many people disdain the possum as food on the grounds of what it eats, but how about the pig, the lobster, and the chicken? And I am not a picky eater anyway, especially when I am sampling something proposed for the world's hungry. Maybe possum would be a little gamy. I was game. Why then did I feel uneasy?

I don't want to sound like an alarmist, but sometimes a situation seems to me just slightly unsteady enough that I begin to anticipate an ontological shift. In this case I began to wonder whether there was such a person as Basil Clark. Maybe the possum would rise up, begin to dance, and become him, or Clark, when he appeared, would be the Almighty or somebody and tell me, "You have been living a dream. In the real world, possums are Life." And *then* the possum would dance.

You never know, on the road, what you are getting into.

Then Clark arrived. He was wearing his hat, boots, mustache, and possum belt. He was of less than medium height and stooped. Answers to several of my questions had been deferred until his arrival. Oh, McAfee had been forthcoming enough. In a regrettable lapse of dinner-table taste, especially in light of what was on the table, I had mentioned that my research had suggested that possums picked up a lot of parasites. "Oh, chiggers and ticks," McAfee had said. "They're not parasites, they're natives. But you better wait for Basil to give you the story on that."

Now Basil trudged across the room amid expectant silence and took his seat next to me. He sat there hunched and gave me a sidelong look. Then he looked away again. "I attended Western Carolina College, where I was served a diet of green eggs and dried bologna," he said, "and it stunted my growth."

With that, McAfee began to carve the possum, which Mrs. Billie Strickland had parboiled for half an hour and then basted while baking it with the sweet potatoes. The possum carved easily. "This is not the little old black possum that roams the wood," said McAfee. "This is a registered possum."

"A registered possum is a better possum," said Clark. "Put that first, and everything else falls into place." My notes for the talk that ensued, as we ate, do not fall into place as neatly as I could wish, but the following will give you an idea:

"I have a documented statement that possum is the most powerful aphrodisiac known to man," said Clark. "Every time I butcher one, that musk gets on me and the girls nearly run me crazy. Like to get attacked right in the post office." Everybody laughed at this except Basil. I was to conclude later that the things Basil really brightened up about were things that were not only astonishing but also true. He broke into an unabashed chortle as he said:

"Other day there was a long-distance call at the post office—'Who knows Basil Clark?' They handed the phone out the window to me. It was a doctor at the University of Ohio; wants to come down and contract possums. Do embryological research on 'em. And psychological. Been using possums in the space program. The valves in their hearts are like a squirrel-cage fan." As I was trying to think what a squirrel-cage fan was, he shifted to a graver, more philosophical tone.

"Possums are the last piece of free enterprise that's left— the government don't know anything about possums. But it'll come. People take cotton allotments, we'll get possum allotments. A hundred active possum growers, we're a minority. The government finds out about a new minority, it's like an itch, got to scratch it. Then Congress finds out people are growing possums, they'll pass a bill not to grow 'em. Give us an allotment. Retire us with a government check coming in every month."

Clark talked fast. I didn't know exactly how to get a journalistic grip on what he was saying, but I felt it would help if I could pin it all down to some specific verifiable program. "With Curtis Smith in the legislature," I asked, "are you going to try to get laws passed on possums here in the state?"

McAfee responded to that. He said, "Curtis is going to introduce a bill to prosecute possum rustlers. You know, these rustlers haul 'em off in trucks and they fall out and get run over by cars. See 'em all over the highway. Basil says it's the biggest loss we face."

"Back in the thirties," Clark said soberly, "I predicted the world would be knee-deep in possums by 1952. What happened? Automobiles.

"The fat in possum," he went on more lightly, "is polyunsaturated—clean your arteries like a Roto-Rooter. There's a husband-and-wife team working on that right now. A possum cools himself in the summer like an automobile—pumps his blood into the tail and licks it and the blood flows back into him cooled." Clark smiled with what I took to be pride in the possum's homely ingenuity. To rig up a radiator out of a tongue and a tail! It was the kind of thing a man who grew up without a great many material resources could identify with.

Still, I needed more background on the PGBA. Pressed for it, Clark said, "Got to kicking this thing around in 1968. Incorporated in 1971. It just come time to register a possum. Had a lawyer said we couldn't do it. I said, 'They register horses, don't they?' I said, 'They register cats and dogs.' I said, 'We done put a man on the moon, you mean to tell me we can't register a possum?' Got another lawyer.

"We got to get the eagle off the national emblem and put the possum up there where it belongs. There's many a person in the United States that between '29 and '48 would've starved to death if it hadn't been for the possum. Had a dog named Katy—me and old Katy, Uncle Billy, Uncle Buck, and Uncle James would go out, and when six or eight other people were chasing the same possum, that's how you could tell that times was hard."

One more point of interest: "You got to know when to breed a possum. You've seen a possum dead in the road, grinning like he knows something nobody else knows? When that grin turns to a smile, it's time to breed."

About then it was time to adjourn. I was beginning to see that you had to go with the flow of this possum thing—that you can indeed communicate with people about the possum, but it takes some getting into. I had, myself, begun to feel basically at home with these folks when I took my second big helping of possum. Possum was sort of like dark meat of chicken, only stronger-tasting and looser on the bone, and stringy, like pork.

Still, I felt the need to nail a few facts down. I went with

Clark to the Clanton Drive-In Theatre, which he manages and which he lives next to in a mobile home. The trucks and cages and things around the mobile home constitute the Big C Possum Ranch.

Clark got out a big floppy briefcase full of PGBA materials and opened it up on the counter next to the popcorn machine. The amount of change going on in the world was amazing, he said. "There's a bigger generation gap between me and my son Frank than between me and Jesus Christ. Animals are dying out. People can't afford to devote two acres per animal to raising cattle. Ten years from now, when you see a cow and a calf, it's going to be in the zoo. When you eat animal protein, it's going to be possum." He produced a letter from Samuel Taylor, Food for Peace Officer, U.S. Agency for International Development, Mission to El Salvador, which said in part: "Here in El Salvador . . . possums are considered a delicacy among the rural populace. At the same time, the prevalence of protein/caloric malnutrition is estimated at over 70% in the age group under five years of age.

"Many people," the letter went on, "still think I am joking when I try to sell the idea that possums could be an added source of protein for many rural families. What I need to get for more acceptance of the idea is scientific data. Could you send me . . ."

I felt bad about certain doubts that had persisted in my mind about the PGBA. Then Clark showed a picture of himself, several possums, and a class of schoolchildren. "Possums are educational," he said. Then he added, "I've had people in the association who've gone right along with me, say, 'Basil, I believe you're *serious* with this thing.' " He shook his head. "I say, 'You *believe* I'm serious!' You know *vision* is what separates men from the animals. I studied to be a doctor. I could always see things other people couldn't see, even in a microscope. But I couldn't pass English. If I had, I'd be a doctor, the worse thing I coulda done. Doctors ain't got time to do anything."

He pulled out pictures of himself, a pretty girl in a fancy gown, a fat and bouffant possum, and a number of politicians in the chamber of the Georgia House of Representatives. "They were reapportioning the districts that day," he said. "You know how important that is to politicians. Well, they was all voting with one hand and petting the possum with the other. Every one of 'em had to come have his picture taken with the possum."

He gave me an EAT MORE POSSUM tag, a certificate for my den wall, and a PGBA wallet identification card. To join, he said, I had to declare two things:

"One, that you either own property, or rent property, or have an idea where you can get some.

"Two, that you can raise a possum full-growed without eating him up."

I so declared.

The next day was show day. "You might have to judge," Basil said, so we went out to look at a lot of possums. I was being swept into the mainstream of the possum, and I didn't know whether I was ready. That was when Basil said, "You can just *tell* a good possum."

He admitted it hadn't been so easy in the first year of the PGBA. Everybody went out into the woods and rounded up the best-looking "range" possum they could and fed it for a while. "How you going to tell a good possum when you haven't got any good possums?" he said.

"We just picked the best we had and named him the Beauregard and judged the others by him. I'd rather have the Beauregard than the world champion."

But then a lady named Mrs. Wilson in Wetumpka, Alabama, was found to have produced a better possum. "She's the one bred the red on 'em," said Curtis Smith, who owns the current Beauregard and also the world champion and whose farm outside Clanton we visited. Curtis is a big ole solid man who played walk-on end for Auburn in the early fifties (until he "sprung both ankles") and looks like he might be chewing tobacco even when he isn't. "We got three from Mrs. Wilson and then started moving toward a larger, more domesticated animal."

We went out back of Smith's barn, and he started pulling possums out of homemade wood-and-chicken-wire cages. "He knows which ones you can pick up and which ones you can't," said Clark. "I don't like to mess around with another man's possums."

"When you wake them up they're just like anybody else—grouchy," said Smith.

"That's old Beauregard there," Curtis said. "No, that's old Stonewall, I guess. See those teeth? They'll cut your finger off just like with the snips." He took out Stonewall II, the world champion, and started grooming him vigorously with a hairbrush. "That possum has been in *National Geographic* and on 'To Tell the Truth,' " said Basil.

"He's been breeding," said Curtis. "He looks a little poor."

"I think that's the best way to lose weight," said Basil.

I asked Curtis whether he thought possums were very intelligent. "They're intelligent if they have to be," he said. "They'd rather just mosey along."

I asked him whether his possums knew him. He seemed to muse. "I got no way of telling," he said.

"At least they can tell a stranger," said Basil, "or they wouldn't be acting this way." They were showing bad character. Stonewall was resisting being groomed. Curtis had brought out his trophy to show me, and Stonewall had hold of it with his teeth, trying to gain a purchase that would help him evade the press.

"Number one rule," Basil announced at the show the next night, "any possum that bites a judge twice will be disqualified." Dr. Johns, the town doctor, who works himself half to death treating people with or without money, got bit by one of his possums. He said it was a considerable nip, and he should know. He takes in hurt animals—eagles, owls, skunks, woodchucks—and nurses them back to health. "I've been bit by a lot of things," he said.

My wife Joan, as I have said, was named Miss Possum International. This was largely because the incumbent Possum Queen had "gotten older and discovered boys" and therefore had a date and couldn't appear, but Joan said simply, "I'm honored."

"We had a hard time getting a Possum Queen to begin with," Basil said. "Then I came up with a prize they couldn't turn down, something their mamas made 'em get in for—an eight-pound bucket of pure lard. Within three days the first Miss Possum was internationally famous. Been on national television and in the legislatures of two Southern states. A Miss Possum is chosen on personality, looks, and poise. Poise is how they hold a possum." Joan held them by the tail. Basil said he was going to get her on the Carson show.

I found that the other two judges and I tended to come up with very nearly the same point totals from possum to possum. "See," said Basil triumphantly, "you can just *tell.*"

One of Dr. Johns's possums, whose name I never caught, won best boar possum, and Pat Cargile's Miss Pollyanna Possum ("We call her April around the house") repeated as best sow. She *was* a pretty little possum.

There were maybe forty possums entered, all of them, as it turned out, from Alabama, though one was alleged to be Mexican. A leading owner from Florida had been unable to appear. "They feed 'em mangoes down there," I was told. In Alabama they tend to feed them Jim Dandy dog food.

The last International Show was criticized as not being entertaining enough for the fairgoers watching from the several rows of bleacher seats. "We're not here to entertain," Basil had snapped. "We're here to judge possums."

But at this show a lot of people enjoyed coming up and talking about the possum. Somebody claimed that his "grandparents used to catch a bunch of possums, turn them loose in the mulberry tree in the backyard, and tie a dog to the trunk. We'd have a dozen or fifteen possums in the tree fattening up on berries, and when we wanted one we'd go out and shake a limb or shoot one.''

A lady described her emotions on seeing a possum in the Clarks' living room. ''One of them came walking in there and I jumped up on Charlotte's couch, feet, shoes, and all. 'He ain't going to bother you,' they said. 'No, I ain't going to let him bother me,' I said.''

None of the show possums played possum—or ''sulled'' as they call it in Alabama. ''I've known possums the last fifty years,'' said a man, ''and some possums sull and some won't. If he's been handled, he won't sull. He'll bite. I've had as many as six or eight in a sack at one time. I love possums.''

Dorothy and Horace Goodman, from Columbus, Georgia, had driven over a hundred miles to the show for a reason. They wanted to replace their pet possum, Punky-Pooh, which had died. ''He got mail at Christmas,'' said Mrs. Goodman. ''He was a wonderful pet. He had his own little bed. He'd go to the bathroom in the bowl and wake up by an alarm clock. He ate bacon and cookies. My daughter found him in the yard, just laid out. At first she threw him in the garbage can. We didn't recognize it was a little possum till we got to looking at his feet. His tail was peeled down like a banana. A dog had got a hold of him and peeled him. But he revived.''

''When I was a boy,'' said Clark, ''the only thing in the world I'd have to look forward to was when I'd be big enough for someone else to carry the possum bag when we went on a hunt.

''Now look where possums have got me. You know the principle of Occam's razor: the solution to a problem is always real simple. Possum's simple.''

All the people present seemed satisfied with the judging. As for the possums, I noticed that they would neither look at you nor seem to make an effort to look away from you. I who had judged them tried to catch their eye, but they were even harder to know than the President.

Possum's more simple than Jimmy is.

More Carters

Ladlow Prud'homme Carter Jr., 40, Crabhandle, Louisiana, who didn't speak a word until he was nine years old and hasn't come out with a full subject or verb to this day.

"Nor fixing to, neither."

Jrs.

. . . a voice heard only in the heart of him who is the substance of his shadow, the son consubstantial with the father.
—Stephen Dedalus

The older I get, the more I realize that people get old pretty young.
—Susan Blount Duff

Hamlet. The President. Me.

Jrs. haunted by the shrouded father.

This problem may by no means be isolated. Call it rebirth, recycling, epigonism, or whatever you want to, but contemporary public life is shot through with Jrs.

I'm not going to name them all. But we haven't had a non-Jr. President since Nixon. (Gerald Ford Jr., the only man to be appointed Vice-President and President, was adopted by Gerald Ford Sr.) And seven Jrs. declared themselves candidates for 1980: Jimmy Carter, Governor Edmund G. Brown Jr., Senator Howard Baker Jr., John Connally Jr., Governor Meldrim Thomson Jr., Senator Lowell P. Weicker Jr., and Lyndon Larouche Jr. Furthermore, the Kennedy who was originally supposed to run for President was Joseph Jr.—Teddy is the third in a line of *surrogate* Jrs. Nationwide bumperstickers nominated J. R. Ewing of "Dallas" (Jock Ewing Jr.).

A few years back there was evidence in this country of a ruling network of HH's. Harold Howe II, Hubert Humphrey, H. R. Haldeman, (E.) Howard Hunt, Hal Holbrook, Senator Harold Hughes, H. L. Hunt, Howard Hughes, Harold Hayes, Hugh Hefner, Huntington Hartford, H. J. Heinz, H. G. Hill, Happy Hairston, Helen Hayes. I'm not going to name them all. Humbert Humbert. But by and large HH's have faded.

Jrs. have filled the vacuum. The Carter administration: Secretary of Health, Education, and Welfare Joseph A. Califano Jr., Cabinet Secretary Jack H. Watson Jr., Directors of Management and Budget Bertram Lance Jr. and James T. McIntyre Jr., Staff Director Alonzo L. McDonald Jr., Secretary of Energy Charles William Duncan Jr., Secretary of the Army Clifford L. Alexander Jr., Secretary of the Navy and Temporary Secretary of Transportation W. Graham Clayton Jr., FBI Director-designate Judge Frank M. Johnson Jr., Ambassador to Moscow Thomas J. Watson Jr., Carter-Mondale Political Director John A. Walsh Jr., White House Day-to-Day Operations Chief Hugh A. Carter Jr., and Department of Interior Herpetologist C. Kenneth Dodd Jr. (who was fired for overzealous defense of the Pennsylvania rattlesnake, then reinstated after a flap). Billy Carter's doctor is Dr. Paul Broun Jr. and his lawyer is Pierre Howard Jr. Jimmy's cross-country coach at the Naval Academy was Captain Ellery Clark Jr.

The Speaker of the House: Thomas P. O'Neill Jr. The Senate Minority Leader: Baker. The House Minority Leader: James C. Wright Jr. (At one of the inaugural parties, I talked to a Fort Worth car dealer who said, "I hear Jim Wright drives a '68 automobile. Hell, I'm going to give him a new car. Lot of the lawyers around town want to go in with me on it, but I tell em, 'No, y'all can do something else for him, but I want to do this.' ") The Supreme Court has Lewis F. Powell Jr. and William J. Brennan Jr.

Richard Bissell Jr. of the CIA conceived the Bay of Pigs fiasco, E. Howard Hunt Jr. and James W. McCloud Jr. led the Watergate break-in, Baker and Senator Sam Ervin Jr. led the Watergate hearings, J. Fred Buzhardt Jr. represented President Nixon, Henry S. Ruth Jr. was deputy special prosecutor, and Alexander Haig Jr. was all but President while Nixon was deciding whether to resign. Sheriff Christopher Look Jr. was at Chappaquiddick and William F. Calley Jr. at My Lai. William Sloane Coffin Jr. visited the hostages in Iran. ABSCAM had Senator Harrison Williams Jr. The Chairman of the Joint

Chiefs of Staff at the time of the aborted Iran-hostage rescue mission is a Jr., and so are the judge who tried Bert Lance and the Export-Import Bank president who gave Rupert Murdoch a low-interest loan just before his newspaper endorsed Jimmy over Teddy.

Variously involved in Southern racial struggles: Martin Luther King Jr., Charles Morgan Jr., Representative Charles C. Diggs Jr., Ivan Allen Jr., Whitney Young Jr., Vernon Jordan Jr., Clarence Mitchell Jr., and FBI infiltrator Gary Thomas Rowe Jr.

John H. Glenn Jr., Edwin E. Aldrin Jr., Alan B. Shepherd Jr., Walter M. Schirra Jr., L. Gordon Cooper Jr., Charles Conrad Jr., James A. Lovell Jr., Edward H. White 2d, Richard F. Gordon Jr., Fred W. Haise Jr., John L. Swigert Jr., Charles W. Duke Jr., and Alan L. Bean Jr. were thirteen of the first thirty-two astronauts in space. Shepherd, Glenn, Schirra, and Cooper were four of the first six.

Mass murderers: John Gacy Jr., Elmer Wayne Henley Jr., and the Reverend Jim Jones Jr.

There are any number of prominent Jr. governors (William P. Clements Jr. of Texas, for example), senators (Joseph R. Biden Jr. of Delaware, for example), mayors (Richard E. Arrington Jr. of Birmingham, for example), and congressmen (Paul N. McClosky Jr. of California, for example). C. C. Garvin Jr. is chairman of the board of the Exxon Corporation, Sam Church Jr. is head of the United Mine Workers, Victor Stello Jr. is the Nuclear Regulatory Commission's director of inspection and enforcement, Roone P. Arledge Jr. is head of ABC News, Alfred A. Marks Jr. is director of the Miss America pageant, and George Gallup Jr. is president of the American Institute of Public Opinion.

On-the-make-under-the-aegis-of-the-glamorous-wife politicians: Governor John Y. Brown Jr. of Kentucky and Governor John W. Warner Jr. of Virginia.

And don't forget: Generoso Pope Jr., Efrem Zimbalist Jr., J. P. Donleavy Jr., Hubert Selby Jr., Evan S. Connell Jr., Arthur

Schlesinger Jr., A. B. Guthrie Jr., Scott Momaday Jr., Vine De-
loria Jr., Ring Lardner Jr., Mike Royko Jr., R. Emmett Tyrell
Jr., Kurt Vonnegut Jr., E. J. Kahn Jr., R. W. Apple Jr., Jason Ro-
bards Jr., Joe Yule Jr. (Mickey Rooney), Cassius Clay Jr. (Muhammad Ali), Joe Gilliam Jr. (not to be confused with the late
Junior Gilliam, to whom the Dodgers dedicated the 1978
World Series unsuccessfully), Dock Ellis Jr., Phil Niekro Jr.,
Angel Cordero Jr., Laffit Pincay Jr., Giuseppe Paolo DeMaggio
Jr. (Joe DiMaggio), Sammy Davis Jr. (I once talked to a man in
a Southern truck stop who claimed that his father had "left
all his money, and his body, to Sammy Davis Jr. He figured it
would piss everybody off, including Sammy Davis Jr. What
was Sammy Davis Jr. going to do with $1,700 and a shriveled-
up old white man? Whereas we could've used the money.
Course we overthrew it and Sammy Davis Jr. didn't even en-
ter into it. But the lawyers charged $2,400.") A friend of mine
went to General George S. Patton Jr. Junior High.

And yet Jr. is not a chic designation. Terry Southern has
written that when he was reading manuscripts for a men's
magazine he would automatically reject any author using a Jr.
in his name. Gore Vidal—who was born Eugene L. Vidal Jr.
but took a new first name from his mother's family—writes
that Alfred Appel Jr., the real-life Nabokov scholar, is "plainly
a Nabokovian invention—the 'Jr.' is one giveaway." Henry
James was a Jr., but you never heard him admitting it, especially in Europe. So is Tom Wolfe.

(By the way, Kansas City Royals first baseman Peter La-
Cock Jr. is the son of Peter Marshall, the host of Hollywood
Squares. "You can't have just any name on television," La-
Cock Jr. has observed.)

A Northerner once informed me that Jr. is a Southern institution—this in the face of innumerable Jrs. among Kennedys,
Rockefellers, Roosevelts, Fords, and Morgenthaus. Okay,
maybe it is more common in the South to *call* somebody "Junior." And, okay, I am at some disadvantage in this chapter

because "Daddy" looks funny in print. But you can't write off the Sr.-Jr. problem as Cracker business.

John McEnroe Jr., the flamboyant young tennis star, is from Long Island or somewhere. He stands accused of being a brat. "He's entitled to his own personality," says John McEnroe Sr., his businessman father. "He's entitled to be John McEnroe." An extraordinary statement. What's your name—Perry Wickwire? Try saying out of your own mouth, about *anyone*, "He's entitled to be Perry Wickwire." Names mean something.

At a mass meeting of Atlanta blacks in the early days of the Civil Rights Movement, Dr. Martin Luther King Sr. is hissed and booed for wanting to go slow. Martin Jr. rises, with tears in his eyes, and defends his father in what a co-worker will recall fifteen years later as "the greatest speech of his life, greater than the one he made on the March on Washington. . . . He talked about 'the cancerous disease of disunity.' " Martin Sr.'s conservatives carry the day: the result of Martin Jr.'s greatest speech is a ten-month deferral of integrated dining in Rich's department store.

Father-son unity confuses roles. Hamlet (like Jimmy Carter) is an ill-focused Jr. in a post-assassination time. The new king, murderer of Hamlet Sr., has usurped not only Hamlet's mother and patrimony but also Hamlet's Oedipal right to kill his own father—something Jrs. are more than normally ambivalent about to begin with.

"Taint not thy mind," Hamlet Sr.'s ghost tells Hamlet Jr. Easy for him to talk. Revenge your father's foul murder that your incestuous mother had a part in, but don't let it upset you psychologically. Okay, right. The kind of guy Hamlet is, I don't think he's been so eager to be King Hamlet anyway. It's been done, for one thing. And for a Jr., there's too much *structure* there. Hamlet would probably rather stay in Wittenberg and be a critic or something—do something more detached. (Axel Springer Jr. was an internationally known photographer under the name Sven Simon. But he was also heir to West

Germany's largest newspaper empire. At thirty-eight he shot himself.)

But now that there is no King Hamlet, Hamlet's father the ghost is *urgently* defining his purpose in life: Kill your uncle. Hamlet can't seem to get motivated. How is he ever going to get the old man out of his head now? In the end, only by getting himself killed too.

T. S. Eliot, although he missed the Jr. angle in *Hamlet*, recognized that something hard to dramatize was going on. Hamlet is "dominated," Eliot wrote, "by an emotion which is inexpressible, because it is in *excess* of the facts as they appear."

Jimmy Carter, on the other hand, has seemed to be dominated by an excess of facts. Dominated, anyway, by something shadowy—as his father was by a suit of clothes that came from out there in the great world beyond Plains.

We know only so much about the relationship between James Earl Carter Jr. and Sr., but that suit is of national interest. "One of the rare times I ever felt desperately sorry for my father," Jimmy writes in *Why Not the Best*, was when Sr. ordered the first tailor-made suit of his life and it came "twice as large as my father." But "no one in the family laughed" when he tried it on.

If that is not a primal Jr. scene, I don't know what is. The suit was some corporation's idea of how large a standard father ought to be—twice the size of a distant and sometimes harshly punitive daddy whom Jimmy says he "never even considered disobeying." It must have been a shock to see an outfit so much bigger than the model that little Jimmy scarcely dared aspire to. At the same time, the sight must have been wickedly stimulating.

As Jimmy grew up, the father who had seemed godlike turned out to be swaddled (unlike the wider-ranging mother) by his little town and by what has traditionally kept Crackers down below national standards: provincial race prejudice.

Jimmy unlearned the prejudice, escaped Plains, went further than the Sr. But he never quite got over the suit.

Jimmy didn't grow into presidential dimensions; he scaled his notion of Presidents down to his level. He lost his "feeling of awe about Presidents" after meeting Nixon and various famed presidential hopefuls. "I have always looked on the Presidency of the United States with reverence and awe, and I still do," he writes in his campaign autobiography. "But recently I have begun to realize that the President is just a human being."

After Jimmy became President, the electorate arrived at the same realization, and didn't like it. The climax of the Carter *Hamlet* was the being elected. Cutting everyone else in the national arena down to size. Then, however, Jimmy had to wear the suit. And people did laugh, hollowly, when he tried it on. Here was a Chief Executive whose chief distinctions seemed to be indistinctness and a failure to execute (except rashly: Hamlet dispatching half the Danish court, Jimmy his Cabinet). His critics said what one of Macbeth's critics says:

> . . . now does he feel his title
> Hang loose about him, like a giant's robe
> Upon a dwarfish thief.

Nobody calls Jimmy a thief, of course, now that the possibility has been looked into by a special prosecutor. Jimmy is not a Macbeth. Macbeth is not a Jr.; his father's name was Sinel. Rosalynn has been likened to Lady Macbeth, but it is not, at bottom, a woman that dominates a Jr.

Incidentally, the out-of-town paternal suit mentioned in *Why Not the Best* may not be the only idealized outfit that both spurs and muffles Jimmy. A popular rumor, proved *factually* false, is that Jimmy resembles John Kennedy because he springs from the illicit union of Joseph P. Kennedy Sr. and Miss Lillian—who was supposed to have been in Boston once when old Joe was there, and who, indeed, often refers to the

Kennedys as if she were one of them. After Jimmy outshone Teddy at the JKF Library dedication (and after Miss Lillian had said that if Teddy were *her* son she was not sure she would let him run), Jimmy told reporters that he had as much right to the Kennedy legacy as Teddy did. What if Jimmy's un-expected drollery on that occasion came from his sense of be-ing a Kennedy himself? Not a legitimate one, though; a pretender. Jackie didn't want him to kiss her. The public has regarded his version of Camelot as if it were Tobacco Road. Jimmy may diminish people, even Kennedys, but there will always be folds and layers between a Cracker and the ruling class. And between a Jr. and his role.

"My father is special," said Jimmy's son Jack in 1977, "but not tops in the country. There are five men in Calhoun who could be President of the United States."

A Jr. would never say that about a Sr. (Incidentally, I hope none of those guys in Calhoun makes it. I don't want to go through all this again.) A Jr. lets people of all ages keep him from getting big enough for his inherited britches. At Hugh Carter's worm farm in Plains, I talked to an old black man who said Jimmy Jr. didn't take after Jimmy Sr. much. Billy did, he said. "To see Mr. Billy walk—that's his daddy, exactly. Course, I never saw his daddy drunk many times." This same man, after fixing me up a bag of worm manure, asked what I did for a living, and I told him, with as little self-importance as possible, that I wrote. "I reckon you can do that in the shade, can't you?" he said.

Jrs. grow up to some extent in the shade. As it happens, however, most public Jrs. achieve broader recognition than their fathers did. (An exception: Frank Sinatra Jr. A young woman once asked him for his autograph and, as he signed, she said, "And leave off the Jr.") This may strike the Jr. as a denial of the Sr. Whatever else he is all his life, a Jr. may nev-er quite get over the idea that he is, or ought to be, a son.

(Elisha Cook Jr. had Sydney Greenstreet; Harry Lillis "Bing" Crosby Jr. had Barry Fitzgerald; Willie Mays Jr. had

Leo Durocher; Vida Blue Jr., unfortunately, had Charles O. Finley; William Buckley Sr. was an oil man.)

It is confusing not only to *be* a Jr. President, but also to have one. The *nation* is traditionally a fractious adolescent, which wants to be a superpower only so it can be free as a kid. Of course, paternalism is a bad word today, worldwide. (I was proud when Andrew Young said, "The difference between Northern liberals and Southern ones is the difference between paternalism and partnership." Jimmy makes a point of his partnerships with Rosalynn, Mondale, smaller countries.) But the President is the nation's father, to the extent that it acknowledges one. And America likes to think of itself—even as it overbears the world—as a toppler of overbearing figures. Abroad and at home.

Lyndon Johnson: there was a great daddy to disparage. Attacking Nixon was more like kicking a mean but crippled uncle. But Nixon did presume to know more than we did, so he yielded a certain amount of Oedipal pleasure. He was a far more gratifying target than Gerald Ford Jr.—who toppled himself, habitually. And Jimmy—well, Jrs. tend, on purpose, not to grow into the kind of people you get a *kick* out of toppling. You don't resent President Carter the way a child resents a parent, but the other way around.

My late father, Roy Sr., came from an even less favored background than Jimmy's, couldn't afford to go to college except for a while at night, never accumulated personal holdings except plenty of insurance and some real estate that went flat as Atlanta's boom subsided, but he was a hell of a president. At one time or another he must have chaired or presided over ten or twelve different bodies, from the church's board of stewards to the National League of Savings and Loans.

My father filled out a size 46-long business suit handsomely, was more congenial and expansive than Jimmy, had at least as much rectitude, and was funnier: once at a banquet, on being presented with a huge silver tray in appreciation of one of his presidencies, he said from the dais by way of thanks, "This is something I've always wanted, but not very much."

My father pushed through the construction of Decatur's tallest office building and its tallest church—the cross on the steeple two feet higher than the Baptists'. (*His* father was a carpenter, with no access to capital.) He had various civic dealings with Governor Carter, who didn't impress my father very much. I have a picture of the two of them smiling at a piece of just-passed legislation, Jimmy looking like a somewhat wizened Brandon De Wilde and my father like an ampler, Southern Methodist Spencer Tracy.

But Jimmy has been a more suitable U.S. President, in these fault-finding times, than my father would have been. Jimmy embarrasses *us*, whereas my father was the type of person who made you worry about embarrassing *him*.

The summer before I went into the Army—Freedom Summer—two other local scions and I got together and decided we were going to appear before the school board and demand total integration. My father was chairman of the school board—undoubtedly the best man in Decatur for the job, though not radical enough for my taste, at that difficult juncture. He was chairing desegregation with his usual burgherish progressiveness. (Decatur High today is sound and 65 percent black.)

There was a scene at home: My father was standing out in the backyard looking stricken and my mother was telling me he'd heard what we scions were planning and he was hurt. I felt callow and disloyal. I withdrew from the scionist plot, which collapsed. I never did discuss all this with my father. I wasn't afraid of him—what I dreaded was exposing the little kid, *disturbingly* like me, who seemed to be curled inside his imposing structure.

Jimmy is like that kid, without the kind of presumption it takes to build the structure. Jimmy *Sr.* must have had the presumption, otherwise his family would have felt free to chuckle when he tried on the suit. There wouldn't have been any *desperation* in his son's sympathy.

But isn't the President supposed to have that kind of presumption? He's supposed to be the Head Honcho! The voice of America! He's not supposed to be uneasy around congressmen and ballplayers, anxious to please everybody, leery of swimming rabbits! He's not supposed to swoon like a possum in the middle of a footrace!

Yeah, but these days anybody in an executive capacity has people all *over* his ass. Upside and inside his head, right up in his face, messing with every least bit of his business. If he tries to stand like a Colossus, he's not going to stand long. That's why we see so many Jrs. in executive positions. We don't want to feel desperately sorry for a President again.

I don't think any article of *clothing* could have made me feel desperately sorry for my father. He had this off-green cap from Disneyland with Donald Duck on it, whose bill (the hat's, I mean—Donald had his usual bill) was so long and green it looked like a one-man awning. He wore it boating because it was the only thing he'd found that would shade his eyes. It flew off his head as he was driving the motorboat, pulling Susan on skis, and I remember my mother sitting up on the porch snapping beans, watching him boat back after it a long ways. Finally he gave it up for lost. My mother said, "Oh, he loved that hat."

We were proud of him for wearing it.

Fishing, my father would bring eels, gar, crabs, toadfish, small furiously thrashing *sharks* up into the boat, with aplomb. He wasn't leery of anything, except dissolution, heart-to-heart talks, and criticism.

When my father served as chairman of the Metropolitan Atlanta Rapid Transit Authority, he was outraged that the press, various pols, and rag-tail citizens' groups rewarded his arduous and farsighted efforts with boisterous criticism. By that time, I had taken my Jr. off to New York. On visits home, I felt silly advising him that in an open society (which Atlanta was becoming, after decades of businessman paternalism) the press, various pols, and rag-tail citizens' groups *always* reward arduous and farsighted efforts with boisterous criticism. I *liked* boisterous criticism. Of course, I didn't have to deal with it, and at the same time run a dynamic savings and loan and be a pillar of a dynamic church. His taking boisterous criticism so to heart contributed to the heart attack that killed him.

Another civic leader wrote to my mother: "There is no need to ask the cause of Roy's death. . . . As you know so well, he carried a heavy, heavy load. He was so able and so willing to assume a responsibility, and was such a natural leader, that the community literally overworked him." Whatever else brings *me* down, it's not going to be that. I am a natural *reader*.

So is Hamlet. So is Jimmy. (So is Billy, but he doesn't want to admit it—refuses to remember the titles.) Inspired by his mother and Miss Julia Coleman, Jimmy seized upon reading— a way around head-to-head conflict with the Sr. Even as President, he avoids personal jousting. He is always reading: memoranda, the polls, his chances, his opposition, his situation. *Books*, even. Give him credit. He may have misread Southern (and Russian) lit, but he did *read* it. And other lit too. He lobbied to get Dylan Thomas into Westminster Abbey. He appeared, offering a reader's tribute, in a good documentary film about James Agee. He skimmed some of his malaise speech from Christopher Lasch on narcissism.

Of *course* we got malaise. Anybody who reads knows that. (Or, anybody who reads has it.) But the *President* is not supposed to say so. The President is not supposed to piss and moan. The President is supposed to be in *charge*. Having a President who tells us we got malaise is like having a doctor who says, "Gosh, you feel terrible." For that we maintain a fancy jet plane with a telephone in it, and all those Secret Service guys and a White House?

Jimmy isn't a take-charge guy. A Jr. isn't innocent enough to think he, or anybody else, can actually take charge. People can only *presume* to take charge, and thereby lose their objectivity, and have people all over their ass. Of course, a Jr. has his own kind of innocence: a whole lot of theoretical structure packed inside a little kid.

Jimmy is heavily burdened, all right, but in a Jr. way. He's heavily burdened with *pulling a lot of things together.* But he doesn't have something off balance on his shoulders that propels him along at a lope. He has a tremendous range of things he is determined to cover adequately, he grinds away earnestly, he agonizes over military solutions admirably.

But guys like Lyndon Johnson, Franklin Roosevelt, my father, Woodrow Wilson, Nixon, Hitler—those guys figured that if they didn't come up with something *good,* and put it *over,* things would go to *hell,* and they would be *personally* humiliated. They were damned if that was going to happen. They pushed things, and themselves, to conclusions. They couldn't *help* it. Much of the time, I think, they were unconscious on stage.

Jimmy is always sitting back and reading the whole situation, collating and editing. He suffers everyday possum embarrassments, not the grander embarrassments of presumption. It makes him hard to topple.

I imagine my father in Jimmy's position: For a month or so my father puts up with the kind of abuse Jimmy has suffered, and then he goes on national television and says, *just by the look on his face:* "Listen here. I know who I am and what I can do and I'm proud of it. I don't know who all of you out there are, but then I don't particularly care to, if you aren't proud of me, if you deny that my faith is good. I got work to do. I got *ideas. I* got to *build* something. Good night."

That would have chastened me. But it wouldn't have suited

the nation. The nation is exclaiming constantly in myriad voices: "You're the President and don't understand us! You're the President and you're limited! So *what* if your faith is good!" It would have royally pissed my father off and broken his heart.

Actually I muttered such things to my father a couple of times myself. But I never had the facility for all-out resentment of authority that many Americans of my age did in the sixties. I hate to admit it, I really do, but I could never shake the feeling that I started out as a gleam in authority's eye.

So why didn't my father and I *see* eye to eye? He was into outlook and I was detached. The first thing my eye lit on after my mother called to say my father had abruptly died (earlier that day a close associate had questioned his good faith, and he had come home feeling stricken) was the spiffy, stiffish raglan-sleeve raincoat he and I had picked out together for my Christmas present, which I deplored but knew was the kind of snappy, forward-looking carapace of a raincoat he loved to think I would love. Because that coat made my father's eyes light up I am grateful. But it's a sad damn garment for me to look at—never mind try on.

My father and I took intimate if qualified pride in each other, were told we *moved* alike, were mistaken for each other on the phone; but I rarely felt that I had pleased my father and myself, or that he had pleased himself and me, with one stroke. Which may be why I hardly ever do anything with one stroke.

"BOY! You sure as hell don't! What is this shit!"

My father *made* me a Bunsen burner once. Just out of the blue. I want to mention that. And at the time I *needed* a Bunsen burner.

"God damn it! Are you going to . . . !"

Kiss my ass, Voice.

More Carters

Retrac Carter, 44, Molar, Utah. "Well, my father, he always said a catchy name is half the battle. Today you see it in Lon Nol and Dudley W. Dudley. My father ascribed his own failure in the hardware, heavy maintenance, and soft ice cream businesses to his own name being—and this is ironical—Jimmy, and the best nickname he could ever attract being Bud. I'm in the Xeroxing, multilithing, T-shirt imprinting, blowing-up-your-snapshot business. 'We Know Our Business Inside Out.' A certain amount of people like to have things copied or printed backwards for some reason and we do that. We run little backwards ads sometimes in the paper.

"Course, when I was in school, people, because of my name, you know, would call me Retread and Retard and Meatrack and Retarc. I'd tell 'em I could stand in the mirror and my name would read the same. They'd go off and think awhile and come running back saying, '*How 'bout the capitals*,' you know real mean, '*How 'bout the capitals*,' like it's my fault. People don't want to give you any distinction, especially if it's something *they* don't have.

"So I don't know, my business is doing fine, I'm a household word here in Molar, the talk shows here locally have had me on a number of times, but there's always that little bitterness there, that loneliness, like the hole in the middle where my C's come together, when I print my last name backwards."

Approaching the White House

I was in the White House once. . . . This was when I was just a kid, still going to college. I was living at the Wardman Park Hotel in Washington and I had some friends there, the Mortimers. They took me to the White House one evening. . . . It wasn't much of a party. It was, well, I'd say an orgy, to a certain extent. Harding, at one point, went over and pissed in the fireplace. Hell, I was shocked. I never saw a President piss in the fireplace before. Haven't seen once since, either.

—RICHARDS VIDMER, the old sportswriter, quoted in *No Cheering in the Press Box* by Jerome Holtzman

I was born in Georgia, and my ways are underground.

—BESSIE SMITH

I have disclaimed any use of drugs in the White House; Georgians, I have suggested, are heir to enough peculiar sensations, hepped-up states of mind, fugue states, and whatnot without recourse to drugs. And when we encounter visions, we take them to heart. We *dwell* on them. We don't want to be able to explain them away as hallucinations.

Back in the late sixties a Georgia legislator went to a rock festival in Byron, Georgia, because of what he was afraid it was going to be like, and sure enough, he came back denouncing it, saying, "I saw one man walking around nude who said he was a doctor." It beat all he had ever heard of.

The legislator also declared that festival visitors "invaded a nearby cattle farm and settled at the edge of the yard. The family was subjected to nudeness." No, not nudniks, "nudeness." Also:

"People not only swam in nudeness in the privately owned

creeks and lakes in the area, they also invaded motels and swam in pools with all their clothes on."

To this day I wonder why a nude man would tell a legislator he was a doctor. Maybe the legislator was so shocked by the general nudeness that he got the hiccups and this man jumped out at him from nowhere hollering "WOOLAWOO- LAWOOLA" and later justified his actions by claiming to be a doctor who knew the best way to cure hiccups was to scare the person.

Or maybe the legislator just overheard someone who'd recently received his M.D. telling someone, "I'm a *new* doctor," and the legislator looked around in the direction from which the remark came and saw a nude person who he *assumed* had just said, "I'm a nude doctor."

I don't know. But simple basic things like nudeness, even if not doctoral, bother Georgians enough that Georgians don't need drugs. If Georgians want to ingest something not merchandised by a Mammoth Corporation, we will grow a big old deep-red tomato and eat it. My goodness, I'd love it if I were ever in the White House and somebody offered me a big old deep-red home-grown vine-ripe tomato. Wouldn't that be nice, sitting there knowing you were in the highest house in the land and eating something that good too?

On the other hand, it might be better to eat that tomato at home. Let me explain.

As I write this, I have not been in the Carter White House at all. I can't even claim to have impacted more than slightly on the administration. I did hear in 1977 that my story about Billy in *Playboy* had caused some worried talk among White House personnel. A bunch of presidential staffers were resting up from softball and wondering whether some of the things I had quoted Billy as saying were going to have repercussions.

"Well," one operative reflected, "after all the things Billy's said already, I don't know that anything else can hurt." (This was before he got involved with Arabs.)

"Yeah," mused another. "But . . ." He cited the part in my story where there is a good deal of talk against the Equal Rights Amendment and sharing toilets, which Billy sums up by saying, "I never did say my shit don't stink."

"What," this operative wondered, "if that is taken out of context?"

Then I heard that Jody Powell had moved in next door to my friend Ruff Fant, who is from Holly Springs, Mississippi, and is now a Washington lawyer. If anybody in the world was a good old boy, Jody was, Ruff said. Jody had come over one evening and fixed Ruff's toilet, and Ruff had turned Jody on to Randy Newman's album *Good Old Boys*, which includes the lines. "We're red . . . necks, we're red . . . necks, we don't know our ass from a hole in the ground." Jody loved it. That was the kind of thing I wanted to hear about a Georgia administration.

No Georgian wants to be pushy, though, even or especially among other Georgians. No Jr. does either. Since I had read right after the election that transition staffers were giving "Shameless Letter of the Week" awards to communications they were receiving from old acquaintances they hadn't heard from in years, I decided not to write to Transition Head Jack Watson, whom I had known in college and Atlanta but hadn't seen since we had gone to a performance of *Dionysus in '69* together in New York in 1969 and a near-naked member of the cast had come over and stood next to us and glared at us and we couldn't think of anything to say to her and it had been an awkward evening.

I never have known what to make of Jack Watson anyway. He was a towering campus figure my freshman year at Vanderbilt. One night during Orientation Week, I walked up to an outdoor Student Christian Association mixer and saw him gesticulating and shouting, "*What* are you going to *think* when *Nietzsche* says GOD IS DEAD!?!"

"Oh my Lord," I thought to myself. "Is this what college is going to be like?" It wasn't. I can't understand why people criticize Hamilton Jordan for having lived in a Volkswagen full of dirty clothes, or whatever it was that he did in college. What if everybody in college avoided doing things like that, for fear that they would want to go into politics someday and their underwear would come back to haunt them?

Hell, I bet world affairs turns out to be a lot like college (which was a lot like high school, which was a lot like grammar school, which was a lot like just hanging out with the other infants) when you get on the inside of it. You remember when that great flap arose over Jordan's looking at that highly placed Egyptian woman's bosom and saying he'd always wanted to see the pyramids along the Nile? You notice the Egyptian woman denied that any out-of-line remark was passed. So maybe that's how everybody talks at these state dinners. The public thinks it's all very stuffy and everyone's concentrating on using the right fork, but maybe representatives of the world's nations are saying to each other, "Hey, how's it hanging, Anwar?" "Gettin' any lately, Menachem?" "Hey, Mrs. Somaliland down there, was that you farted?" "I'd like to present to you the Premier of Tunisia, who I understand has a dick on him the size of your arm. How about it, Premier?" If diplomatic relations are not in fact like this, then maybe they ought to be. Nations might work out their feelings with resort to 3.5 percent less bloodshed.

What do you want for your political leaders? Guys who in college wore a fresh tie every day and addressed Tacitus, planerium, and Tri Delt with consistent gravity? What do you think John Kennedy was probably like in college?

It was too late for me to get to know any of the Carter administration in school. But I figured we were of near enough the same provenance to wind up together somehow, and I'd get to go to the White House. Not that it would be any big deal.

Then one weekend in '78, Ruff invited Jody and me and Billy Yancey of Somerville, Tennessee, to go goose-hunting on the Chesapeake Bay in Maryland. We all four drank a strong stream of beer, talked about entering a Duroc retriever in the National Field Trials (a Duroc is a kind of hog), sat around in a goose blind for several hours, shot one goose simultaneously (actually I didn't shoot it, because I had accidentally flicked my safety on instead of off, but I let everybody believe I did), and wound things up by going deep-sea fishing with Carl Perkins, who wrote "Blue Suede Shoes."

Nobody did any real fishing when we went out with Carl Perkins, but we did see something come down out of the sky and land in the water near the boat. I don't know what it was; it looked like a message. A message with some kind of a rudder or aileron or something on it. Just came floating down out of the heavens as if from space. Jody got the boat pilot to go back after this thing that fell out of the sky. But when we got to where it had landed, it was gone. Must have sunk. I was disappointed, thinking that some alien intelligence had messed up a chance to communicate with Ruff, Yancey, Carl Perkins, me, Jody, and, in turn, the President. I guess you think *that* wouldn't have been something to tell my grandchildren.

"Granddaddy, you were right there on the *boat* when the first word came down from the Outer Galacticans?"

"Yeah, and I'll never forget it. I was the one actually who scooped it out of the water."

"*Aw!*"

"Yeah! Just go on up to the U.S. Supreme Court and ask Justice Ruff Fant if it ain't so. He was there too, *trying* to grab it. His arm was shorter."

"And you were the first to realize what it said?"

"Well, yeah, I was. Old Carl Perkins *thought* he had it figured, he claimed it said something about pie. I told him, 'Naw, Carl, I admire your place in musical history and appreciate what you said when Elvis died'—you know, he said about Elvis, 'He had to wait till the world was in bed to ride his motorcycle.' 'But what this is,' I said, 'is something about

Pi.' Course what it was, we all know now, was 'Pi equals 56295141.3,' which meant they had a completely different kind of circle up there, which explained why it took them so long to get around to contacting us."

"Granddaddy?"

"Yeah."

"What was Billy Yancey really like?"

But, like I say, the thing, whatever it was, sank. And I was disappointed. But Jody said, "Anybody who sends a message that don't float to a planet that is three-fourths covered by water is too damn dumb to communicate with anyway."

That was the kind of thing I liked to hear from a Georgia administration. Some might impute unto it an arrogance, but I call it common sense. I liked Jody fine. He was just what I had in mind: just as plain as dirt but plenty sharp enough to help run the country. At one point during the weekend he told about how George McGovern got nominated in 1972 because of a fight he—Jody, not McGovern—and Hamilton Jordan got into with a lot of people in a bar, but I was making a point of not being in the capacity of a reporter—I may have been singing, too—and I can't recall the details.

Jody also said that during the long campaign for the nomination Jimmy traveled around meeting with Americans and telling them how he had met with Americans all over the nation, in their homes and at factory gates and beauty parlors and county fairs and feeder-pig sales. These remarks went over fine, Jody said, until Jimmy started using them in suburban Connecticut, where people would shift around and look at each other bemusedly and whisper, *"What are feeder-pig sales?"* So Jimmy dropped "feeder-pig sales" from his remarks.

I could theorize that the dropping of the feeder-pig sales was the end of something for Jimmy Carter. But no, I can see how a man going for President of the whole country would feel a responsibility to make his remarks intelligible to Connecticutters, or whatever you call them, when he was in Connecticut. I don't object to that, assuming he didn't start saying he had been meeting with Americans all over the nation in their Yale clubs and country clubs and prep schools.

Anyway, now that I had met Jody, I figured I had a foot in the White House door. I had already met Billy and Miss Lillian and Hugh Carter Sr. (Hugh, the worm farmer, told me, "You know how the mail is. I get a lot of Jimmy's White House mail down here, and he gets a lot of my worm mail up there.") And I figured I had observed the proper amenities—I had got drunk with the press secretary—so that I could go ahead and meet Jimmy.

Of course, I realized that a lot of people were trying to get in to see the President. A Baptist lay minister from Marshall, Texas, had crawled sixteen hundred miles to the gate of the White House, and Jimmy hadn't had time to see him. It was probably a particularly hectic day, and he said, "If I talked to everybody who crawled here from East Texas, I'd never get anything done."

Then there was Anthony Philip Henry of Dayton, Ohio, who believed it was blasphemous to have the words "In God We Trust" on U.S. currency and was wearing karate-fighter's baggy white pants and blouse and carrying a well-thumbed Bible. He had scaled the fence outside the White House lawn and charged toward the North Portico, "keeping up a stream of shouts, most of it apparently critical of the U.S. government," according to the UPI, and he had pulled a three-inch knife from his Bible and cut two White House guards before being subdued.

The approach of Milton Cashmore of Illinois had been to just drive his car up to the White House gates and demand to see the President. When he was told the President was out of the country, he had stood beside his car with the aid of crutches and yelled, "Open the gate and let me in. Jimmy Carter is fired. I'm going to sleep in the White House tonight." He was arrested. I knew too that Bo Diddley, the historic rock-and-roll figure, was wanting to talk to Jimmy about an idea he had for an electric car. Diddley had told Bob Greene, the syndicated columnist, "I don't trust nobody now. Who can do you the most damage, your friend or your enemy? I've invented an electric car. Yeah. An electric car. It's a real good electric car. You don't have to stop and charge it up. It charges its own self. But I'm not telling no lawyer about it. He'd just cheat me. I'm waiting to talk to President Carter. I'm going to ask him if he can work a way for me to bypass the patent office. That way my electric car can be American instead of Japanese. Yeah."

I was aware that at least two people had buried themselves just so they could *hear* from Jimmy. Stunt man Bill Shirk had done it and wound up with a ten-foot python coiled around his neck. He had risen from the grave where, according to the Atlanta *Constitution*, he had "spent three days with snakes and spiders in order to raise money for the retarded. When he emerged, Shirk seemed to be in a struggle with the python. He was . . . immediately shown a White House telegram he had demanded as a condition to being dug up from the grave in front of his radio station. . . .

"Asked what went wrong at the last, Shirk explained: 'Well I want to be real honest with you. I thought I'd get the python out and kinda mess with him a little bit, and all of a sudden he got up around my neck area. Man, I—seriously—he choked me.' "

Digger O'Dell down in Phenix City, Alabama, had come up out of *his* grave after a few days even though he hadn't gotten an answer to the letter he'd written to the President—asking him, because of the oil shortage, to make it illegal for any student in America to drive to school.

It seemed to me, as I read about Digger, that if I'd been the redneck President I would have answered the man's letter. I might even have encouraged more of that kind of demonstration. But I knew that James Wieghart was writing in the New

York *Daily News* that "a host of unmet needs and unresolved issues is converging on the Carter White House, chipping away at the foundation, raising the specter of an administration near collapse."

Who was I to come on as one more unmet need? Jimmy didn't need any more of those. And I knew he was busy. I figured that when Jody went to tell him I wanted to meet him, he'd say, "Jody, I got to work on the Holy Land. And inflation."

But I figured Jody could tell him, "I know it, I know it, but just meet this old boy for a minute. You knew his daddy. And him and I went out on Carl Perkins' boat and saw something fall into the sea."

After all, Jimmy had said before he was elected that being born again "changed my feelings toward people I see—for example, on elevators. I want to help people on elevators, to see what I can do for them, rather than what I can derive from them or just blotting them out of my mind." I was willing to get into any elevator in the land with Jimmy.

Then at one point Jimmy was going to give everybody in America fifty dollars, including four million people not even listed in the federal files. I was willing to pass up my fifty dollars for a few minutes of his time.

So I wrote old Jody a letter, told him I was writing a book and wondered if I could come drop by the White House at everybody's convenience. It's a good thing I didn't bury myself, because I never heard one word in reply. I did run into somebody who said, "I was out with old Jody till all hours the other evening in Washington and I nearly but not quite got him to give me the number in Teheran so I could call up them Iranians and tell them to fuck theirselves, and Jody spoke well of you," but that wasn't enough to make me feel that I had *gotten in on* anything.

While I was waiting for some access, Jimmy was photographed in the White House, all in one day, with (1) three members of the new Nicaraguan junta, (2) Lou Brock of the

St. Louis Cardinals (who gave Jimmy a pair of shoes and the bat he used to get his three thousandth hit, but wouldn't tell reporters his choice for President), and (3) the Bee Gees, who, according to the Boston *Globe,* said that Jimmy "astounded them by singing a few bars of 'The Sound of Music.' " Jimmy had the exact same expression in all three photos.

While I was waiting, I read where Jimmy told his Sunday-school class in Plains that they should list the persons from whom they were "estranged" and figure out the reasons for their feelings and perhaps telephone those people.

"I will do it if you will," he said.

He never called me.

Maybe I should have bundled up my ten-year-old boy and a boa constrictor and a Bible with an orange crayon mark down the middle of it and hitchhiked thirty miles in the rain to see Jimmy and give him the Bible. That's what a lady from Gulfport, Mississippi, did when Jimmy was in Tampa, and it worked. He met them, and took the Bible, although the Secret Service was uneasy about the snake. It was those people's *family* Bible. I wonder where it is now.

While I was waiting to hear something from Jody, the President coptered out to Rock Hill, West Virginia, and met with a group of residents at the home of Marvin and Virginia Porterfield. "He agreed with pretty much everything we said," said Marvin, a sixty-one-year-old retired beef cattle farmer. "He seemed to know what was going on."

Hell, I could have told Jimmy all kinds of things he could have agreed with.

While I was waiting, I read a column by somebody named Jimmy Townsend in the Atlanta *Constitution.* " 'Make yourselves at home' was the message President Jimmy Carter left for us at the White House when we went there for an all-night visit. My wife Geri, my daughter Tracy, her husband Doug Vaughn, and our grandson Chris, who is almost six, entered the White House grounds with me at 2:30 P.M. Sunday, June

24. Jack Carter, the President's oldest son, met us and escorted us to the elevator where [no, the President wasn't in it] we rode to the second floor for what would become the most unusual visit that ever happened to anyone in any century."

Well, Townsend's account does not entirely justify that characterization of the visit, but he mentions that "we made over a hundred and fifty pictures" and "I was . . . roaming all over the White House. That's not just literally speaking, either, because I went up to the sun room where I was soon joined by the family and Jack's sister-in-law, Lucy Langford. We were allowed to go up on the roof and walk across the catwalk." Jimmy is supposed to be such a stickler for good English usage, and here he is letting a man roam all over the White House who doesn't even know what "literally" means.

Finally, I saw where Billy Graham and Oral Roberts had gotten in.

By this time, to be truthful with you, I was losing my need to visit the White House. I had already devoted a lot of time to a number of theories about the administration, and if I went to the White House and met Jimmy I might decide, "Well, he's not a bad old boy. And in fact he knows more than I do." And where would that leave me? You can study a President a lot more intimately from a distance.

Even if I had gotten a chance to *hang around* the Georgia White House for a while, I probably wouldn't be any more an authority on it than I am now. In that case, if people were to ask me whether I believed in the Carter administration, I'd be like the old boy when they asked him if he believed in infant baptism. He said, "*Believe* in it. Hell, I've seen it *done.*"

I have come to realize that I *don't believe* in approaching the White House, and the reason is that we have all seen it done.

That may be a lesson we could learn from the Carter Years: approaching the White House is not some kind of ultimate trip. It's not healthy for people to want to approach the White

House the way they want to visit Lourdes or Hawaii or go on "The Dating Game" or shake hands with Harry Belafonte or take a drug. People want to approach the White House who couldn't handle approaching the houses up and down their own street, much less across the tracks. They want to transcend the polity. What we ought to do is *boycott* the White House, on the one hand, and give it a little breathing room, on the other. We ought to go visit feeder-pig sales.

People don't stop to think that there has been a lot of grief associated with approaching the White House. In fact, any President who is going to be an *inspiring* person to meet in the White House, somebody will probably have shot him before you get there. Or before *he* gets there. If such a President is not inspiring, an increasing number of analysts will probably already have concluded about him what Christopher Lasch has about Kissinger and Nixon: that he is "fatally removed from American life."

And if there is a profound reason for you to visit him there, somebody will have probably shot you.

I looked old Nixon in the eye once, the day of Martin Luther King's funeral. Dr. King had been shot before he could approach the White House one more time with a host of unmet needs. During the funeral service, I was standing in Auburn Avenue outside the church among a multitude of people. "Somebody still reading the Scripture in there," groused one of the thousands, but a little after twelve-thirty the service that was supposed to be over at eleven let out. The people made way for the mules and the casket to get through and head toward the burial, and then they squeezed back in solid except for a narrow passageway that was cleared for the celebrities.

The first to leave the church was Harry Belafonte. "Harry! Hey, Harry!" a woman kept crying, until finally he looked her in the eye, annoyed. The show-business people were the ones that the people forming the long gauntlet were most excited by, and the show-business people were the least pleased to see them. Eartha Kitt and Sammy Davis Jr. came out clinging to each other and crying. People reached out for Davis' arm, but he jerked away. Sidney Poitier came out comforting Nancy Wilson, and he scowled at the crowd when they exclaimed or whispered, "Sidney Poitier with Nancy Wilson!"

The politicians were different. John Lindsay came out smiling, striding, looking the most presidential of all. Nelson and Happy Rockefeller were grinning and nodding and trying to stay together. Romney, Percy, and Javits looked hale. Only Bobby Kennedy looked grim. He was the only one of them who had a man going ahead fending people off. Ethel Kennedy looked scared and vulnerable. ("Honey, can I help you any way at all?" a big black woman in a light blue church dress asked her later as she and Bobby were walking to the burial.)

Stokely Carmichael was the liveliest mourner. "Ohhh, Stokely," the crowd said, and his eyes flashed and he grinned and pumped several hands. Dick Gregory came out thin and stooped from fasting, and the crowd regarded him uncertainly; folks don't identify too readily with a hunger artist.

The easiest reception was given the sports figures, who looked subdued but philosophical, the way athletes should look after a loss. "Why, there's Floyd Patterson," said someone almost tenderly. "Hey, Floyd," several people said, and he nodded amiably, shyly, and shook some hands. Jackie Robinson looked more like a busy executive than a fevered baserunner, but the people said, "Hey, Jackie," and he gravely pressed flesh.

The most striking juxtaposition was when Nixon came through, with Wilt Chamberlain, four or five heads taller, right behind him. People murmured, "Nixon," and cried out, "Wilt, hey, Wilt!"

"Hey, Stilt!" hollered a man delightedly. "One time, baby!" and Chamberlain smiled and reached down over Nixon's shoulder and took the outstretched skin.

Nixon—this was before he was President—looked from under the overhanging limb at me, the only white face in sight, and I swear the message I got was this: "Could you please find it in your heart to cry, 'Dick! Hey Dick!'?"

I couldn't.

"Raymond!" somebody yelled at the man who'd shaken hands with Chamberlain. "You got Wilt!"

The celebrities stopped coming, and members of the crowd said disappointedly, "That must be it."

"But Bill Cosby ain't been by," someone said.

Then one of the SCLC field workers who admirably kept the crowd somewhat organized—they were ceded absolute authority by the police, who did their bidding—began to clear a way so that the cars carrying the family could get through. "With dignity, with dignity," the worker said calmly over the bullhorn. "That's right. Isn't that beautiful? We're doing it of our own free will. So just stand there for Dr. King. This is a memorial service. It's a religious activity. Holding fast for Dr. King."

Dr. King may have retired the title of great Georgian. If he'd lived, he'd be fifty-one now, and how could anybody excuse, morally, his not being the first Georgian President? We can see now that he led the tactically most disciplined, the morally least impeachable, and the media-wisest movement in the history of America, with the FBI against him. And all along firmly grass-rooted and honoring the essential system. His being a Jr. was important: he didn't presume. He wasn't out to *supplant* anybody, or to defend a worldly position. (Except his father's.) He stood up naked and didn't fight back. He stuck with being objectively *right*. Not always, it must be said, a workable program.

Strangely enough, Jimmy Carter was a surrogate Dr. King. As Howell Raines writes in his history of the Movement, *My Soul Is Rested*, Carter said all over the country during the '76 campaign that "I could not stand here today as a candidate for President of the United States had it not been for Martin Luther King Jr.," and when Carter was elected, former SNCC chairman John Lewis "wept for joy and wished aloud that his mentor [Dr. King] had lived to see what the Movement had accomplished." Dr. King Sr. told the Democratic convention, "The Lord sent Jimmy Carter to come on out and bring America back to where she belongs."

I looked Dr. King in the eye twice in a journalistic capacity. Of course, Dr. King's home-town papers were too responsible to give him more than minimal publicity when he was alive. John Askins, then of the Atlanta *Journal*, did a long interview with him in '67, but the paper wouldn't run it for fear, Askins was told, that it might stir things up. Georgians could get so excited over a nude doctor, there was no telling how they would carry on if a great black man were thrust upon them. The Movement would never have worked if rednecks hadn't been so innocently excitable.

Dr. King's rhetoric was old-fashioned, Baptist; Stokely Carmichael's was more thought-provoking. But there was never any doubt about where Dr. King's rhetoric was coming from or heading; how many other great Americans have there been about whom such a statement could be made? When I talked to him after press conferences, he had all the presence he needed and no bearing at all. He discussed his projected multiracial Poor People's Campaign as if it went without saying that he, the poor people, and I were all the same kind of folks.

At a meeting of delegates to a preliminary Poor People's Campaign conference, I saw a big broad-faced Indian woman, a lank country white woman in a loose frizzy pink sweater, a middle-aged Mexican-American man, a jittery squat Puerto Rican man, and a black woman with a straw hat on, all standing around in a hallway of Paschal's Motor Hotel drinking Cokes and talking *policy*. "Nobody wasting nobody. It is a miracle. And a miracle is the way things ought to be," as Cyrus in the movie *The Warriors* tells the peaceably assembled gangs of New York moments before somebody shoots him.

"I call on men of good will," I heard Dr. King proclaim in the Vanderbilt gymnasium, "to be maladjusted. Let us have a creative maladjustment, which will speed that glad and beautiful day when *all* God's children will be able to join hands and sing, 'Free at last, free at last, thank God Almighty we are free at last.' "

This was at an all-star symposium, which also featured Allen Ginsberg, Stokely Carmichael, and Strom Thurmond. While Thurmond spoke, Ginsberg put some kind of hex sign on him from the crowd. Later Ginsberg frugged with the editoress of the literary magazine, talked in the rec room of the Women's Quadrangle about how it felt to come, chanted a long poem, and asked to meet Allen Tate, who wasn't interested. Stokely gave a liberal intellectual speech to us mostly white folks and then went over to Nashville's black colleges, told them to kill Whitey, started a riot, and left town. "The important thing about man is not his specificity but his fundamentum," Dr. King told us, the same as he would tell any other audience, the same as he would be telling everybody today. But before he could lead his many-hued campaign up to confront the White House, one of God's specific maladjusted children shot him.

The fundamentum. My friend Holt Smith told me that once when he was a boy he couldn't stand looking at the hauteur of his neighbor's huge fluffy Persian cat one minute longer, so he got it and shaved it with an electric razor. "And this *pink little animal* ran home." Holt felt terrible. (In later life Holt was featured in a big spread in *People* for marrying Julie Newmar.) It's dangerous for a public figure to cut too close to that quick.

It was the Movement that brought the Kennedys close to the fundamentum. In 1963 the building superintendent of my graduate dorm came by, carrying a stepladder and light bulbs, to say that John Kennedy had been shot. We turned on the radio. A very peculiar Indian mathematician and a student of Polish who on other occasions would fling open his door and

yell, *"Who stole my laundry! Christ! Who stole my laundry!
Christ!"* or *"All right! Christ! Who stole my flip-flops!
Christ!"* listened with us as we heard Kennedy was dead. The
super said, "Poor soul. He had such an *appeal*," and we all
agreed.

The day Robert Kennedy died, I overslept and didn't know
anything had happened until my office mate at the *Journal*
handed me a radio—I assumed to listen to late returns from
the California primary—and said, "Last thing I heard he was
still in surgery." It just took a second to guess who it was.
"Let me explain! I can explain!" Sirhan Sirhan was quoted as
saying. Bobby appealed across the board, to eggheads and construction workers. He showed his personal feelings, weak-
nesses, and aggression right there on television, to the point
almost of nudeness. When he went by in a parade, people
couldn't restrain themselves, they pulled him out of his car,
tousled his hair, chipped his tooth. People don't want to do
that to Jimmy.

When the news came that Dr. King had been killed, I was
with some white people I didn't know, middle-class Atlan-
tans, and one of them agreed that it was awful and then she
added, "If they were going to do it, I just wish someone had
done it sooner." Didn't say they *should* have done it: she was
a moderate. I spent an hour with those people for my sins.
Real hard-core rednecks—people who never said their shit
don't stink but who believed that Dr. King (who beat all they
ever heard of) was out to expose them to abysmal funk and to
jump the niggers up ahead of them in society—would have
been more interesting though scarier company. But exposure
to these moderates was sufficient to keep the rind fairly tough
on my fundamentum.

The multiracial coalition had dissolved by the time Dr.
King died; when the Poor People's Campaign came through
Atlanta on its way to the White House the Poor People were
all black. But Father James Groppi told ten thousand people

packed into the Civic Center for a benefit show, "Unless the man in Washington deals with us, he isn't going to be able to deal with anything in Washington."

The show was held up for over an hour because the Poor People were late. When they did arrive, some four hundred of them up from Mississippi and other points south, crowd marshals cried, "Make way for the Poor People," and they filed in, aged eight weeks to eighty years. One old man was dragging himself along on crutches, and there was one woman with fourteen children, another with eight, and another with seven.

A good many of the Poor People were heavily scarred about the face and head, and there was a high incidence of bad teeth. Each of them wore a tag, "Hello, My Name Is," printed, and "SCLC Number 309," or some other number, written in. Many of them, including very Bible-reading-looking old ladies, were wearing armbands reading "Mississippi . . . God Damn." A camera crew shined a light on some of them and they waved—eventually, since the camera crew was Italian, to the people of Italy.

The Motown singers sang to them (Diana Ross and the Supremes: "That's the Sound of the Men Working on the Chain Gang" and "I Know You-oo-oo Send Me"; The Temptations: "Swanee"). The SCLC leaders welcomed them, had the ladies with the most children along stand, and affirmed their, the leaders', leadership. The Reverend Ralph Abernathy, Dr. King's successor: "My children say I'm a better daddy than LBJ. They say my kisses are sweeter and my hugs are the best in the world. . . . If you recognize my leadership, everyone here will stop talking." Everyone stopped for the time being.

After the Poor People reached Washington, Billy Graham told a packed crowd in San Antonio that Bertrand Russell had said the world would end within five years. "Everybody knows it, everybody feels it. It's in the air," Graham said. The question was, who was responsible.

Governor Lester Maddox summed up the destructive forces

as "these satchel-toters [i.e.: Health, Education, and Welfare officials] who are coming into our communities and burning down our schools."

For James Baldwin it was white power, white ignorance, and white fear. Which, he said, made it reasonable for black youths in the city to think the system was tending toward their murder and the rape of their sisters. Baldwin pointed particularly toward the steel industry, the real estate lobby, and the Texas oil millionaires.

For the New Left, it was the corporate structure, technology rampant, the CIA. An East German had just written a book that said President Johnson, Arthur Schlesinger Jr., Arthur Goldberg, George Meany, Dean Rusk, Robert S. McNamara, Clark Clifford, Cyrus Vance, Bill Moyers, a New York *Daily News* reporter, the ambassador to Tunisia, the curator of the Museum of Modern Art, a sociology professor at MIT, and McGeorge Bundy were all agents of the CIA.

Flapdoodle, sure, but almost everybody was able to find some institutional force or body of men, working undercover or inadvertently or by inertia, that was out to get him and his kind. Conservatives were rushing us to destruction; liberals were impeding change. People were feeling strongly that they wanted to destroy the System because the System, whether it knew it or not, wanted to destroy them.

At Resurrection City, which the Poor People had set up in Washington, Poor People were stoning passing cars. Friendly reporters had been beaten unconscious there and one almost raped. Demonstrating Poor People complained that they were tired of picketing the Capitol all day and coming back to find that their huts had been looted and their wives raped by neighboring Poor People. The System was being lost sight of.

The Poor People never got the satisfaction they craved from the Great Society's White House (and statistics show poor people to be further behind today than then), although there were reports that the federal bureaucracy was learning a few things and responding according to its lights. Directives were being sent down from the White House, to be toted in satchels.

Dr. King was gone and the textbook-perfect Movement was over. In fact, its being perfect may have kept it from being a good textbook. It may have encouraged us to think we could go in with a strong federal presence and straighten out the South of Vietnam. It may have encouraged too many people to think they could solve their problems by catching the TV's and the White House's eye. ("The Whole World Is Watching.") It may have made getting hit over the head by a policeman voguish for a while among white youths. It may have made us assume too easily that impositional school-mixing, which made sense in Southern towns, would work in less civilized places like Boston. It may have encouraged nationally ambitious white Southerners like Jimmy Carter to nationalize their standards according to some idealized liberal media version of national standards.

That the Movement was a sweet, noble uprising most of America has acknowledged, in retrospect. Jimmy Carter's derivative sequel to it, being electoral, has put a lot more priority on being acknowledged contemporaneously—or *in advance*—as noble and sweet. The Carter Phenomenon picked up on the Movement and spread it broader and blander—with an unthreatening, unsexy, therefore unlikely-to-be-shot vague white man up front. Not a despicable formula, nor rousing either. (I say "unlikely-to-be-shot," but there was that perhaps farcical episode when one low-life whose last two names were Lee Harvey and another one whose first name was Osvaldo were arrested, and the Lee Harvey one claimed that the two of them were planning to shoot Jimmy. Why is it that even something of that seriousness, when it is focused on a Cracker, seems a little too something or other to be . . . high?)

Jimmy's pop white version of folksy, abuse-suffering, sympathy-seeking, high-minded, love-invoking Christian nonviolence (plus fiscal conservatism, adjusted for inflation) is sweeter and more noble than Nixon's counter-Movement music, but Nixon got *down*. Nixon tapped into something fundamentally distressing about American self-government—as Jerry Brown may be doing by looking away toward Outer Galactica—and the System knew what to do with him. Jimmy—although commentators accuse him of self-destructiveness, a great way to avoid explaining why somebody does something—has a lot of self-preservative reserve.

Jimmy tends to cut into the fundamentum only when he slips and reveals himself as a peculiar vulnerable little old boy (still worrying about lustful thoughts, still telling people about what happened between him and a little rabbit), and when that happens people don't like it; it's embarrassing; nobody really wants to behold a nude little pink Cracker.

What people used to want up there in the White House was a big old *lightning rod*, which glowed while taking everybody's heat and could be mourned with luxurious warmth after a bolt struck it down. Jimmy's not like that. You want to lay into him. But when you do, you feel like you're picking on someone smaller and more earnest than your image of yourself.

More Carters

Credo Tenet Carter, 71, Solid Mount, Alabama, who believes in laying down basic principles. "There are certain things that go without saying, and I believe in saying 'em. That don't mean put 'em on your T-shirt. Anything you see on a T-shirt, short of sweat, ain't in earnest.

"Working hard for the Devil is better in *some ways* than sitting around on your ass for the Lord. Working hard for the Lord is better in *some ways* than sitting around on your ass for the Devil. The Lord knows sitting around on your ass is better in some ways.

"There is a heaven, some kind, somewhere.

"Ain't here.

"Ain't *going* to be here.

"Even if you never saw it before, a dog's probably not going to bite you if you address it squarely and in a way that *a dog can identify* as congenial but not ridiculous. A dog has an awkward position in the world. It can't talk, gets in trouble if it bites, and ain't supposed to lick people. But that is the dog's problem. Except you got no call to aggravate it.

"The same with people.

"Unless there's something funny about them.

"There is *something* funny about every single soul. But sometimes you run into something funny you'd just as soon do without. And might enjoy chasing off.

"Figuring out that we are all ruled by the unconscious is fine as far as that goes. But tell everybody Hidy. Why not?

"Whatever don't taste good, spit it out or swallow it.

"Some people are just existentialists by nature.

"Anything you can break down, is not what you think you're breaking down. Just because you got something figured out, don't mean you know it.

"Nothing you can say is peculiar enough to stretch the truth. Assuming you realize that fact.

"There is such a thing as being honest. Up to a point. No point in admitting something that everybody would just as soon you didn't.

"If you've got it, don't flaunt it. Deny you have it. Flaunt something else. Something you don't have. But do it in a way that denies anybody the chance (which they'd dearly love) to say, 'Where does he get off flaunting that?'

"Nobody *has* anything.

"It's not so much who you know, and it's not so much what you know, and it's not so much who knows you know it. And it's not so much what you know you don't know. And it's not so much how well you know whoever knows what you don't know or whoever knows *that* you don't know it. But all of these things prove handy.

"It's always something. If it's not one thing, it's another. A nihilist has a ready argument, but he ain't going to amount to nothing.

"Only things that are 'only' something—like it's only make-believe, or it's only me—are anything.

"Meanness is a thing of the soul. Don't indulge it, but don't try to smother it, either. If it wasn't for pure D meanness, Eve wouldn't've eaten the apple. And we'd all be sitting around nekkid eating figs. Which would be all right if it wasn't for meanness.

"Don't get ahead of yourself. Stay a beat or two behind yourself if anything.

"There are several different signs that you can count on to promise rain. But all signs fail in case of dry weather.

"We just don't know. We just don't know."

The Curse of Georgians

[Burt Lance] sits here being tried for the imbecile optimism that is the curse of Georgians.
        —MURRAY KEMPTON, in the New York *Post.*

"Now I, like you, am an American," I heard Jimmy Carter tell a crowd of conceivably redeemed Southerners at the Yazoo City airport back in 1977, when he still had his grin. That's what Jimmy wants to be: National. International. Humanitarian. No Cracker.

He doesn't want anybody ever to be able to accuse him rightly of being wrong. He grew up being deplorable on the national level, by birthright—a Cracker. But he's not going to get caught being distinctly deplorable again.

He's going to regard the Russians no more reactionarily than God does. He's going to suffer the Iranian Moslems to holler unto him. Until the Russians and the Iranians prove to *any objective person's* satisfaction that they don't know what it means to act right.

Then, even when he's fighting deplorable foes, he's going to do it in undeplorable ways. He combats the Russians by boycotting their Olympics. He tries to rescue the American hostages in Iran by sending over a military mission so resolutely non-violent that its only casualties are accidental and American. The Iranians, who seem to be taking on the redneck role internationally, desecrate the American dead on television. "That is a demonstration," responds Jimmy on television, "of the type of people they are."

The Civil Rights Movement seemed to demonstrate what type of people Crackers are. The Vietnam War, Americans.

Now, though, a Crackro-American is not the brutalizer, he is aligned with the brutalized. (In fact, although Jimmy is too national to point this out, six of the eight victims were Southern whites.) George Wallace never could look better nationally than Martin Luther King Jr., nor Lyndon Johnson internationally than Ho Chi Minh. But the Ayatollah makes Jimmy appear enlightened by contrast—the same service Lester Maddox provided Jimmy back in Georgia. It's not just that Jimmy is lucky in his revolutionary. He must also have learned a little something about moral positioning, down in Georgia watching TV news in the sixties.

But that kind of learning doesn't necessarily translate into executive achievement. If you are always bending over backward, and in every other direction, trying to be demonstrably undeplorable from any angle, it is hard for anyone to make out what you are driving at, if anything. When you're President, policy is the best honesty, and Jimy doesn't seem to have one—except a personal *inverse* Crackerism. For all Jimmy's efforts, "a Georgia Cracker" is how Mayor Byrne of Chicago's husband summed up the President recently. And although I doubt seriously that the mayor's spouse knew what he was talking about, he was indirectly right.

Jimmy *became* President by seeming to be a new creature: a Kennedyesque Baptist, a tight-fisted Democrat, a white Georgian who could race-relate better than broad-minded Northerners. For a sort of liberal to arise from the least liberal depth of the national polity seemed a radical infusion, a lifting of the muck up into the liberal mix, which was getting thin.

"So far as liberalism moves toward organization, it . . . unconsciously limits its view of the world to what it can deal with," wrote Lionel Trilling. Being a white Georgian—something that liberalism had never been able to deal with—gave Jimmy the element of surprise. "Says he's going to lift the downtrodden *and* balance the budget," the moderate voter mused. "Who knows, maybe he can. Before I saw him, I'd have bet a south Georgian couldn't say a sentence on television longer than 'Git 'em.'"

But Jimmy didn't bring a new vigor to U.S. affairs; he brought a new, not very hearty, pathos. Internationally, this may have done us some good. It must be hard for uncommitted Third World people to take seriously any demagogue who decries Jimmy as the Devil. And back when our allies thought the U.S. was on top of everything, they didn't see much point in giving us a lot of help. Under Jimmy, it has become clear that we *need* it.

Jimmy has also brought us some new confusion. An American President today has to be inexplicable to have any elbow room. If you're explicable, people will be swarming all over television explaining you to everybody's satisfaction, and everybody will be saying, "Oh, that's what he's up to. *That* ain't going to work." People around the world will be making livings or revolutions out of explaining what's wrong with what you're up to, and the Iranian clergy won't let their government get away with going along with it, whatever it is. So here we have an old Georgia boy who is globally inexplicable.

He has us voting in the United Nations against Israeli settlements and then calling the vote a slip-up. My explanation of that is as follows. Jimmy had understood the Egyptians! He had understood the Israelis! And by doing what he does best—hovering alertly between both sides of an issue—he had brought them to an accord. Could somebody who's just an old Cracker pull off something like that? But those settlements violated the accord, so we voted against them. On reflection, though, that seemed construably anti-Semitic. A reconstructed Cracker can't risk being construed that way. So Jimmy said the vote was a mistake. That way, the vote was on the record, sort of, but so were his qualms about it. The vote-plus-retraction was probably representative of the national consensus:

Israel ought to be less aggressive, but we don't feel right about saying so. A vote resonant with qualms is surely more interesting—in a way more of a statement—than just a plain vote.

A vote with qualms is the kind I am willing, though not thrilled (and I may declare it a mistake), to cast for Jimmy.

Jimmy over Ronald Reagan. It has long been clear to Reagan just what an American is. I believe an American ought to be wondering. Jimmy, I think, does do that.

Jimmy over John Anderson. As a young congressman, Anderson sponsored a bill to make Christianity the national religion. Non-Christian officeholders would have been required to take a kind of loyalty oath. The resolution no longer reflects his thinking, Anderson says. Well, deliver me from the kind of Christian who has ever had any such thoughts beyond puberty. What if it came out that *Jimmy* once harbored such a notion? Everybody would be yelling, "Uh-huh! Uh-huh! CRACKER CRACKER CRACKER!"

Jimmy over Teddy Kennedy. It has long been clear to Teddy just what a liberal is. And I don't want to go back to the kind of President that people want to shoot.

Sitting here well fed in Massachusetts on April 29, 1980, inflation eating me up, a God knows how tenuous but highly desirable peace out my window, I would like to note that the first Georgia President, though a letdown, *still* hasn't caused any shooting anywhere. If I can't vote for Sadat or Robert Mugabe or Willie Nelson or maybe Edmund Muskie or Mo Udall, then I'm not too proud to vote for Jimmy—although quite often when I say so, people say back: "Because you're from Georgia."

"Now I, like you, am an American." Tell *me* there's not some poignance to my ethnos.

"*WHAT?* Poign. . . . *What in the. . . . Boy! GOT DAMN.* POIGNANCE! *You going to show them* Russians *some of that* poignance?"

By the time the Russians come, I figure I, like you *and* the

Russians, will be soot. And somebody in Africa who doesn't know a Cracker from an Ohioan will be viewing the remains on TV and remarking, "That's the type of people they were."

"How much more of this liberal bullshit . . ."

And some of the soot will be saying, "Soot? I'm anything *but*." And some of it, "I never did say my soot don't stink."

More Carters

Dogsbody Carter, no telling how old, Tuberangle, Arkansas, has always got by. "No. There doesn't nobody like me. Ain't ever has. Momma took one look at me, said 'There's just something. . . . I just don't like that baby.' Her judgment was bore out. Go into some place and ebbody just kindly sliiiides away, to me that's like the sploop when a rock hits the water. How you count on it going.

"I go my way. Do some work, I get paid. Got some money, I get furnished. Eat, it goes down.

"I got one wife living, one wife that died. Six children, ten-leven grandchildern, one gret grandbaby, one dog living, twenty-three dogs died. There hasn't none of 'em liked me yet, and none of 'em lied.

"Course, now, if I was to bump into somebody this afternoon. A utter stranger—that said, 'By Glory it's just a pure-to-Goodness pleasure to meet you, Dogsbody. You're a right likable old man.' I wouldn't argue with him.

"Dumb son of a bitch."

The works of Roy Blount, Jr., include the memoir *Be Sweet: A Conditional Love Story*, the novel *First Hubby*, the screenplay for *Larger than Life*, the edited anthology *Roy Blount's Book of Southern Humor*, and such collections as *Now, Where Were We?* and *Not Exactly What I Had in Mind*. Blount is a frequent guest on Garrison Keillor's *A Prairie Home Companion* and a columnist for *Oxford American*. He lives in New York City and western Massachusetts.